HIPPEIS

HISTORY AND WARFARE

Arther Ferrill, *Series Editor*

HIPPEIS: The Cavalry of Ancient Greece
Leslie J. Worley

The SEVEN MILITARY CLASSICS of Ancient China
Ralph D. Sawyer, *translator*

**FEEDING MARS: Logistics in Western Warfare from the
Middle Ages to the Present**   John Lynn, *editor*

FORTHCOMING

ON WATERLOO
The Campaign of 1815 in France by Carl von Clausewitz
Memorandum on the Battle of Waterloo by the Duke of Wellington
Christopher Bassford, *translator*

THE CHIWAYA WAR: Malawians in World War One
Melvin Page

**THE ANATOMY OF A LITTLE WAR: A Diplomatic and
Military History of the Gundovald Affair, 567–585**
Bernard S. Bachrach

**THE HALT IN THE MUD: French Strategic Planning
from Waterloo to the Franco-Prussian War**
Gary P. Cox

THE HUNDRED YEARS WAR FOR MOROCCO:
Gunpowder and the Military Revolution in the
Early Modern Muslim World   Weston F. Cook, Jr.

**ORDERING SOCIETY: A World History of
Military Institutions**   Barton C. Hacker

**WARFARE AND CIVILIZATION IN THE
MEDIEVAL ISLAMIC WORLD**   William J. Hamblin

HIPPEIS

The Cavalry of Ancient Greece

Leslie J. Worley

WESTVIEW PRESS

Boulder • San Francisco • Oxford

History and Warfare

Copyright © 1994 by Westview Press, Inc.

Published in 1994 in the United States of America by Westview Press, Inc., 5500 Central Avenue, Boulder, Colorado 80301-2877, and in the United Kingdom by Westview Press, 36 Lonsdale Road, Summertown, Oxford OX2 7EW

Library of Congress Cataloging-in-Publication Data
Worley, Leslie J.
  Hippeis : the cavalry of Ancient Greece / Leslie J. Worley.
     p.   cm.
  Includes bibliographical references and index.
  ISBN 0-8133-1804-1
  1. Cavalry—Greece—History.   I. Title.
UE75.W67   1994
357'.1'0938—dc20   93-29067
                                                                              CIP

UE
75
.W67
1994

Printed and bound in the United States of America

The paper used in this publication meets the requirements
of the American National Standard for Permanence of Paper
for Printed Library Materials Z39.48-1984.

10   9   8   7   6   5   4   3   2   1

To

Marjorie C. Worley,

my mother

Contents

List of Figures   xi
Acknowledgments   xiii

1. Introduction   1

2. The Mycenaean Mounted Warrior   7

3. Greek Cavalry in the Archaic Period   21

4. Greek Cavalry in the Periclean Age   59

5. Greek Cavalry in the Peloponnesian War   83

6. Greek Cavalry in the Fourth Century B.C.   123

7. The Cavalry of Philip II and Alexander III   153

8. Conclusion   169

List of Abbreviations   173
Notes   177
Selected Bibliography   219
About the Book and Author   229
Index   230

Figures

2.1 Mycenae terra-cotta horseman (fourteenth century B.C.), 10

2.2 Horsemen fresco from Mycenae (late Mycenaean period), 10

2.3 Dark Age Greek mounted warrior (Geometric period), 14

2.4 Mounted warrior wearing bell-shaped corslet following chariot (late Geometric Attic amphora), 16

3.1 Spartan hippeus (seventh century B.C. ivory fibula-plaque), 25

3.2 Thessalian cavalry troop and squadron rhomboid or diamond formations, 31

3.3 Light cavalry depicted on terra-cotta revetment from Thasos (Archaic period), 37

3.4 A light cavalryman advancing in front of a hoplite (early Protocorinthian aryballos), 37

3.5 Light cavalry attacking hoplites (sixth century B.C. Attic black-figure band-cup), 39

3.6 Greek light cavalry attacking barbarian mounted archers (mid–sixth century B.C. Attic black-figure dinos), 40

3.7 Corinthian heavy cavalry riding into battle (early seventh century B.C. Corinthian wine-jug), 42

3.8 Athenian heavy cavalrymen, each equipped with two spears, metal helmet, and greaves (mid–sixth century B.C. Attic black-figure mastos), 42

3.9 Two Greek heavy cavalrymen engage in combat (late sixth century B.C. Attic black-figure vase), 43

3.10 Corinthian heavy cavalrymen ride toward battle (early seventh century Middle Corinthian vase),   44

3.11 Greek heavy cavalryman equipped with complete panoply, including hoplon, or large circular shield, engages in heroic combat with Amazon (late seventh century B.C. Attic black-figure amphora),   45

3.12 Battle scene with cavalry and infantry (early sixth century B.C. Attic black-figure band-cup),   46

4.1 Athenian cavalry phyle formation,   76

4.2 Athenian cavalrymen practice throwing javelins at suspended shields (fourth century B.C. Attic red-figure crater),   79

4.3 Light cavalryman throwing his javelin (not shown) at a fallen hoplite, Stele of Dexileos (fourth century B.C.),   80

5.1 Spartan cavalry mora formations,   91

5.2 Syracusan cavalry squadron in formation,   101

5.3 Siege of Syracuse,   105

6.1 Battle of Leuctra (371 B.C.),   143

6.2 Battle of Mantinea (362 B.C.),   147

7.1 Macedonian wedge-shaped cavalry formation,   158

7.2 Battle of Chaeronea (338 B.C.),   161

7.3 Battle of Issus (333 B.C.),   164

Acknowledgments

As with any literary endeavor, there are a number of people whose assistance and suggestions were most helpful. I wish to thank them all, from my fellow history graduate students at the University of Washington to the members of the faculty of the Department of History. Special thanks go to Professor Arther Ferrill and Professor Carol Thomas. Arther Ferrill suggested the topic of this book, provided valuable insights and comments early in the writing process, and helped me in the search for a publisher. Carol Thomas read much of the first draft, pointed out a number of inconsistencies and weaknesses, and proposed solutions for these various problems. Further, I wish to acknowledge the support and help of Charles D. Hamilton, professor of history, San Diego State University. He also read much of the first draft and made significant comments, but more importantly, he constantly encouraged me in my work and was someone to whom I could always turn for advice and professional dialogue.

Finally, I wish to acknowledge the assistance of the staffs of the British Museum, the Buffalo Museum of Science, the Heraklion Museum, the Herzog Anton Ulrich Museum, the Louvre Museum, the Martin von Wagner Museum at the University of Würzburg, the National Archaeological Museum of Athens, and the Staatliche Museum of Berlin. It was through the efficient, prompt, and courteous assistance of these people that I was able to obtain the photographs for this book.

Leslie J. Worley

1

Introduction

In modern works on the military history of ancient Greece, the hoplite has received far more attention and praise than any other warrior. To a degree, this focus is justly deserved because the heavily armed infantryman dominated the battlefields of the Greek world from the Archaic period until the rise of Philip II of Macedon and the Macedonian phalangite. At Marathon, Thermopylae, Plataea, and Cunaxa, the hoplite defeated both Persian infantry and cavalry; at Delium, Coronea, Leuctra, and Mantinea, hoplites were the principal soldiers in the opposing armies. When commanded by such leaders as Leonidas, Pausanias, Agesilaus, Epaminondas, and Pelopidas, the hoplite clearly demonstrated his prowess. And yet, other types of soldiers took part and contributed to victories as well: Light-armed skirmishers known as peltasts played the dominant role at Sphacteria and Corinth, and cavalry was important at Delium, Leuctra, and Mantinea. The modern preoccupation with the hoplite has led to a disregard for or misunderstanding of the roles played by other types of soldiers on the battlefields of the Greek world. Greek cavalry has been especially subject to this neglect.

Although there is evidence that the Greeks used cavalry throughout the Archaic and Classical periods, many scholars and writers have ignored or discounted the Greek *hippeis* in their works. Capt. L. E. Nolan, writing in the nineteenth century, stated that "[while] the Athenians, and most of the Greeks imbibed a passion for beautiful horses and horse-racing ... it does not appear that the Greeks at this

period made any extensive use of cavalry on the actual field of battle."[1] More than one hundred years later, J. M. Brereton took much
the same view: "Greek cavalry did not shine until after Xenophon's
day; it was Philip of Macedon who organized the Greek cavalry into a
formidable fighting arm."[2] This view has also been expressed by various well-known ancient historians. George Cawkwell believed that
"true cavalry" developed very slowly until the time of Philip, because the Greeks did not have the stirrup and their horses were
small.[3] W. Kendrick Pritchett, the leading authority on Greek warfare, virtually ignored cavalry in his multivolume work. He stated,
"The issues of battle were settled on level ground between two armies of hoplites, and cavalry and light-armed forces played only minor, defensive roles."[4]

Although several works have appeared in recent years dealing
with Greek cavalry exclusively, even these efforts have focused on aspects other than either the general military role or the specific combat role of Greek horsemen. P.A.L. Greenhalgh's excellent book detailed the evidence for the existence of cavalry in the Archaic period
of Greek history (800–500 B.C.). But he seemed to be concerned
principally with establishing that cavalry existed in the Archaic
period along with mounted hoplites.[5] Glenn Bugh analyzed in some
detail the Athenian cavalry in both the Archaic period and the Classical period (500–323 B.C.) but concentrated on the political and social aspects of this force.[6] Thus, the military role of Greek cavalry
needs careful examination.

In this work, I trace the evolution of cavalry on the battlefields of
ancient Greece. Like many of the eastern Mediterranean peoples,
the Greeks began to experiment with the mounted warrior toward
the end of the Bronze Age, known in Greece as the Mycenaean
period (1500–1100 B.C.). The evidence shows that this experimentation took place in Crete, Cyprus, and the Peloponnesus. Although
the fall of the Mycenaean civilization no doubt slowed the development of cavalry, several factors indicate the process continued
throughout the Dark Age (1100–800 B.C.).

In the early Archaic period, aristocratic cavalrymen were prominent in Greek *poleis* and on Greek battlefields. Magnesia, Colophon,
Eretria, Chalcis, and Thebes all produced notable cavalry forces.

The Thessalian cavalry was the decisive factor in the Lelantine War, beginning its long tenure as the finest mounted force in Greece. As a rule, the cavalrymen were aristocrats because commoners could not afford expensive war-horses. Even though the cost involved limited the size of armies and cavalry forces, it did not hinder diversity. Three types of cavalry became common: light cavalry, whose riders, armed with javelins, could harass and skirmish; heavy cavalry, whose troopers, using lances, had the ability to close with their opponents; and dragoons, whose equipment allowed them to fight either on horseback or on foot.

As the Archaic period progressed, the age of the hoplite arrived and the role of this warrior matured. Most hoplites were commoners who could afford the panoply of the heavy infantryman, and larger armies—larger than several hundred aristocratic horsemen on each side—took the field, with phalanx fighting phalanx. Although the hippeis typically could not break the well-disciplined phalanx, cavalry did not disappear from the battlefields of the Greek world. If anything, the employment of cavalry became more complicated and demanding, and mounted warriors, who once had the single role of attack, assumed the multiple roles of scouting, screening, skirmishing, attacking, harassing, and pursuing. These tactical activities had to be performed against heavy infantry and the phalanx, as well as against rival cavalry forces. The Battle of Plataea clearly demonstrated the merits, and limitations of Archaic cavalry.

By the end of the Archaic period, cavalry was so effective that the postwar era saw both Boeotia and Athens, two of the rising powers in the Greek world, strengthen their mounted forces. The former organized the Boeotian Confederacy, with a federal military that included a strong and proficient cavalry. Athens created its cavalry virtually from nothing by subsidizing the purchase and mainte- nance of cavalry horses. Later, during the Peloponnesian War, the wisdom of these moves and the importance of effective mounted forces were demonstrated as cavalry was employed in a variety of tac- tical roles: to serve as the first and principal line of defense against invasions or incursions; to gain victory by surprise; to prevent the en- velopment of a phalanx; and to defeat a withdrawing foe.

As the fourth century B.C. dawned and unfolded, Greek cavalry

assumed an increasingly important role on the battlefield. To be victorious, Greek commanders campaigning in Asia had to have a
strong and effective cavalry force to counter the Persian horsemen.
In Asia and Greece, the coordinated infantry-cavalry attack made its
debut and proved decisive when properly employed. The hippeis
could open the battle with a charge to disrupt the opposing cavalry
and infantry, as in the Theban victories at Leuctra and Mantinea, or
wait for an opportunity or weakness to appear and then exploit it, as
in the Macedonian victories at Chaeronea and Issus. In either situation, the cavalry charge became an important tactical option.

In fact, throughout its history, Greek cavalry followed the same
stages of development as did almost all cavalry in the ancient eastern
Mediterranean. At first, the horse was used simply as a means of
rapid conveyance to the battlefield; then, it was used as a fighting
platform; finally, the cavalry charge appeared, adding the weight and
speed of the horse as elements of force and victory.[7]

Strangely, the definition of the word *cavalry* has not always been
consistent. According to J. H. Crouwell, "The term may only be properly applied to mounted troops when these are trained to the degree
where they can function with precision 'as a unit'—not only advancing on command but changing gaits, turning, deploying, and reas-
sembling in their proper positions in the ranks."[8] Col. D. H. Gordon
gave a simpler definition: "Cavalry consists of a large number of
mounted men capable of concerted action."[9] While both of these
definitions have some validity, neither is acceptable for the purposes
of this work, in part because each reflects ideas which have caused
historians to ignore Greek cavalry in the past. Crouwell implied that
cavalry could only fight mounted, a view that is also expressed in the
argument that "mounted hoplites" were not cavalry. This definition
ignores the dragoon, a cavalryman equipped and trained to fight
both mounted and dismounted. Colonel Gordon qualified his definition with the phrase "large number of mounted men." However,
large is a relative term, and Greek cavalry, whose numbers ranged
from a few hundred to a few thousand, paled to insignificance in
comparison to the massive cavalry units in the other areas of the
eastern Mediterranean. Yet the Greeks did deploy cavalry, and at
times—most notably under Philip II and Alexander III—it was the

finest cavalry in the world. Thus, for this work, *cavalry* will be used in its broadest sense and defined as any group of men, including dragoons, who use the horse for combat mobility and are trained and equipped to fight mounted.

I hope that this work will have an impact on the study of warfare in ancient Greece, but more important is the need to open debate and call attention to a military element that has too long been ignored or bypassed. Clearly, the hoplite was important. But hoplites did not fight alone. Nor was infantry the only force to make a contribution on the battlefields of the Greek world. Warfare in ancient Greece was not monolithic, not the exclusive realm of a single type of soldier, at any point. The hippeis were present in all periods and played their part in the tactical operations of their day.

2

The Mycenaean Mounted Warrior

In the eastern Mediterranean during the late Bronze Age, the chariot was the principal means of achieving mobility on the battlefield. The Egyptians used a lightweight chariot drawn by a pair of horses as a mobile firing platform for an archer armed with a composite bow. The Hittites preferred a slightly heavier vehicle whose pair of horses pulled a crew composed of a charioteer, a shield-bearer, and a spearman. Because the spear was not of the throwing variety, the Hittite crew was apparently meant to close with and assault the enemy. The Greeks, if one believes Homer and considers the topography of Greece, used the chariot as a battle-taxi—a vehicle to transport the warrior to and from the battlefield.[1] Yet in the midst of this widespread and diverse use of the chariot, the Greeks began to experiment with the first phase of cavalry, in which the horse was used as a conveyance for the armed, mounted warrior.[2]

Although the evidence is sparse, it appears that mounted warriors were used in various areas of the Aegean from as early as 1400 B.C. Among the tablets found in the palace at Knossos, two record the issue of a corslet and a horse to separate individuals. This contrasts markedly with the majority of the so-called chariot tablets, which record the issue of equipment obviously meant for charioteers or chariot warriors—namely, a corslet, a chariot, and a pair of horses. Sir Arthur Evans believed that the scribes of the two tablets

7

that lacked the chariot sign had simply been in a hurry and abbreviated their notations by omitting the chariot character or sign.[3] Although plausible, this explanation is not convincing. In fact, if one considers how little time would have been saved by deleting one or two Linear B characters, this explanation seems highly improbable. If ancient scribes wrote such characters as easily and rapidly as modern authors or secretaries write words, then each character took no more than a second or two, at the most, to form or scribe on the clay tablet. Thus, the omissions on the two tablets in question amounted to a savings of about four seconds. Only if the enemy were at the very gates of the palace would a few seconds seem to matter—and in that case, the warriors' equipment probably would have been issued without accounting for it at all.

Some scholars have argued that the Linear B tablets recording less than a complete equipment issue simply indicate the equipment the warriors lacked; thus, the soldiers in question each had a chariot and a single horse but needed a second horse and body armor.[4] Again, this is a plausible explanation, but it is not very persuasive. If some of the tablets do record replacement issue, then one would expect to find more variety in the combinations of needed equipment. Considering that the most vulnerable parts of a chariot were the wheels and axle, for example, these items should have been disbursed regularly. Similarly, because unshod horses went lame easily, a horse or two should appear consistently on replacement equipment lists. We might expect to see a combination of a wheel and a horse or perhaps the corslet, an expendable piece of armor often damaged in combat.

Because the chariot tablets as a group seem to show the disbursement of complete issues, the most plausible explanation here is that the complete issue for the two individuals in question was a corslet and a single horse. Thus, the two recipients wore armor and were mounted on horseback.[5]

Representations of various kinds and from diverse locales enhance the picture and give us a clue as to the appearance and capabilities of these mounted warriors. An amphoriod crater with Cyro-Minoan script dating to the fourteenth century B.C. shows a chariot with three unarmed occupants preceded by a rider who wears a coni-cal helmet and body armor. Although the rider has no visible weap-ons, he is obviously meant to be an escort, or horse guard, for the chariot and its occupants.[6]

Two figurines of mounted warriors have been recovered from Mycenae, showing that, although Agamemnon may have used a chariot at Troy, the mounted warrior had apparently made his ap-pearance at Mycenae by 1300 B.C. The best-preserved piece (Figure 2.1) depicts a rider wearing a conical helmet. He is clasping some sort of weapon in his right hand—a sword or dagger in a sheath or possi-bly a quiver.[7] Two other mounted warriors (Figure 2.2) apparently ap-pear in the shards of a fresco found in the remains of the Megaron. Both warriors wear body armor. One is leading two horses by their bridles, and the second stands on the far side of the horses, holding a spear. The second warrior is also wearing a helmet and greaves.[8]

A mounted warrior figurine has also been found at Prosymna, near Argos, by Carl Blegen. This figure differed from the others only in that the horse was missing; the warrior has his legs astride, clearly indicating that he was originally mounted.[9] Nonmilitary riding figu-rines have also been found. In a tomb at Spata in Attica, for instance, figures of both male and female riders were discovered, proving that horseback riding was not confined to Greek males alone.[10]

One can speculate on the military capabilities of the Mycenaean horsemen based on the equipment they are known to have used. The fact that body armor is prevalent among the represented figures and in the Linear B records indicates that close combat was a possi-bility. In most of the known representations, shields are not present, and because some figurines are fully intact, this seems to rule out dismounted combat. A. M. Snodgrass has demonstrated that through-out the Mycenaean period, a variety of shields were used by the in-fantry soldiers. For the late Mycenaean period, the Warrior Vase shows an infantry formation with all the soldiers carrying identical shields.[11] The weapons visible with the mounted figures are the sword and the spear. Several types of spears were prevalent in the Mycenaean period, and virtually any of these could have been used on horseback. The one exception is the massive weapon whose

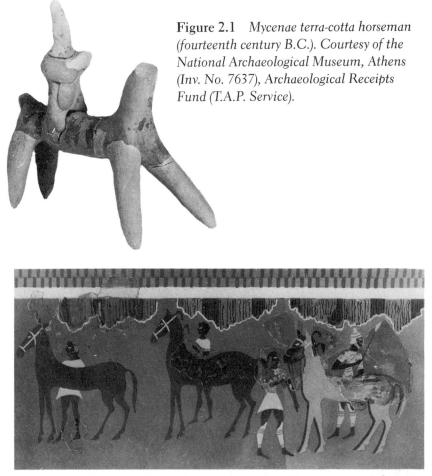

Figure 2.1 *Mycenae terra-cotta horseman (fourteenth century B.C.). Courtesy of the National Archaeological Museum, Athens (Inv. No. 7637), Archaeological Receipts Fund (T.A.P. Service).*

Figure 2.2 *Horsemen fresco from Mycenae (late Mycenaean period). Courtesy of the National Archaeological Museum, Athens (Inv. No. 2915), Archaeological Receipts Fund (T.A.P. Service)*

spearhead was 2 feet long, probably having an overall length of about 10 feet.[12] The size of this weapon would have made it extremely difficult to wield on horseback.

The swords shown on the figurines are sheathed, with the sheath attached to the chest of the rider diagonally from the left shoulder area toward the lower right torso area. This rather unusual arrangement limited the length of the sword to something less than 24 inches. Although this appears to be a rather short weapon for a mounted warrior (unless his opponent was also mounted or the cavalryman was going to dismount and fight close combat on foot), the *kopis* used by later cavalrymen was about the same length.[13] It is also possible that longer swords were used when they became available and hung in a different scabbard arrangement, unknown to us today. In fact, it may be that the needs of the mounted warrior led to the development of the longer swords common in the Mycenaean period.

Archaeological sites on both Crete and Greece have yielded long rapier-type weapons of the necessary length for use as slashing weapons on horseback. These rapiers were of Minoan origin, and many exceeded 3 feet in length.[14] Regardless of their length, spears and swords were close-combat weapons. Thus, the mounted warriors of this period who wore body armor and fought with spears and swords were equipped to fight mounted and at close range. Although none of our sources indicates the use of mounted warriors as a group or unit of cavalry, the possibility exists that a few small cavalry units were formed and employed. Whether the Mycenaean mounted warriors rode as individuals or in small groups, this marked the beginning of cavalry for the ancient Greeks.

The interest in mounting an armed man on a horse was not unique to the Greeks but seems to have been part of a trend throughout the eastern Mediterranean toward the end of the Bronze Age. Perhaps the true limitations of the chariot were recognized, and another method of mobility on the battlefield was sought. After all, chariots bogged down in loose sand or soil, broke wheels on rocks, were restricted in their movements, and were stopped completely by rough terrain, hilly country, and narrow passes. In contrast, the horse and rider could cross loose sand and soil, and traverse difficult terrain and narrow passes quite easily. In short, although the chariot at times was a better, more stable firing platform, cavalry was superior because of its greater mobility.[15]

Mounted warriors appeared in Egypt by the fourteenth century B.C., as they had in the Aegean. A battle-ax from the Eighteenth Dynasty has a decorative, open-worked blade depicting a rider mounted on a mare. Considering this decoration, it is likely that this battle-ax was used by a mounted warrior, and the depiction may represent the man who actually carried this ax.[16] A more graphic piece of evidence appears on a plaque of glazed steatite from the reign of Thutmose III. The scene on the plaque shows an Egyptian mounted warrior armed with a mace and a bow. The warrior's horse is shown trampling a fallen foe.[17]

By the time of the Battle of Kadesh (c. 1285 B.C.), the Egyptian army had at least one unit of mounted scouts or perhaps the first mounted archers in the Near East. The various reliefs depicting the battle show a number of mounted riders. Several of them are armed with bows, bows and quivers, or quivers alone, which indicates they were mounted archers. One of the horsemen armed with a bow is identified by the accompanying inscription as "the scout of the army of Pharaoh."[18] Another armed with bow and quiver was an officer. A. R. Schulman believes that these horse-archers were part of a unit of mounted scouts. Although this group was small and new at the time of Kadesh, its mission was important and included scouting and messenger duties.[19] The reliefs also show a group of dismounted archers leading their horses. Though the exact intent of these archers is unclear, dismounting would enable them to shoot more accurately and farther than they could on horseback or to lower their profile while scouting the enemy during battle.[20]

Egypt's neighbors also had mounted warriors. The tablets discovered at Nuzi, dating from the fifteenth century B.C., record that the army of Mitanni was composed of infantry, chariots, and cavalry.[21] Egyptian reliefs from the reign of Seti I (c. 1318–1304 B.C.) display armed and mounted Syrian and Hittite warriors. The Hittite horsemen wore plumed helmets and quivers slung over their backs. One of the representations shows a fleeing warrior with his shield transfixed by an arrow from the pharaoh's bow. Although the fleeing man has no weapon, the presence of the shield rules out the possibility that he was a mounted archer; most likely, he carried a spear or javelins.[22]

Later evidence regarding Syria and other parts of the Near East demonstrates that the mounted warrior had progressed to true cavalry a hundred years or so after the Battle of Kadesh. From Ugarit in northern Syria, the fragments of a crater in the late Mycenaean style (end of the twelfth century B.C.) show a frieze of horsemen, one of whom is clearly armed with a poniard. This group has been identified as a file of Ugarit cavalry, and here, for the first time, is the representation of a group of horsemen riding together, apparently in formation.[23] By the tenth century B.C., cavalry was not uncommon in the Near East. The Aramaic cavalry was equipped with helmets and small round shields that could be slung over the backs of the riders to free their hands and armed with spears or javelins.[24]

As the Bronze Age drew to an end, warfare erupted throughout the eastern Mediterranean and affected all the societies and cultures of the area. In Greece, this time marked the beginning of the Dark Age. As with virtually every other aspect of Greek life and culture, there is little evidence from the Dark Age to help us understand mounted warfare and the development of Greek cavalry. J. K. Anderson concluded that the aristocrats and nobles of that age employed war chariots in combat in the fashion portrayed in Homer: The warrior, driven to the battle in his chariot, dismounted and fought on foot, with the charioteer remaining close by to allow for a quick withdrawal.[25] Yet chariot warfare was the product of fairly sophisticated, complex societies, whether in Egypt, Hatti, Assyria, or Greece. Did that structure exist in Dark Age Greece? Most ancient historians agree that the fall of the Mycenaean palace centers in the twelfth century B.C. destroyed the fragile network that included court and religious officials, public servants, military officers, merchants, craftsmen, and scribes. In short, only the routines of those in the lowest level of society—farmers and shepherds—were likely to have endured in much the same fashion as before. And it is probable that the people needed to build and maintain the chariots were unavailable in the depopulated, fragmented, and impoverished village society of the Dark Age.

No doubt, the conditions of the Dark Age also adversely affected the development of the mounted warrior or cavalryman, yet there is some evidence that indicates a continuation of the mounted warrior in the Greek world. A vase from Mouliana in Crete (Figure 2.3), which is variously dated as Sub-Mycenaean, Proto-Geometric, or even early Geometric, contains the only surviving representation of a mounted warrior before the mid–eighth century B.C. The warrior

Figure 2.3   *Dark Age Greek mounted warrior (Geometric period). Courtesy of the Heraklion Museum, Heraklion, Crete.*

wears a conical helmet, is armed with a spear, and carries a shield that has a telamon or strap. The shield appears as a convex targe or small, circular, outwardly curved buckler, with a flat extension on the lower edge, possibly representing a leather flap or apron similar to those used on hoplite shields for a time.[26] Snodgrass proposed that this figure depicts the infancy of Greek cavalry.[27] Crouwell concluded that because of the shield, this warrior had difficulty controlling his horse and fighting mounted, and therefore that he may have been the predecessor of the mounted hoplite.[28]

In fact, this cavalryman probably was able to fight equally well mounted or dismounted and thus may have been a dragoon. The presence of the spear shows that he was equipped for close combat, either on horseback or on foot. Since only one spear is present, the warrior apparently had no intention of throwing the weapon but probably used it as a thrusting spear. The presence of the shield clearly indicates that he was equipped to fight dismounted, but this cannot be used to rule out mounted combat. Although the earlier Mycenaean mounted warriors and the later Classical period cavalrymen did not, as a rule, carry shields, other ancient peoples fighting on horseback did carry and use shields. As mentioned earlier, the Aramaic cavalryman of the tenth century B.C. was equipped in a similar fashion to the Mouliana warrior. The Greek cavalrymen of Cumae also carried shields and passed this practice on to the early Roman cavalry.[29] And at the end of the ancient era, the standard equipment for the mounted Gothic noble was body armor of ring mail or scale armor, crested helmet, sword, dagger, lance, and round shield.[30] Further, the fact that the Dark Age warrior's shield had a telamon and was fairly small meant it could be used while mounted or pushed around and fastened on the rider's back, thus freeing both of the warrior's hands if necessary.

Equipment consistent with that represented on the vases from Mouliana and suitable for mounted warriors has been found in various Dark Age grave sites. A bronze, conical helmet with cheek pieces dating to the mid–eleventh century B.C. was found at Tiryns.[31] There are remains of spears and spearheads at Tiryns and Athens and in Macedonia. Interestingly, according to Snodgrass, from about 900 B.C. onward, it was the practice to inter multiple spears or spearheads with the deceased warrior. Considering that warriors were buried with their personal weapons—weapons they carried into battle—the multiple spears may, indeed, represent a shift in warfare to an emphasis on the thrown spear, or javelin.[32] Greek mounted warriors and cavalry carried javelins at various times. A grave at Tiryns yielded spearheads of approximately 9.5, 10, and 12.5 inches.[33] The two smaller ones are no doubt javelin heads, and the longer is the appropriate length for a thrusting spear. A warrior grave at Athens contained various iron objects, including a long sword, a large and a small spear, and a pair of horse bits.[34] A spear found in a Macedonian grave had an iron head of approximately 11 inches, a 2.5-inch iron butt, and the remains of a shaft 6 feet 2 inches in length; the overall length of this spear was 7 feet 3 inches.[35] An iron slashing sword with an ivory handle was found at Fortetsa in Crete.[36] This sword type marked a real change in the design of swords, which previously had been thrusting weapons for the most part, and it was particularly useful to a man on horseback whose natural motion with a sword was a slash, as opposed to a thrust.[37] Finally, several sites mentioned earlier, including Tiryns, Athens, and

Figure 2.4 *Mounted warrior wearing bell-shaped corslet following chariot (late Geometric Attic amphora). Courtesy of the Buffalo Museum of Science, Buffalo, New York.*

Mouliana, have yielded the metal fittings and bosses associated with Dark Age shields, made largely of perishable materials.[38] Such shields were light enough for use by horsemen.

Evidence directly links the aristocrats with cavalry warfare toward the end of the Dark Age and the beginning of the Archaic period. A late Geometric Attic amphora (Figure 2.4) shows a scene with chariots in a procession. Following these vehicles is a mounted warrior with a spear. While the amphora warrior may be wearing a helmet, he is definitely wearing a bell-shaped corslet with a jutting lower rim. The warrior rides on one horse; another has been drawn on the warrior's far side, but no second rider is shown. The general opinion concerning this lack of a second rider is that it was convenient for the artist to draw only one and that the second rider was the squire of the amphora warrior.[39] Of course, it is possible that the warrior was a cavalryman leading a spare mount or even that the artist did not paint the second figure because he was identical to the first and riding exactly parallel to him. Thus, this vase painting was perhaps meant to show a pair of aristocratic mounted warriors riding side by side or in formation. In any case, the amphora warrior was an aristocratic cavalryman who was, at the very least, prepared to use his mount for combat mobility at this stage.[40]

The evidence of the Attic amphora is strengthened considerably by artifacts from a tomb in Argos that was contemporary with the amphora. This tomb contained armor identical to that worn by the amphora warrior, proving that the armor was available at that time and used by aristocrats. Interred with the dead warrior were a bronze helmet with a high crest, as well as both the front and back halves of a bronze, bell-shaped corslet obviously meant for a mounted warrior.[41] The bell corslet, as its name implies, flares outward toward the waist area. This allowed for the expansion of the stomach and lower torso area while the horseman was sitting on his mount. Moreover, the armorer who constructed it took special care to roll up or round the bronze of the jutting lower edge. Although no armorer would have left any sharp edges, the special care given the rim clearly indicates that it would come into contact with the wearer's lower torso and upper thighs—a type of contact that would obviously occur while riding a horse.

One of the contemporary Greek literary sources may well have given a description of some of the ways in which a Dark Age aristocratic mounted warrior employed his horse in combat. In the *Iliad,* Homer showed the Greeks preparing for battle, with Agamemnon deploying the army:

> The Achaians again put on their armour, and remembered, their warcraft. Then you would not have seen brilliant Agamemnon

asleep nor skulking aside, nor in any way a reluctant fighter, but driving eagerly toward the fighting where men win glory. He left aside
his chariot gleaming with bronze, and his horses, and these, breath-
ing hard, were held aside by a henchman, Eurymedon, born to
Ptolemaios, the son of Peiraios. Agamemnon told him to keep them
well in hand, till the time came when weariness might take hold of
his limbs, through marshalling so many. Then he, on foot as he was,
ranged through the ranks of the fighters.[42]

Later, Agamemnon was wounded and withdrew:

As the sharp sorrow of pain descends on a woman in labour, the bit-
terness that the hard spirits of childbirth bring on, Hera's daughters,
who hold the power of the bitter birthpangs, so the sharp pains began to break in on the strength of Atreides [Agamemnon]. He sprang
back into the car, and called on his charioteer to drive him back to
the hollow ships, since his heart was heavy.[43]

And when the Trojans broke before the onslaught of Achilleus,
the Greek hero pursued:

So before great-hearted Achilleus the single-foot horses trampled
alike dead men and shields, and the axle under the chariot was all
splashed with blood and the rails which encircled the chariot, struck
by flying drops from the feet of the horses, from the running rims of
the wheels. The son of Peleus was straining to win glory.[44]

Obviously, Homer had Agamemnon and all his heroes using the
chariot, but it has been argued that this great epic poet intentionally
introduced this anachronistic vehicle in order to give his work more
of a heroic character. In fact, some say, Homer was showing how the
mounted war-horse was used in his own day.[45] One of the leading pro-
ponents of this argument, Greenhalgh, pointed out that such a practice—the introduction of anachronistic elements by Homer—occurred in other areas also; Homer had all his warriors use bronze
weapons, despite the fact that archaeological evidence for the Dark
Age reveals that almost all weapons were made of iron.[46] Further,
Homer's language, Greenhalgh continued, showed a familiarity with
the practice of the mounted warrior accompanied by the mounted
squire.[47] "Finally there is the fact that the Homeric chariots were rep-

resented as transporting individual warriors in the thick of the fighting on the field of battle itself, and there is no doubt that its greater
mobility, simplicity and maneuverability make that role a far more
practical possibility for the mounted horse than for the chariot."[48]

Thus, the Dark Age mounted warrior used his horse as transportation to the battlefield. After dismounting, his squire kept the war-
horse close by, perhaps just behind the front ranks of the army and
just out of harm's way, in readiness for the hippeus to remount. The
warrior remounted his horse to leave the combat if he was tired or
wounded or perhaps when he needed to pursue the enemy. This
means that Dark Age cavalry was in the first stage of development,
in which the horse was used as a rapid conveyance to the battlefield.

While there is some uncertainty about this interpretation of
Homer, it is certain that aristocratic political organization and cavalry warfare were both sufficiently well established in Greece in the
eighth century B.C. to be transplanted to one of the first Greek colo-
nies. Cumae, founded about 750 B.C., was the colony of Chalcis in
Euboea. Aristotle acknowledged that the government of the *hip-
pobotai*, the equestrians or horsemen, sent out this Chalcidian colony.[49] Although the Euboeans did not sail west in order to breed
horses, the wide Campanian plain must have been very inviting, in-
fluencing settlers from a horse-breeding Greek aristocracy. The earliest Greek settlement no doubt was concentrated on and around the
acropolis at Cumae (as an earlier pre-Hellenic community had been),
but within a short period of time, Greek Cumae spread its control
outward. Tombs of the wealthy Greeks have been found extending
north from the city gate more than 2 kilometers. By the sixth century B.C., Cumae controlled territory as far north as Naples and
across the plain to the Clanis River.

The tombs of Cumae have yielded horse bits from the earliest
settlement until well into the Greek period. One fairly typical Hel-
lenic tomb contained gold, silver, and bronze ornaments, a large
round shield, a dagger, a Greek iron sword, a number of spearheads,
and an iron horse bit.[50] The association of shield and horse bit seems
to imply that the deceased may have fought in the Homeric fashion,
but later cavalrymen from this area carried shields and fought
mounted—a practice that clearly started at this early date. Without a

doubt, this hippeus was equipped to fight either on horseback or dismounted. The city's influence in warfare, controlling territory from Cumae to Naples, spread ever farther north. Capua, for example, adopted Greek-style cavalry as a direct result of the Cumaean mounted tradition,[51] and Rome later followed suit. Polybius recorded the reasons for this:

> Since therefore their arms did not stand the test of experience, they soon took to making them in the Greek fashion, which ensures that the first stroke of the lance-head shall be both well aimed and telling, since the lance is so constructed as to be steady and strong, and also that it may continue to be effectively used by reversing it and striking with the spike at the butt end. And the same applies to the Greek shields, which being of solid and firm texture do good service both in defence and attack.[52]

Other sources attest to the size and the proficiency of the Cumaean cavalry. In Dionysius of Halicarnassus' account of the struggles between the Cumaeans and the Etruscans about 524 B.C., Cumaean forces consisted of 4,500 infantry and 600 cavalry. Although heavily outnumbered, the Cumaeans defeated their enemy largely because of superior mounted forces. The prize of valor was awarded to Hippomedon, the *hipparchos,* or cavalry commander.[53]

Hippomedon and his hippeis were the product of seven hundred years of cavalry development. The first phase of this evolution was over for the Greeks: The horse was no longer simply a means of conveyance to and from the battlefield. The Mycenaeans probably began the use of the mounted warrior as an experiment, a means of more conveniently transporting the armored soldier. Ultimately, cavalry survived the hardships and instabilities of the Dark Age to emerge as an institution that was so much a part of the Greek social, political, and military life that it was transplanted with Greek colonization. Now, the mounted warrior was ready to assume a place of importance and prominence on the battlefields of the Greek world.

3

Greek Cavalry
in the Archaic Period

According to Aristotle, "After kingship the earliest governments among the Greeks gave political rights to the warrior class, and in the beginning were made up of the *hippeis,* for with the *hippeis* rested strength and superiority in war at the time."[1] Although Aristotle's evidence has been questioned by some scholars, events in the Archaic period seem to justify his assessment. This period opened with two wars, the First Messenian War and the Lelantine War, in which cavalry played important, if not decisive, roles. Throughout the period, cavalry developed in various localities in Greece, but the hoplite and the phalanx gradually became the principal forces on the battlefield. Yet Greek cavalry did not disappear; instead, it altered its tactics to take into account the speed and mobility of the horse and concentrated on harassing, screening, and pursuing.

One of the earliest twentieth-century works on Greek cavalry set the tone for later scholars who disregarded or ignored Aristotle's evaluation of warfare in the early Archaic period. W. Helbig argued the hippeis were simply mounted hoplites or mounted infantry and never fought on horseback. Much of the evidence he used consisted of pictorial representations on vases. The typical warrior vase shows a mounted man arrayed in the complete hoplite panoply, including metal helmet, breastplate, greaves, large circular shield, and a single spear. This warrior is accompanied by a second rider, who is usually unarmed and unarmored. Helbig's conclusion was that this pair represented an aristocratic warrior and his squire; for combat, the warrior dismounted and fought on foot while the squire kept the horse close by but out of danger. Thus, he concluded, there was no cavalry in Greece at this time.[2]

More recently, Greenhalgh defended Helbig's conclusions. He asserted that Aristotle said virtually nothing about cavalry and mounted combat and did not relate how the horses were employed by the hippeis. According to Greenhalgh, the strength in warfare lay with the hippeis because they alone used horses—as means of transport in wars waged against their neighbors, before there was a hoplite force and phalanx organization with the necessary techniques and tactics. Aristotle may have assumed the early Archaic warrior class was true cavalry, but how much could he have really known about warfare three hundred years before his own time? For Greenhalgh, the weight of archaeological evidence, vases similar to those Helbig used, and the Homeric epics clearly indicated that Archaic hippeis used their horses principally for transportation.[3]

J.A.O. Larsen was also convinced that Aristotle's hippeis did not exist as a cavalry force. He argued that they rode chariots into battle in earlier periods of Greek history but usually dismounted for actual combat. This practice may have continued to the time when the Homeric epics were composed. After chariots disappeared, according to this view, there were absolutely no mounted troops in Greece for a while, but the name hippeis continued to be applied to a few privileged warriors. This name was then transferred to those individuals who started to use horses as transport but fought as infantrymen. Larsen contended that cavalry appeared late in ancient Greece, beginning in Thessaly. Mounted warfare then spread south to the areas closest to Thessaly; Thebes adopted cavalry sometime before 480 B.C., and later, other Greeks followed suit.[4]

All of these scholars have made interesting arguments. However, it seems necessary to comment briefly on several points. First, Helbig's pictorial evidence was almost exclusively from a hundred years or more after the beginning of the Archaic period. The hoplite reform or revolution had already taken place, and warfare, as well as politics and society, had changed dramatically when the vases he analyzed were made and decorated. It is true many practices in warfare carried on unchanged for centuries, but the hoplite reform was fundamental and far reaching. Evidence that dates from a period after the reform, such as the vase paintings mentioned previously, may not accurately reflect practices in the earlier period of warfare and cannot support the conclusion that all mounted warriors served only as mounted infantry.

With regard to Aristotle's statement and the extent of his knowledge, which Greenhalgh questioned, almost all scholars recognize the truth of this philosopher's views about the end of Greek monarchy insofar as political control and power are concerned. Most basic texts on Greek history depict the early Archaic period as one dominated by aristocracies. It seems unlikely that Aristotle could be so correct about the political environment and yet so completely incorrect about the military environment. Finally, Larsen seemed to completely ignore the evidence for horsemen in warfare before the Archaic period, and thus he saw no basis for continuity.

Pausanias' account of the First Messenian War, which can be dated to about 740–720 B.C. or the early part of the Archaic period, showed that both the Spartans and the Messenians possessed and employed cavalry in the war, thus confirming Aristotle.[5] In the third year after the fall of Amphea, Euphaes, the Messenian king, took the field because he believed his forces were disciplined enough to confront the Spartans. The army was commanded by Cleonnis, and Pytharatus and Antander commanded the cavalry and light infantry, together numbering about 500 men. The Messenian army was drawn up on a field that had a *charadra*, or deep ravine, running down most of its length. One scholar has identified this charadra as the Charadros River and placed the battlefield site near the Karnasion grove.[6] To strengthen their position, the Messenians constructed a palisade to reinforce and protect an exposed area. When the Messenian and Spartan armies advanced, the deep glen prevented the main bodies from closing. Because the glen did not run the entire length of the field, the cavalry and light infantry of both armies fought above that glen. This combat was not decisive because the Messenians and Spartans were evenly matched in horsemen and light-armed troops.[7]

This short surviving account indicated that both sides not only had about the same number of cavalry and light infantry soldiers but also that they fought in similar fashions. Obviously, the mounted and light troops of the opponents were positioned on a single wing of their respective armies, facing each other above the glen. Since Pausanias seemed to show that Euphaes or Cleonnis chose the field of battle, it is clear that the Messenian army was drawn up first and that the Spartans deployed their troops in response to their opponent. Possibly, the Messenian commanders chose the field because the glen was an obstacle to the main body of the enemy: It would break up any advance by the Spartan heavy infantry. If the Messenians felt their cavalry and light infantry were equal or superior to the Spartans, the glen was not a hindrance to victory but a tactical asset to be exploited.

The First Messenian War apparently took a heavy toll on the horsemen of both sides. During a later battle in the fourth year after the fall of Amphea, cavalry was once again employed by the opposing armies. However, Pausanias stated that the bulk of the fighting was done by the infantry because the mounted troops of both sides were very few in number.[8] This attrition may well have been severe by the end of the war; in the last battle, fought at the foot of Mt. Ithome, no cavalry was present.[9]

Due to the lack of sources, it is impossible to discuss the Messenian cavalry, but some information about the Spartan horsemen can be discerned. The Spartan hippeis had a traditional strength of 300 men. This number probably represented equal recruitment or selection from the three Dorian tribes of Spartan society; thus, the tribes of Hylleis, Dymanes, and Pamphyli each supplied 100 men. At some early time, the hippeis were undoubtedly close followers of the king or kings; they were aristocrats who advised the king and accompanied him in battle, and they may have used chariots. However, by the Archaic period, the chariot had been replaced by the horse, and these mounted warriors, as Pausanias' account of the First Messenian War showed, functioned as cavalry.[10] The military reforms of Lycurgus that were enacted about the time of the First Messenian War—or at least those credited to him—saw the Spartan cavalry organized into 6 *oulamoi,* or troops, with each

Figure 3.1 *Spartan hippeus (seventh century B.C. ivory fibula-plaque). Courtesy of the National Archaeological Museum, Athens (Inv. No. 15355), Archaeological Receipts Fund (T.A.P. Service).*

troop composed of 50 men.[11] It seems reasonable to assume that each troop was commanded by a troop leader, that each tribal squadron of 2 troops had a commander, and that, at times, the regiment of hippeis had an overall commander, possibly one of the kings or an appointee.[12]

Plutarch told us the standard formation for each troop was a square. By that, he might have meant that each troop formed with a depth and a front of 7 men, totaling 49 without the troop leader. More probably, Plutarch referred to distance rather than to the number of men or horses. Logically, a troop of 50 men could form a square that consisted of 10 files of 5 men each. With a distance of 2 horses' widths or 2 yards between files and an interval of 1 horse's length or 3 yards between ranks, the formation would have been a square measuring about 27 yards on each side.[13] The only evidence that possibly reveals the equipment of the Spartan hippeis is an ivory fibula-plaque (Figure 3.1) from the early seventh century B.C. The plaque was found in the sanctuary of Artemis Orthia at Sparta. The representation on the plaque shows a tunic-clad rider, armed with a spear and carrying a round shield. The shield does not appear to be the large *hoplon* of the later hoplite but rather a smaller, round buckler. Both the spear and the shield are carried on the left side, thus presumably freeing the right hand to hold the horse's reins.[14] A cavalryman armed in such a fashion would have been capable of engaging in mounted shock warfare against either cavalry or infantry, prior to the hoplite reform and the advent of the phalanx, or of dismounting and fighting on foot. Thus, the fibula warrior could very well be considered a dragoon.

It seems likely Sparta's cavalry ceased to exist as a functioning mounted military unit when the Spartans embarked upon their most egalitarian reforms, namely, the elimination of the obvious signs of wealth from their society and the compulsory training of all their males as professional soldiers and hoplites. An elite, privileged, mounted force would have, in fact, shown that equality of hardship and service was a falsehood. This move may well have occurred during the Second Messenian War (c. 640–620 B.C.). Tyrtaeus, who apparently was a Spartan general as well as a poet, certainly spoke of hoplite warfare in his poetry when he exhorted, "To die, fallen in the front line, a brave man fighting for his fatherland, is honorable; but to leave one's city and its rich fields and live as a beggar is the depth of misery."[15] Further, the threat to Sparta at this time was grave enough to make drastic change acceptable to the population. For at least part of the war, the Messenians, the Arcadians, and the Argives were all hostile to Sparta, posing a threat on three fronts. In the face of this danger, the Spartans might readily have accepted mandatory, strict, and harsh military training for all males.

Although there was a time of visible Spartan prosperity in the immediate postwar period—made notable by the poetry of Alcman, the construction of the temple to Artemis Orthia, and the Scias adorned with sculpture by Theodorus of Samos—this faded as the sixth century B.C. progressed. Before the middle of the century, Sparta became laconic and Spartan. The name *hippeis* was now applied to the foot-guard of the king in battle. And the tradition and history of cavalry warfare were lost, thus leading Thucydides to report one hundred and fifty years later, that during the Peloponnesian War, the Spartans deployed cavalry for the first time.[16]

Other areas of Archaic Greece, however, continued to use cavalry in war. The sources for the Lelantine War, at the very end of the eighth century B.C., clearly showed the use of cavalry in Euboea by Chalcis, Eretria, and the Thessalians. This war was fought by the cities of Chalcis and Eretria over the Lelantine Plain on the island. The strength of Chalcis at this time is unknown, but had the citizens of the city not felt comparable in strength and ability to Eretria, they would not have entered into a war that was seemingly lost from the start. Aristotle did say Chalcis and Eretria both raised and used horses in war.[17] The Eretrian military strength for this period, as recorded on a pillar dedicated to Artemis Amarynthia, encompassed 3,000 heavy infantry, 600 cavalry, and 60 chariots. By Greek standards, this was a fairly high percentage of cavalry to infantry. Later, Athens had 1,200 cavalrymen and 29,000 hoplites, and the Boeotian League fielded 1,100 hippeis and 11,000 infantrymen.[18]

Strabo informed us that the Eretrians and the Chalcidians had reached an agreement prohibiting the use of long-range missiles by both sides in this conflict.[19] This agreement may well have been aimed at protecting the horses of the hippeis. Although mounted warriors of this period wore body armor and helmets and at times carried shields, as did the infantry, Greek cavalry horses were never armored. Thus, they were highly susceptible to wounds from arrows and sling bullets or stones. The effectiveness of archers and slingers against mounted troops was clearly evident in later times. Nicias, for example, asked the Athenians to send large numbers of archers with the Sicilian Expedition in order to counter the Syracusan horse.[20] Xenophon used Cretan archers and Rhodian slingers as part of the rear guard for the "Ten Thousand" to keep the Persian cavalry at bay.[21] Alexander supported the Thessalian cavalry with his Cretan archers on the left wing of the Macedonian army at Issus when they faced the numerically superior Persian horsemen.[22] And in the Middle Ages, the Second Lateran Council banned the use of the bow and crossbow from the field of combat when Christian armies contended, due to the deadly missile fire.[23] As it was, the Euboeans may have inflicted a considerable amount of damage on both men and horses with short-range missiles—namely, javelins.

Snodgrass wrote that the javelin's introduction into general use, starting in the Geometric period, was a major alteration of the pattern of warfare.[24] Other evidence seems to indicate that the islanders were still using the javelin extensively in the seventh century B.C. Archilochus, a soldier and poet from Naxos who lived in that century, commented on the use of the javelin in warfare between Paros and Naxos.[25] When writing about the Lelantine War, he said, "Not many bows will be stretched tight, nor frequent slings be whirled, when Ares joins men in the moil of war upon the plain, but swords will do their mournful work, for this is the warfare wherein those men are expert who rule over Euboea and are famous with the spear."[26] This quotation seems absurd to some scholars because, in hoplite warfare, the sword was an emergency weapon to be used only when the hoplite's spear broke. However, if the Euboean hippeis were armed with javelins and fought mounted, it makes perfect sense. At least one of the javelins would be thrown, and the second might be used as a spear for a time, but it, too, would be thrown or possibly broken because of the lightweight construction.[27] Then, the sword would be the mounted warrior's principal weapon for close combat. In the hands of a skilled cavalryman, the sword was a truly fearsome weapon, even in ancient times. Cleitus the Black saved the life of Alexander the Great at the Battle of Granicus when, using a sword, he cleaved off the arm of Spithridates.[28] In fact, Chalcis was the center for the production of the finest iron swords in Greece.[29]

In the ensuing war over the Lelantine Plain, both Chalcis and Eretria drew allies to their sides. Chalcis was joined by Samos and possibly Corinth. Eretria, which controlled Andros, Cos, and Tenos, received Megarian assistance. Thucydides said that all the rest of the Greeks took sides in this struggle.[30] The decisive victory was achieved by Chalcis when Cleomachus and some Thessalian mounted units joined the Chalcidians and defeated the Eretrian horsemen.[31]

Judging from the results of the Lelantine War, it would appear that by the end of the eighth century B.C., the Thessalian cavalry was well on its way to becoming the finest cavalry in ancient Greece, a reputation it retained until the time of Philip II and Alexander III of Macedon. Some credit the Thessalians' ability to their early acquaintance with the horse. Virgil wrote that the Lapithae, a people of Thessaly, were the first to mount on horseback, to apply the reins, to turn the horse in the ring, and to teach the armed horseman to spurn the plain.[32] Although they disagree with Virgil's assessment, some scholars believe that the Thessalians were the first Greeks to acquire the "great horse," a horse capable of carrying a man on its back in battle. Such horses came from the Kimmerioi, who moved off the steppes and poured into Asia. They passed on their line of horses to their kinsmen, the Thracians, who, in turn, gave them to the Greeks of Thessaly.[33]

Actually, the proficiency of the Thessalian horsemen should be seen as the result of emphasis and organization. Thessalian society was largely feudal in nature, with classes of serfs, *perioikoi*, or subordinate free people who dwelled in the foothills, free peasants, and the nobles. A few noble families, possibly numbering no more than 150, lived on large estates that encompassed most of the best land; they dominated their smaller neighbors.[34] As in the Middle Ages in Europe, the nobles set the tone for the society and emphasized riding and horsemanship. In part, this may have been due to practicality because the horse made it possible for the noble to get around his estate and supervise his serfs and dependents. But the horse was also the principal means of recreation. The national sport of the Thessalians was *tauroxathapsia*, or bullthrowing. This sport, which was similar to bulldogging in the U.S. rodeo, called for excellent horsemanship, good coordination, and superb physical conditioning. The rider chased a bull, reached over and clasped its horns, slid off his mount, and pulled the bull to the ground. Of course, the Thessalians also practiced and enjoyed horse racing. The Thessalians' early acquaintance with and skill in this sport is clearly demonstrated by the fact that the first horse-racing competition in the Olympic Games was won by a Thessalian.[35]

The organization of the Thessalian cavalry at the time of the Lelantine War is still not known precisely, but it seems to have been fairly rough and feudal in nature. The cavalry was composed of the lords, nobles, wealthy landowners, their free retainers, and, possibly at times, their *penestai*, or serfs. In times of conflict, each lord apparently gathered his followers and formed a mounted unit, for military service was part of the general obligations owed to the nobles by their followers. It was sometimes possible for an individual lord to assemble a small cavalry army, numbering as many as 200 or 300 men, from among his own retainers.[36] If the various lords' cavalry units were grouped into larger organizations, these composite units may have been based on the *moirai*, or districts. Thessaly was divided into four such districts in the seventh century B.C.[37]

The first known formal organization of the Thessalian army and cavalry occurred at the end of that century. Although Aleuas the Red is given credit for this, it is likely that many of his reforms were mere formalizations of practices that had been carried on for some time, possibly as long as a hundred years. With this new organization, each *kleros*, or division of land, was required to furnish a set number of military personnel—40 cavalrymen and 80 infantrymen—to the national army.[38] It seems logical to conclude that each 40-man contingent formed a troop, the lowest or basic unit of cavalry, and was led by a troop leader. Because the kleros was the basis for recruitment and the feudal nature of Thessaly remained strong, the local noble was probably still the troop leader. Several troops were almost certainly grouped into a squadron, and all the squadrons of a district no doubt formed a regiment with the tetrarch, or district leader, or someone appointed by him in command. The *tagos*, the supreme military leader, was the only one who could mobilize the Thessalian national army, and he commanded it in the field. If traditional numbers can be trusted, the strength of the army of the tagos was 6,000 cavalrymen, 10,000 infantrymen, and numerous light-armed troops.[39]

The corps of 6,000 horsemen was by far the largest of any political entity in ancient Greece. At some point, the squadrons of the Thessalian cavalry adopted a rhomboid, or diamond-shaped, formation. Aelian, though noting that the credit for this was given to Jason of Pherae, believed this formation was much older and was attributed to Jason falsely. It seems possible that this unique formation could have been adopted as early as the seventh century B.C. because this would explain the early success of the Thessalian horse. Obviously, a single troop could deploy in such a formation, and it may have been the basis of larger ones; the number of men in each line of the rhomboid formation would progress from 1 to 3 to 5 and so forth, as represented in Figure 3.2, for a total of 41 men. Four troops were probably united to form a squadron: It would be a simple matter to unite 4 small diamond formations into a squadron rhomboid of about 160 men.[40] Officers rode at the four points of this formation, and the squadron was led by an *ilarchos*, or squadron com-

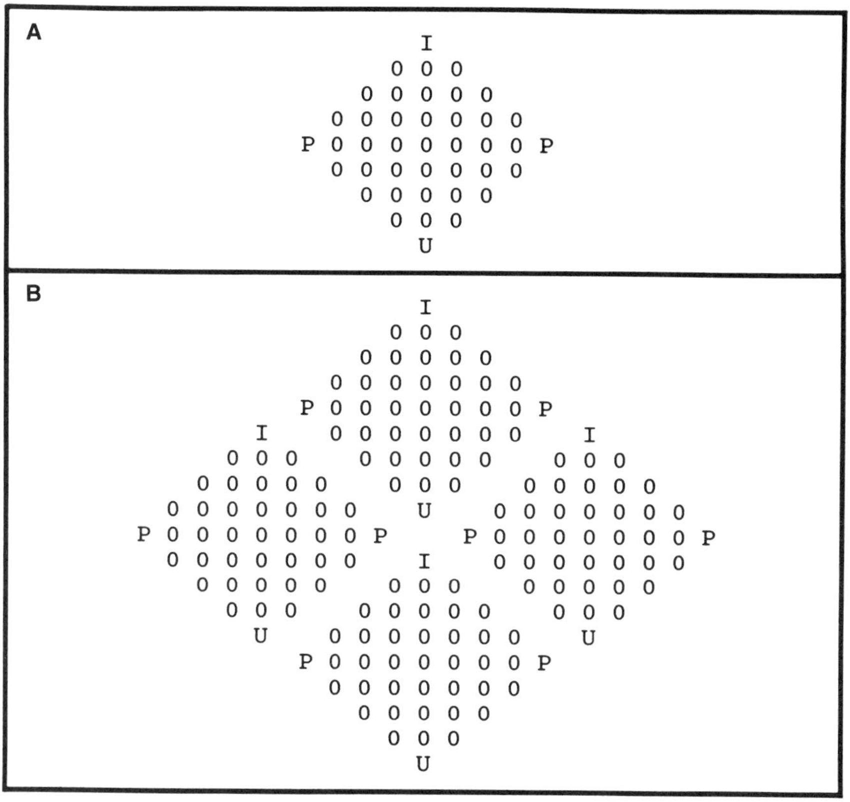

```
A                                   I
                                  0 0 0
                                0 0 0 0 0
                              0 0 0 0 0 0 0
                          P 0 0 0 0 0 0 0 0 P
                              0 0 0 0 0 0 0
                                0 0 0 0 0
                                  0 0 0
                                    U
```

```
B                                   I
                                  0 0 0
                                0 0 0 0 0
                              0 0 0 0 0 0 0
                          P 0 0 0 0 0 0 0 0 P
              I               0 0 0 0 0 0 0              I
            0 0 0               0 0 0 0 0             0 0 0
          0 0 0 0 0               0 0 0           0 0 0 0 0
        0 0 0 0 0 0 0             U             0 0 0 0 0 0 0
      P 0 0 0 0 0 0 0 0 P               P 0 0 0 0 0 0 0 0 P
        0 0 0 0 0 0 0             I             0 0 0 0 0 0 0
          0 0 0 0 0             0 0 0             0 0 0 0 0
            0 0 0           0 0 0 0 0               0 0 0
              U           0 0 0 0 0 0 0              U
                        P 0 0 0 0 0 0 0 0 P
                          0 0 0 0 0 0 0
                            0 0 0 0 0
                              0 0 0
                                U
```

I Ilarchos
P Plagiophylakoi
U Uragos
0 Cavalry Troopers

Figure 3.2 *Thessalian cavalry troop (A) and squadron (B) rhomboid or diamond formations.*

mander, who rode at the fore-point. At the rear-point rode the *uragos,* and the *plagiophylakoi* rode on the side angles. The best cavalrymen rode on the outsides, while the inexperienced and weaker occupied the center.[41]

Our ancient sources tell us this formation was very successful because it was hard to throw into disorder. It could be led by simply having all the horsemen follow the ilarchos. The wedge-shaped formation used by the Scythians and Macedonians was praised for this same reason for "all have their eyes fixed on the single squadron commander, as is the case also in the flight of cranes."[42] But in the case of the rhomboid, the whole formation could also turn at the same time in almost any direction as a single entity and still be led by an officer, thanks to the formation's shape and the fact that officers were positioned at all four points. Finally, the rhomboid was very suitable for shock tactics. When attacking another formation, whether a square or rectangle, infantry or cavalry, the initial penetration was made by a point and gradually expanded. This may have been effective even against the early hoplite phalanx.

Although the Thessalian cavalry was the best in Greece, it was small and one dimensional by comparison with cavalry in other parts of the eastern Mediterranean. By far the best mounted force at this time was the Assyrian cavalry, and when it is compared to various Greek cavalry units, the latter fade almost to insignificance. In fact, some scholars give the Assyrians credit for developing the first true cavalry. Richard A. Gabriel said, "A major Assyrian revolution in battlefield capability was the invention of cavalry."[43] Similarly, Arther Ferrill commented that "the Assyrians were the first major power to use regular cavalry units."[44]

Cavalry was introduced into the Assyrian army by Tukulti-Ninurta (c. 890–884 B.C.). The first Assyrian cavalry was composed of mounted archers or light cavalrymen, who wore helmets but no body armor. Apparently, the mounted archers had trouble controlling their horses at crucial moments when both hands were needed to draw the bow and shoot the arrow. Therefore, the horsemen operated in pairs; as the archer busied himself with his bow, his companion riding to the left reached over and grasped the reins of the archer's horse in order to control the animal. This arrangement worked satisfactorily for some time. While mounted archers would normally not be thought of as shock troops, the reliefs of Ashurnasirpal (c. 883–859 B.C.) show the Assyrian mounted archers trampling their enemies under the hooves of their horses.[45] This would seem to indicate the Assyrians at times rode into and over their opponents, which is clearly a shock tactic.

By the end of the eighth century B.C., three distinct changes had occurred in the Assyrian cavalry. First, the mounted archers had acquired the necessary skills to manage their horses while using their weapons, and thus there was no need for companions. Second, the bow was no longer the only weapon of the cavalry; cavalrymen were armed with bows, bows and spears, or spears alone. Finally, all cavalrymen were equipped with conical helmets, iron-scale body armor or corslets, greaves, and boots.[46] These changes not only allowed for a doubling of the effective strength of the cavalry (because all riders could be employed as combatants), they also greatly increased the effectiveness and the potential use of shock tactics.

The Assyrian horsemen finally had the necessary arms to charge their enemy and inflict damage with a short-range weapon—the spear—and the equipment to ride into the thick of battle with a fair degree of confidence in the protection afforded by their armor. In fact, even the horses were given protective equipment. By the reign of Esarhaddon (c. 680–669 B.C.) and probably before, the horses were protected by large saddlecloths that completely covered their backs. Although it is difficult to determine the makeup of these cloths exactly, the depictions seem to indicate that they were very thick and heavy, possibly composed of multiple layers of material, and they may have had metal scales or plates sewn onto them at intervals to provide added protection. These cloths were connected to breast-pieces that protected the chest and neck areas of the horses.[47]

Concern for the horses' safety surely reflects two things. First, protection was necessary. Horses in mounted warfare, particularly where shock tactics were employed, were exposed to all the hazards of combat and suffered substantial casualty rates. The losses could be reduced with some protection. Second, horses were valuable. Proper treatment of the horses was important because the demands of the large Assyrian cavalry and chariot corps no doubt created an ongoing supply problem. To meet these demands special horse procurement officers, called *musarkisu*, were employed. Usually, there were 2 such officers assigned to each province, reporting directly to the king (and bypassing the provincial governor). Obviously, obtaining horses was a royal concern, and each procurement officer was assisted by a scribe and several other lesser officials. Judging from the surviving records of the officer in charge of the royal stables, the musarkisu performed their duties very efficiently. During a twenty-seven-day period, the reports show 2,911 animals (mostly horses, but a few mules were included) arrived at the royal stables at Nineveh; of the horses, 1,840 were designated for the chariot corps and 787 were assigned as cavalry mounts.[48] These figures seem to indicate that roughly 36,000 horses and mules were procured each year for the Assyrian army, with the chariot corps receiving about 23,000 horses and the cavalry about 10,000. These figures may seem excessively high, but it should be remembered that the Assyrian army was very large, with proportional chariot and cavalry components.

Although there are no exact figures for the total strength of the Assyrian army, the best estimates range between 100,000 and 200,000 men. Probably the latter figure is closer to the actual size. Assyrian records show that Shalmaneser III crossed the Euphrates River in 845 B.C. with an army of 120,000 men and that Sennacherib had 185,000 men in the army that captured Jerusalem in 699 B.C.[49] If it is reasonable to accept a ratio of 1 chariot to 10 cavalrymen to 100 infantrymen, then Shalmaneser III had 1,100 chariots and 11,000 cavalry, and Sennacherib had 1,600 chariots and 16,000 cavalry.[50] These totals seem to coincide with the horse procurement figures, particularly when one considers that there were spare mounts and teams—possibly 1 spare mount for each cavalryman and 1 spare team for each chariot—because combat and shock tactics were hard on horses.

That the Assyrian cavalry used shock tactics seems almost certain. In 714 B.C., Sargon II mounted a campaign against Ursa, king of Urartu. As Sargon's army approached the enemy after a hard march, the Assyrian soldiers were tired, hungry, and thirsty. The Urartu king had formed a battleline of archers, spearmen, and horsemen. Not wanting to fight a prolonged engagement with tired soldiers, the Assyrian king did not bother to deploy from line-of-column into a battleline but instead personally led a charge with his leading chariot and mounted units. Ursa's army broke as the Assyrian infantry, inspired by the leading cavalry and chariot units, joined the battle. In commemorating the role his cavalry played in this victory, Sargon wrote, "I plunged into [the enemy's] midst like a swift javelin,"[51] clearly indicating an assault and shock tactic. He also named and praised his cavalry commander for his conduct.[52]

Of course, the Assyrian horse sometimes played roles dictated by its mobility, which was greater than that of either the infantry or the chariots. At a battle near the Ulai River in 653 B.C., Ashurbanipal met the Elamites under King Teuman. The Assyrian king had his chariots charge into the Elamite army in order to cause breaks and confusion in the enemy formation. The Assyrian infantry followed the chariots to exploit these opportunities, and to drive the enemy back toward the river. Ashurbanipal employed his cavalry on the flanks where the ground was too broken and unsuitable for chariots. The Assyrian horse raced down the flanks of the Elamite army, containing the enemy soldiers and preventing any escape or breakout. Some of Ashurbanipal's horsemen were armed with bows, and others had spears. Thus, various cavalry units were trained and equipped either for missile fire or close combat. It appears that, at times, assaults were launched against the flanks of the Elamite army by Assyrian cavalry units. As the Elamites broke and fled, the Assyrian cavalry participated in the pursuit and subsequent slaughter of the enemy. The depictions of this battle on the reliefs at Nineveh once again show the Assyrian horsemen riding down and over the enemy infantry.[53]

Although none of the Greek poleis or *ethne* (ethnic groups or tribes or nations of peoples) could match or equal the Assyrian cavalry, many city-states outside Thessaly did maintain and field cavalry forces. These forces apparently were of three types: light cavalry, which consisted of men who wore little or no armor and used javelins or light spears; heavy cavalry, which, as its name implies, was composed of men who often wore the complete hoplite panoply but usually did not carry shields; and dragoons, whom some scholars have identified as mounted hoplites and who were equipped as hoplites, accompanied by squires, and capable of fighting mounted or dismounted.

With regard to cavalry strength, Aristotle placed the city of Magnesia on the Maeander in the same category as Chalcis and Eretria. It appears that horsemanship and cavalry duty were the price of citizenship in Magnesia.[54] Each hippeus equipped himself as a heavy cavalryman and was accompanied by a mounted squire or servant who was lightly armed and carried a javelin and thus served as a light cavalry soldier. In addition, each pair brought along a hunting hound.[55] The tactics of the Magnesian cavalry apparently were to use the hounds and the light-armed troops to attack the enemy initially and disrupt their formation, whether infantry or cavalry. When sufficient disorder resulted, the Magnesian hippeis charged and delivered the decisive blow.[56] In fact, shock tactics must have been the norm in Asia Minor. The Lydian cavalry, accustomed to fighting skillfully on horseback with long spears, used shock against Cyrus and the Persians.[57]

Other Ionian cavalry units may have been even more formidable than the Magnesians. Strabo reported that the reputation of the cavalry of Colophon was so great "that wherever in wars that were hard to bring to an end, the cavalrymen of the Colophonians served as allies, the war came to an end; whence arose the proverb, 'he put Colophon to it', which is quoted when a sure end is put to an affair."[58]

Hounds and light cavalry were also used by the citizens of Thasos. A terra-cotta revetment (Figure 3.3) gives a clear depiction. The horsemen apparently wear light corslets but no helmets. They are armed with spears or javelins, which they hold in their right hands in an overhand throwing position. In the left hand, each cavalryman carries a small, circular shield held slightly in front of his body. Hounds race along beside, as the horses gallop forward.[59]

Judging from the evidence of vase paintings, Athens and Corinth both developed all three forms of cavalry in the Archaic period. An early Protocorinthian aryballos (Figure 3.4) painted no later than c. 700 B.C. shows a man on a horse preceding a heavily armed infantry-man, possibly an early hoplite. The mounted figure does not appear to be wearing a helmet or body armor, in contrast to the infantryman who is wearing a high-crested helmet, corslet or breastplate and greaves and carrying a large, round shield. Both figures are armed with spears; the rider's spear, which is very faint, is held in his right hand in an almost vertical attitude. If the artist meant, as seems likely, for each figure to be symbolic or represent more than one, then the scene shows light cavalry troops advancing in front of hoplites or a phalanx.[60]

Figure 3.3   *Light cavalry depicted on terra-cotta revetment from Thasos (Archaic period). Photograph by the author.*

Figure 3.4   A *light cavalryman advancing in front of a hoplite (early Protocorinthian aryballos). Courtesy of the Trustees of the British Museum, London.*

A later Athenian black-figure lekanis-lid shows much the same scene, except with greater detail. On this piece, unlike the earlier vase, one figure does not represent several; rather, the skilled vase painter clearly drew an advancing hoplite phalanx preceded by light cavalry. The horsemen wear chitons but no helmets or hats. They are preparing to throw their javelins and have them raised over their heads in their right hands.[61] The light horsemen probably screened the phalanx in the initial stages of its deployment and advance and then attempted to disrupt or create gaps in the opposing phalanx with their javelins. Obviously, the phalanx was going to deliver the decisive blow because light cavalrymen would never attempt to rupture a hoplite phalanx by direct assault.

An Athenian black-figure band-cup (Figure 3.5) may, indeed, show precisely one of the ways in which the Archaic light cavalry attacked hoplites. The artist depicted 4 light horsemen attacking 5 advancing hoplites. Although the limitations of perspective make it appear as if the light cavalry is going to charge right into the heavy infantry, the lead horseman is actually passing down the left flank of the hoplite phalanx (the front legs of the lead horse are shown in front of the first hoplite's shield). The lead horseman apparently intends to throw his javelin across the top of his horse's neck, to his left and down at one of the infantrymen. As long as the horsemen did not venture too close to the phalanx, this maneuver would have been very effective. First, the cavalry horses were too fast for the hoplites; the infantrymen weighted down with the panoply would not have been able to move quickly enough to dash out and strike the horsemen, even had it occurred to them to break formation. Second, by attacking the left of the phalanx, the horsemen attacked inferior hoplites because the best always held the right wing. And finally, this maneuver forced the infantrymen to either leave their left side exposed to attack or shift their shields and expose their front.[62]

Of course, another way for light cavalry to attack a phalanx was to charge across its front, from the right wing toward the left. The horsemen could then throw their javelins in the same manner as mentioned earlier—across the neck of the horse and to the left and down. This meant attacking the best hoplites, but the assault would be made against the exposed or unshielded side. The infantrymen

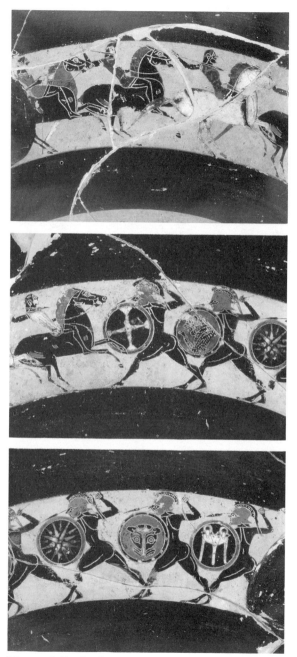

Figure 3.5 *Light cavalry attacking hoplites (sixth century B.C. Attic black-figure band-cup). Courtesy of Antikensammlung, Staatliche Museen zu Berlin. Photograph by Jutta Tletz-Glagow.*

Figure 3.6   Greek light cavalry attacking barbarian mounted archers (mid–sixth century B.C. Attic black-figure dinos). Courtesy of the National Archaeological Museum, Athens (Inv. No. 15116), Archaeological Receipts Fund (T.A.P. Service).

would have a difficult time protecting themselves without breaking the integrity of the phalanx. The most effective way to counter these maneuvers was for the phalanx to have a screen of cavalry or archers.

Of course, light cavalry did go head to head against other light cavalry. An Athenian dinos (Figure 3.6), contemporary with the previously mentioned lekanis-lid, shows a battle between Greek and barbarian light horsemen. A dozen bearded Greek horsemen wearing chitons and felt hats charge 10 barbarian horse-archers. As the mounted archers prepare to shoot, the Greeks are shown in the act of throwing their javelins. The right hand of each Hellene is drawn back in the overhand throwing position, while he holds the reins of his horse and a spare javelin in the left hand.[63]

The Greeks also developed heavy cavalry at this time. The ancient Corinthian and Attic vase painters clearly portrayed the variation in equipment used by the Archaic heavy cavalrymen. The avail-able equipment included the helmet, breastplate, greaves, shield, sword, and spear or javelin. Considering that the cavalrymen equipped themselves at their own expense, some degree of variation is understandable, and there were many combinations used within the two extremes—from the cavalryman who wore only a helmet and used a spear to the one who wore the complete panoply. A large Co-rinthian oenochoe (Figure 3.7) from the seventh century B.C. with a continuous battle scene running around it shows heavy cavalrymen riding into battle. Each rider wears a helmet and carries a spear, but no other armor or weapons are visible.[64] An Attic black-figure mastos (Figure 3.8) from the mid–sixth century B.C. shows four individuals; two are infantrymen, and two are cavalrymen. Each cavalryman is wearing a helmet and greaves and carrying a pair of spears, but nei-ther is wearing a breastplate, nor carrying a shield or sword.[65] An-other black-figure Attic vase (Figure 3.9) displays a combat scene be-tween two horsemen. Both riders wear helmets, breastplates, and greaves, and they are armed with spears and swords.[66] The work of a middle Corinthian vase painter (Figure 3.10) portrays heavy cavalry in two different fashions on the same vase. One cavalryman is equipped with helmet and spear, and three others are more heavily armed with helmets, shields carried on their left arms, and two spears each.[67] Finally, an Attic black-figure amphora (Figure 3.11), which obviously depicts a legendary scene, shows a cavalryman fighting an Amazon. The cavalryman has the complete panoply, in-cluding the large, round shield.[68]

These battle scenes provide some clues as to the styles of fight-ing and tactics employed by the heavy cavalry. The cavalryman ap-parently gripped the spear in two ways: overhand and underhand. Obviously, the former grip was used for throwing the spear or jave-lin, as can be seen on many of depictions of light horsemen in action. Heavy cavalrymen also used the overhand grip at times. An Attic black-figure band-cup (Figure 3.12) from the sixth century B.C. shows a battle scene with hoplites, and both light and heavy cavalry. One heavy cavalryman in the top panel, wearing a helmet and possi-bly greaves and with a shield held in front of his body, has his spear in his right hand in the overhand throwing position. His arm is drawn

42

Figure 3.7 (Above) *Corinthian heavy cavalry riding into battle (early seventh century B.C. Corinthian wine-jug). Courtesy of the Trustees of the British Museum, London.* Figure 3.8 (Below) *Athenian heavy cavalrymen, each equipped with two spears, metal helmet, and greaves (mid–sixth century B.C. Attic black-figure mastos). Courtesy of the Trustees of the British Museum, London.*

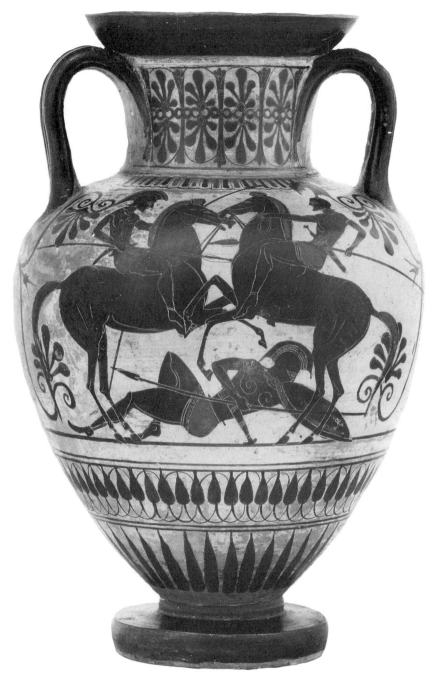

Figure 3.9 *Two Greek heavy cavalrymen engage in combat: Both use the underhand grip for their spears (late sixth century B.C. Attic black-figure vase). Courtesy of the Antiken-Abteilung of the Martin von Wagner-Museum der Universität Würzburg, Braunschweig.*

44

Figure 3.10 *Corinthian heavy cavalrymen ride toward battle (early seventh century Middle Corinthian vase). Courtesy of the Herzog Anton Ulrich-Museum, Braunschweig.*

Figure 3.11 *Greek heavy cavalryman equipped with complete panoply, including hoplon, or large circular shield, engages in heroic combat with Amazon (late seventh century B.C. Attic black-figure amphora). Photograph by the author.*

back, ready to throw the spear at either a hoplite or a mounted archer. The other mounted figures appear to be light horsemen; four are holding their spears in the overhand position, and two are using the underhand grip.[69]

Apparently, when the cavalryman used the underhand grip, he intended to employ his spear as a thrusting weapon only. This grip would allow for a range of motion but was best employed against targets level with the rider's waist or below, such as another horseman or a standing hoplite. The cavalryman could use a swinging motion of his right arm to impart more momentum to the spear, giving it greater penetrating power at the crucial moment. This grip could even be used against an opponent who was low to the ground and close to the horseman, as in a melee, because it allowed the cavalryman to strike down with the butt-spike of his spear without having to change his grip. This was done simply by raising the spear in a vertical attitude and striking downward with the butt end.[70] A previously mentioned vase (Figure 3.9) clearly shows the underhand grip in use

Figure 3.12 (Above and facing) *Battle scene with cavalry and infantry (early sixth century B.C. Attic black-figure band-cup)*. *Courtesy of the Musée du Louvre, Paris. Copyright R.M.N.*

by two heavily armed riders engaged in single combat. The band-cup in Figure 3.12 displays cavalrymen using the underhand grip against both infantry and cavalry. While one cavalryman (panel three) is attacking the hoplite or possibly another horseman in front of him, a second cavalryman (panel four) is riding past the hoplite (the front legs of his horse are behind and past the hoplite's leg) and toward the first horseman.

Interestingly, Archaic heavy cavalrymen at times carried and used shields in combat. Those equipped with the large, round hoplite shields likely either passed them to squires or servants to hold before they took part in mounted operations or discarded them, with the intention of retrieving them later, if they felt the shields were a potential disadvantage. However, as Figure 3.12 indicates, it appears the cavalryman could manage his horse's reins with his left hand, hold his shield on his left arm if necessary, and still fight. It may sometimes have been useful for the rider to swing his shield forward to protect his body while mounted (Figures 3.3 and 3.12). Although some riders may have done this with the hoplon, it is likely that the weight and size of the hoplite shield made this very difficult; thus, some cavalrymen may have used a light shield, or *pelta*, for this purpose. This was not a widespread practice in any case, and the use of the shield while on horseback seems to have been sporadic and short lived, at best.[71]

Obviously, the direct assault or use of shock against one's enemy was a tactical option for the Archaic heavy cavalryman. This probably occurred most often in cavalry-versus-cavalry battles. Individual cavalrymen (Figure 3.9) or groups would simply ride almost head-on at one another with leveled spears. Because the spear was held in the right hand and on the right side of the horse, each horseman attempted to pass his opponent on the right, so that his spear could be brought to bear on the enemy or possibly the enemy's horse. Predictably, the intent was to inflict as much damage as possible, while receiving as little as possible in return.[72] The direct assault was also used by the heavy cavalry against infantry formations, although this tactic was probably employed less frequently as the hoplite phalanx became more widely deployed and better disciplined. If the infantry formation was loose or broken, the cavalry could force its way into and between the files or simply attack and ride down individual infantrymen (Figure 3.12).

There is a chance an intact phalanx could have been broken by a determined cavalry charge, but such a charge and break would have resulted in high casualties for both riders and horses. A contingent of Thessalian cavalry, for example, lost 40 men in a brief assault on a Spartan army.[73] Unfortunately, ancient sources rarely distinguished how casualties occurred, so it is usually impossible to know the number of lives lost in a cavalry attack on a phalanx formation. But to see the kinds of casualties ancient horsemen might have suffered in direct assaults against the phalanx, the Medieval period offers a parallel in the cavalry attacks against the phalanx of the Swiss confederation. At the Battle of Arbedo in 1422, the condottiere generals Carmagnola and Angelo de la Pergola used 6,000 mercenary horsemen against the Swiss phalanx: The result was 400 piked horses and men in the first hour of combat. In 1444, Dauphin Louis launched the Armagnac squadrons at the Swiss in the Battle of St. Jacob. Louis's force suffered 2,000 dead, who lay heaped before the Swiss pikes.[74]

These high casualty rates would have been unacceptable to the ancient Greek political and social entities, whether poleis or ethne, because the hippeis were members of the aristocratic and wealthy class that provided much of the leadership for the community. With regard to Archaic Athens, for instance, Aristotle recorded:

[Solon] divided the people into four property classes according to wealth, as had been done before; the four classes were: *pentako-siomedimnoi, hippeis, zeugitai,* and *thetes.* He distributed the other magistracies to be held by the *pentakosiomedimnoi, hippeis,* and *zeugitai,* allotting the nine Archons, the Treasurers, the *poletai,* the Eleven, and *kolakretai* to various classes in accordance with their property qualification. The *thetes* received only the right to sit in the *Ekklesia* and the *dikasteria.* The property qualification for the *pentakosiomedimnoi* was a minimum yearly return from his own property of 500 measures, dry or liquid. The *hippeis* had a minimum of 300, and some say that the class was also restricted to those able to maintain a horse. ... The minimum qualification for the *zeugitai* was 200 measures, wet and dry combined, while the remainder of the population formed the *thetes* and were not entitled to hold office.[75]

There is much debate about this passage, but one thing is clear: The men in the top two economic categories—the *pentaco-siomedimnoi* and the hippeis—were the ones who held the most important political offices. In fact, at this time, only members of the pentacosiomedimnoi were eligible to be *tamiai*, or state treasurers. The archons, the chief magistrates of Athens, were selected only from the members of the top two classes. These same classes also provided the cavalry. Members of the hippeis and the pentacosiomedimnoi served as cavalrymen, with a minimum qualification of 300 wet or dry measures, and the zeugitai served as hoplites, with a lower economic qualification.[76] Thus, heavy casualties among the cavalrymen was potentially a dire threat to the political and economic health and stability of the community. And so, more prudent cavalry tactics against the phalanx were necessary.

Without a doubt, the tactic preferred by cavalry in attacking a phalanx was the flank or rear attack. A Corinthian wine-jug battle scene (Figure 3.7) shows hoplites engaged in combat and three cavalrymen riding toward the battle. The horsemen are apparently attacking the rear of one of the hoplite groups; the lead rider raises his spear in the overhand position in preparation for driving it into the back of the infantryman ahead of him.[77]

Of course, it was possible for the cavalryman to dismount and fight on foot, if the tactical situation seemed to warrant it and he was equipped appropriately. It is conceivable that the horsemen became so proficient at this that they could easily slide off the left side of their mounts and be ready to fight immediately. An early Corinthian aryballos apparently displays just such an action. The cavalryman has both legs on the left side of his horse, in what seems to be a side-saddle position, and is in the process of sliding to the ground.[78] In this case, one has to wonder what would become of the cavalryman's horse without a squire or servant to hold it. The typical cavalryman probably had at least one servant to accompany him, and some may have had a half dozen or more.[79] Thus, the common practice was for

a servant or squire to go into battle with each hippeus in order to assist the cavalryman with his equipment and mount. An Attic black-
figure lekanis-lid may, indeed, show a scene that was common on
Greek battlefields after the hoplite revolution. The dragoon, having
slid off the left side of his mount, rushes forward to take his place in
the phalanx, while his squire attends to the riderless horse.[80] Obviously, the hippeus could remount very easily and quickly to resume
his duties as a cavalryman.

By the end of the Archaic period, the hoplite and the phalanx
dominated the battlefields of the Greek world. The change that this
necessitated in cavalry tactics and warfare—namely, forsaking the direct assault or shock in favor of harassment and exploitive tactics—
was clearly illustrated by two battles. The first of these occurred in
511/510 B.C. at Phalerum in Attica. A Spartan army under the command of Anchimolius, a leading Spartiate, sailed across the Saronic
Gulf and landed at Phalerum to liberate Athens from Hippias, the
tyrant of the city and the son of Pisistratus. Hippias, forewarned
about the Spartan expedition and its landing site, consequently
sought aid from the Thessalians. In response to Hippias' request,
Cineas of Conium arrived with 1,000 Thessalian cavalrymen.
Hippias had also ordered the plain of Phalerum cleared and leveled
to make it more suitable for cavalry operations. When the Spartans
arrived and began to march toward the city, the Thessalians attacked, killed Anchimolius and many others, and drove the remaining Spartans back to their ships.[81]

Herodotus' account of this battle was, unfortunately, lacking in
details and did not give a clear picture. A question thus arises: Were
the Spartans caught by surprise, either in their camp or marching in
column when the Thessalians attacked, or was this a regular battle
with both sides prepared? The latter seems to have been the case. It
is unlikely that the Spartans were ignorant of the Thessalian presence and thus unaware of the cavalry threat facing them. A number
of prominent Athenians had gone into exile to escape the tyrant,
and all had friends or relatives inside the city who would have had little reason to keep information about Hippias' allies confidential.
Also, cavalrymen and their horses obviously make noise and raise
dust when they move, and a thousand cavalrymen and their mounts

would have created a din and a cloud of dust sufficient to alert anyone.[82] Finally, while Anchimolius was no Alexander, the Spartan commander must have been cognizant that the plain of Phalerum had been manicured. Common sense dictates that any commander would observe his surroundings and the terrain features, whether on the march or forming for battle. Anchimolius must have noticed that bushes had been cut down, rocks moved, and holes filled in, even if a Spartan sympathizer had not provided this information.[83]

Additionally, if a surprise attack—an attack on the Spartans while they were disorganized—was the plan, why wait until the entire army was ashore? Phalerum, after all, was simply a suitable beaching site for ships, with an adjacent plain. There were no fortifications (even simple earthworks) to protect ships and men and impede an attack on the beach. An army disembarking from ships would certainly have been disorganized and vulnerable to attack. In fact, it probably would have been possible for the Thessalians to deny the beach to the Spartans completely and thus prevent a landing in the first place, had they appeared just as the ships approached the beach. Indeed, a few Athenian soldiers and sailors did precisely that when Brasidas attempted to land at Pylos during the Peloponnesian War.[84]

Actually, the Battle of Phalerum was almost certainly a standard battle, with the Thessalian cavalry successfully attacking a phalanx. Several factors undoubtedly were key to the Spartan defeat and the Thessalian victory. First, the Spartans had no screening force. They had no mounted contingents of their own because they had disbanded their cavalry about the time of the Second Messenian War. Further, their arrival by sea meant that no allied cavalry could accompany them; horse-transport ships did not appear in the Greek world until the time of the Peloponnesian War. And Herodotus did not mention the presence of any archers, slingers, or other light-armed troops with the Spartan army. Without the impediment of screening cavalry or light-armed soldiers, the Thessalian horse was able to close at will and maneuver freely. Second, the Spartans were probably not accustomed to fighting against cavalry of any kind, let alone the Thessalian horsemen. Few of the Peloponnesian poleis maintained mounted forces of any size, and those that did most likely did not risk them against the finest hoplites in Greece. Psychologically and tactically, the Spartans were probably not prepared to face the onslaught of 1,000 horsemen riding at them in a series of 5 or so diamonds—horsemen who could advance, throw javelins, and wheel out for another attack without losing their cohesion and formation. And finally, the Spartan army was rather small: Had the army sent to liberate Athens from Hippias been of any size, one of the Spartan kings would have been in command. This meant that either the phalanx could not stretch across the entire plain and thus that the flanks were unprotected and the phalanx subject to flanking attack or encirclement or, alternatively, that to stretch across the plain, the phalanx was deployed thinly, less than the normal 8 men deep that the Spartans preferred. A thin phalanx was a weak one and one that could be broken. If there were a few casualties in the front ranks, gaps appeared that could not be closed—gaps that horsemen could charge into and exploit to their own advantage. In fact, this is almost certainly what happened to the Spartans at Phalerum for Herodotus clearly implied that they were ridden down by the Thessalians.[85] Therefore, Archaic Greek cavalry had successfully charged a hoplite phalanx, something that would not happen again for another hundred years or so, but it was a phalanx that was not as strong and as prepared as it should have been.

Later in the year 511/510 B.C., at the second battle, the Spartans marched a larger army across the isthmus and into Attica. Cleomenes, one of the Spartan kings, commanded this force, and he was well aware of the mounted threat that faced him. As his army entered Attica, he apparently had his phalanx deployed for battle because, when he was immediately attacked by the Thessalian cavalry, the latter suffered a defeat. This cavalry assault against a large, well-prepared phalanx cost the Thessalians 40 dead. This was not an exceptionally costly battle by the standards of the day, but it was so clearly a defeat and Cleomenes was so clearly prepared to meet the mounted threat posed by Hippias' allies that the Thessalians returned home without attempting another engagement.[86] Although cavalry alone could charge and defeat a weak, disorganized phalanx, horsemen were typically unable to successfully employ the charge or shock against properly deployed, massed hoplites.

The Battle of Plataea (479 B.C.) certainly confirmed these lessons. The Persian army, under the command of Mardonius, was composed of Persians, Medes, Sacae, Bactrians, and Indians and contained both infantry and cavalry units. The barbarian mounted units were predominately horse-archers. The Indians formed a true light cavalry, armed with only bows and arrows and wearing virtually no armor. The Bactrians supplemented the meager Indian equipment with a short spear and metal helmet, and the Medes and Persians augmented the Bactrian arms and armor with iron-scale body armor. Thus, the Medes and the Persians were the best equipped. Mardonius also had a number of medized Greeks in his army, including units of Macedonian cavalry, Thessalian cavalry, and Boeotian cavalry and hoplites. With the possible exception of the Macedonians, the medized Greek horsemen must have been equipped in the contemporary fashion of Greek heavy cavalry, with helmet, body armor, possibly greaves, sword, and multiple spears or javelins. Herodotus recorded that the total strength of the Persian force was 300,000 men.[87] If his figure is accepted and the proportion of 1 cavalryman to 10 infantrymen is used, Mardonius' cavalry numbered a maximum of 30,000. In contrast, the Greek army commanded by Pausanias contained 40,500 hoplites and 69,500 light infantrymen but no cavalry.[88]

The first confrontation between cavalry and the hoplite phalanx took place shortly after the Greek army arrived on the battlefield. Pausanias had his forces take up a position in the foothills of Mt. Cithaeron. When the Greeks stayed in the hills and off the plain, Mardonius had all his cavalry attack. Although this attack hit as much of the Greek line as the horsemen could reach, the main thrust fell on 3,000 Megarian hoplites who apparently occupied an exposed position, possibly astride the road leading south into Attica. Mardonius' horsemen attacked by squadrons; each squadron advanced toward the hoplites, fired its arrows or threw its javelins when the range was right, and then retired in order to allow the next squadron to attack. The Megarians were in desperate need of help and sent the following message to Pausanias: "From the men of Megara to their allies: we cannot alone withstand the Persian horse, although we have until now held our ground with patience and valor though hard pressed, in this post where we were first appointed; and now be well assured that we will leave our post, except you send others to take our place."[89]

As a result, 300 Athenian hoplites led by Olympiodorus and accompanied by a contingent of archers (perhaps as many as 1,600 men) took the place of the Megarians. The Athenian hoplites probably formed a solid line that presented nothing but shields and spears to the opposing horsemen, behind which the archers loosed their arrows. The cavalry of the Persian army then attacked the Athenians by squadrons. After some time, the horse of Masistius, the Persian cavalry commander, was hit by an arrow, causing it to rear and throw him to the ground. The Athenian hoplites rushed forward and killed the Persian. Upon realizing that their commander had fallen, the cavalry charged as a single mass.[90] As Herodotus reported:

When the Athenians saw the horsemen riding at them, not by squadrons as before, but all together, they cried to the rest of the army for help. While all their foot was rallying to aid, there waxed a sharp fight over the dead body. As long as the three hundred stood alone, they had the worst of the battle by far, and were nigh leaving the dead man; but when the main body came to their aid, then it was the horsemen that could no longer hold their ground, nor avail to recover the dead man, but they lost others of their comrades too besides Masistius. They drew off therefore ... and resolved, as there were none to lead them, to ride away to Mardonius.[91]

It should be noted that Herodotus directly stated that Mardonius ordered all his cavalry to attack the Greek army; thus, the Theban, Thessalian, and Macedonian mounted units were involved in this confrontation, along with the barbarian horsemen. And yet, the cavalry could not break the phalanx. What seems to have demoralized the Megarians were the casualties caused by the missiles of the attacking horsemen, the inability to strike back, and the feeling of being alone and unsupported. Even though the Megarians were hard pressed, the attacking cavalry made no attempt to employ the direct assault or shock tactic.[92] The Athenians, who replaced the Megarians, had an advantage over their fellow Greeks because they had the supporting fire of their own archers. Without a doubt, Athenian missiles kept the horsemen at bay to a degree because of the superior range and accuracy of foot-archers, as compared to horse-archers who shot from moving, unstable platforms. Yet what stands out is the ineffectiveness of the direct assault by the cavalry against the phalanx. Three hundred hoplites withstood the massed charge of several thousand horsemen. And though the Athenians were pushed back, they were not broken, nor did they break, and eventually, once they were reinforced, the Athenians forced the horsemen to withdraw. Herodotus noted that Mardonius' cavalry suffered many casualties.[93]

Direct assault against a prepared phalanx was costly and ineffective, but cavalry still had a role to play on the battlefield, and Mardonius' mounted units executed the tactics of harassing, exploiting, and screening very well. The mobility of the mounted forces proved highly effective at interfering with Greek logistics. After Pausanias had shifted the Greek army's position to the area around the Asopus Ridge, a detachment of Mardonius' cavalry that probably included the Thebans (because they were familiar with the country) rode around behind the Greek lines in the night. This force attacked and captured a supply train that included a number of wagons and 500 pack animals.[94] Pausanias now faced the loss of his lines of supply or, alternatively, the need to guard them, which meant dissipating his strength.

Mardonius' horsemen also interfered with Greek efforts to obtain water. Any individual or group of individuals who approached the Asopus River was attacked. This meant that all the Greeks had to draw water from the Gargaphia spring, on the right wing of the Greek army. For the Athenians and the others on the left wing, this meant sending men a considerable distance, several times a day, in order to satisfy the daily demands for drinking water. On about the tenth day of this standoff, the spring was ruined by the Persians as a source of water. An all-out cavalry attack was mounted along the entire Greek line, pinning it down. In the confusion and turmoil, some mounted units got behind the Spartan position on the right wing and rode through the spring, fouling the water with dust and dirt. As a result, the Gargaphia became totally useless as a source of drinking water.[95]

This, among other considerations, forced Pausanias to move the Greek army to another position, but during the move, the Greeks became divided. When Mardonius saw that his enemy had abandoned the Asopus Ridge position, he ordered his cavalry to pursue. The barbarian horsemen caught the Spartan section of the Greek army in the open plain and attacked. The Spartans were forced to halt and form a battleline in order to protect themselves from the missiles of the mounted archers. Consequently, the Spartans were prevented from reaching the foothills of Mt. Cithaeron and safety. This gave Mardonius a chance to attack them with the Persian infantry and to engage in the decisive battle he wanted. Although this ultimately led to the Persian commander's death and a Greek victory, Mardonius' cavalry had done its job and provided at least an opportunity for a Persian victory.[96]

At the end of the battle, with Mardonius dead and the Persian army in disarray, the cavalry covered the retreat of the fleeing soldiers. Herodotus praised the efforts of the horsemen in this operation: "Thus they all fled, save only the cavalry, Boeotian and other; which was very advantageous to the fleeing men since it kept constantly between them and their enemies, and shielded its friends from the Greeks in their flight."[97] Though there were numerous mounted units involved in the screening and skirmishing that took place—and many must have performed well—the only unit of horse singled out for special attention by Herodotus was Greek, the Theban cavalry. His description of an encounter between the Thebans and some Megarian and Phliasian hoplites clearly demonstrates how the cavalry screened, as well as the disadvantageous position of the pursuing infantry and the potentially disastrous results for the foot-soldiers: "But when the Megarians and the Phliasians came near to the enemy, the Theban horsemen, whose *hipparchos* was Asopodorus, the son of Timander, saw them approaching in haste and disorder, and rode at them; by which assault they laid 600 of them low, and pursued and swept the rest to Cithaeron."[98] The Megarian and Phliasian hoplites had not maintained their formation, and the Theban horsemen had been able to charge them. The lesson for both cavalry and infantry was clear. Cavalry could successfully charge any infantry unit that pursued so fast it became disorganized, as well as inflict heavy casualties on the foot soldiers. The mounted threat could be lessened by a slow pursuit that maintained formation and good order, but this ensured the escape of the fleeing enemy.

Though the Persians had lost the battle, the mounted units, including the Greek horsemen, had performed their assigned tasks well; they had disrupted the Greek supply lines, deprived the enemy of water, caught an exposed infantry unit in the open and forced a decisive engagement, and, finally, covered the retreat and successfully prevented an even greater slaughter.

The Battle of Plataea marked the end of the Archaic period for Greek horsemen. During this period, the role of cavalry on the battlefield had changed dramatically. At the beginning of the era, the hippeis were the preeminent force—the force that decided the outcome of the battle, by shock, if necessary. The use of cavalry was widespread in the Greek world, with Eretria, Chalcis, Magnesia, Colophon, and Thessaly all having powerful mounted forces. Further, Greek cavalry developed its various manifestations—light cavalry, heavy cavalry, and dragoon—and the corresponding equipment and tactics. However, the hoplite revolution changed the role of cavalry, as shock tactics against the hoplite phalanx proved too costly and ineffective. By the end of the Archaic period, cavalry therefore played a more complicated, multifaceted role on the battlefield, and the principal tactics became harassment, screening, and pursuit. Although the hoplite dominated the battlefield, the importance of the mounted force and its diverse roles were recognized, and at least two Greek political entities—the Boeotian Confederacy and Athens—consequently sought to improve their cavalries in the years ahead.

4

Greek Cavalry in the Periclean Age

The period between the Battle of Plataea (479 B.C.) and the start of the Peloponnesian War (431 B.C.) saw the birth of the Delian League and its transformation into the Athenian Empire, the emergence of the Boeotian Confederacy, and the polarization of Greece into two armed camps. For both camps, the principal implements of war were the hoplite phalanx and the trireme, or warship. The Peloponnesian League's strength lay in its army of heavy infantrymen, while a respectable fleet was maintained by certain of Sparta's allies, notably Corinth. On the other side, Athens developed the most powerful navy in the Mediterranean but had only a respectable army. Yet the Athenians did organize and train a very good cavalry force. This was an intentional policy subsidized by the city of Athens, apparently in response to the employment of cavalry by the Persians, the threat posed by the Boeotian cavalry, and the recognized deficiency of Athenian mounted military assets.

It seems certain that the Persian cavalry made an impression on the Athenians and the other Greeks. Xerxes invaded Greece with a mounted force of 80,000 men.[1] By the standards of any day, this was a huge cavalry force; by comparison, Alexander invaded the Persian Empire and defeated Darius at Arbela with only 7,000 cavalry, Hannibal crossed the Rhone with 9,000 horsemen, and William the Conqueror successfully subdued England with only some 2,000 knights.[2]

In fact, the Persian cavalry was almost as large as the entire Greek army at Plataea. Even if the figures were exaggerated, Xerxes' horse was superior to anything the Greeks had.[3] But the superiority was not only in numbers. Many of the Persian horsemen were mounted on specially bred animals. The satrap of Babylon alone maintained a stud farm which had 800 stallions and 16,000 mares.[4] If every satrap had a similar arrangement, 16,000 stallions and 320,000 mares were on stud farms in various parts of the Persian Empire that bred stock for military purposes. The Persian mounts did, in fact, surpass the best of the Greek horses. When Xerxes raced his horses against those of the Thessalians, the former easily outdistanced their competition.[5] Further, at least some of the Persian horses were specially trained for war—trained not simply to walk, trot, and gallop at the appropriate times but also to use their hooves and weight as weapons.[6]

Probably more than any of the other Greeks, the Athenians had the opportunity to study the Persian cavalry at Plataea. On the first day of the battle, 300 Athenians relieved the beleaguered Megarians and withstood a series of assaults that included Persian mounted units. This action culminated in an all-out assault by all of Mardonius' horse.[7] Later, when the Athenians held the left wing of the Greek battleline, Persian cavalry denied the Athenians and their right wing allies access to the Asopus River. For eight days, the Athenian hoplites were forced to travel to a distant spring to obtain drinking water because the enemy horsemen harassed anyone who attempted to draw water from the river. Thus, for eight days, the Athenians confronted, clashed with, and observed the effectiveness of the enemy's mounted units.[8]

Of course, not all the cavalry serving under Mardonius at Plataea was barbarian. Thebes had medized, and Boeotia was occupied territory. Consequently, the Boeotian cavalry served the Persian cause and took part in several actions against the Greek forces at Plataea, especially against the Athenians. Certainly, Boeotian horsemen were involved in the all-out assault against the 300 Athenian hoplites in the attempt to recover the body of Masistius.[9] Later, when Mardonius deployed his army in battle order, the Boeotian infantry was positioned to face the Athenians, and the Boeotian horsemen almost certainly supported their own hoplites.[10] In the final confused combat, the Boeotians and Athenians fought long and hard until the former lost 300 of their best men, which had to include some caval-rymen because they were members of the best or upper class; at that point, the Boeotians withdrew. Then, the Boeotian horse covered the withdrawal of their hoplites, in the process attacking and routing a pursuing group of Megarian and Phliasian infantry.[11]

The Boeotian cavalry was considered one of the best in Greece and was probably only surpassed by the Thessalian cavalry.[12] The ex-act organization of the Boeotian horse in 479 B.C. is uncertain. Herodotus did identify both Boeotian and Theban mounted units at Plataea, and he showed that the latter was commanded by a hipparchos. This seems to imply that the Boeotian cavalry was orga-nized in a fashion similar to its later federal or confederacy organiza-tion.[13] All the cities of the later confederacy, with the exception of Plataea (which had not medized and fought on the Greek side) prob-ably furnished units for the Boeotian cavalry. At any rate, by the mid–fifth century B.C., the Boeotian Confederacy had emerged, and its army was organized as a federal force.

In the federal organization, Boeotia was divided into 11 districts, with each district providing 1,000 hoplites and 100 cavalrymen to the league's army.[14] Thus, the Boeotian cavalry totaled 1,100 men. Of course, in times of emergency or need, a larger army and cavalry could be called up; Diodorus reported that in 396 B.C., the Boeo-tians mustered 12,000 hoplites and 2,000 cavalrymen.[15] The Boeo-tian cavalry was commanded by the federal hipparchos, an officer se-lected or elected by and subject to the orders of the Boeotarchs, who made up the governing council of the league.[16] A district hipparchos, elected or selected by a local district assembly, commanded each of the 11 district contingents, or regiments.[17] In 447 B.C., at the time of the emergence of the Boeotian Confederacy, Thebes, Plataea, Orchomenus, and Thespis each contained 2 districts; thus, each city provided 2 regiments of cavalry. Tanagra was 1 district and contrib-uted 1 regiment. The remaining 2 districts were combinations of Haliartos, Lebadeia, and Coronea and of Akraiphai, Kopai, and Chaeronea.[18]

Each district regiment was composed of 2 *ilai* or squadrons of 50 men. Ilarchs commanded the squadrons.[19] Considering the size of the squadrons and the fact that there was no mention of any special Theban formation in the ancient sources, it seems likely the normal formation was a square or rectangle.[20] This formation was probably 5 men deep, with a 10-man front. If the interval between ranks was 1 horse's length and the distance between files was 1 horse's width, the rectangle had a front of 19 yards and a depth of 27 yards. Of course, this formation could have been made almost square in appearance by simply increasing the distance between each file to the width of 2 horses; then, the dimensions of the rectangle would have been 28 yards across the front and 27 yards in depth. The distance and interval were likely altered to fit the tactical situation: If the cavalry was attempting an assault, the distance was narrowed to 1 horse's width for a more concentrated mass formation; at other times, the distance was expanded.

Because the Boeotian cavalrymen were armed with javelins, a more open formation was probably used most of the time. This would allow sufficient space for each cavalryman to advance to the appropriate range, throw his weapon, and then wheel or maneuver his horse to reform with his unit.[21] The open formation would also have been more suitable when the Boeotian horsemen were supported by light infantry. By the time of the Peloponnesian War, a special unit of Boeotian light infantry had been formed to accompany the horsemen into battle. At times, each rider had a *hamippe* who fought beside him as a foot soldier. The hamippe accompanied the horseman into battle either by running alongside the horse, holding on to the horse's mane or trappings, or possibly by riding behind the cavalryman on the back of the horse.[22] This type of special infantry appeared later in history on several occasions. Caesar, for example, supported his cavalry with a special infantry unit at Pharsalus, and certain Germanic horsemen were accompanied into battle by foot soldiers who held onto the horse's mane.[23] In fact, Caesar provided the best surviving account of this type of cooperative combat when describing the Germanic tactics:

> The kind of fighting in which the Germans had trained themselves was as follows. There were six thousand horsemen, and as many footmen, as swift as they were brave, who had been chosen out of

the whole force, one by each horseman for his personal protection. With them they worked in encounters; on them the horsemen would retire, and they would concentrate speedily if any serious difficulty arose; they would form round any trooper who fell from his horse severely wounded; and if it was necessary to advance farther in some direction or to retire more rapidly, their training made them so speedy that they could support themselves by the manes of the horses and keep up their pace.[24]

Its organization and standard tactical formation allowed the Boeotian cavalry to meet a variety of challenges on the battlefield. Organized in squadrons that were commanded by ilarchs, cavalry units as small as 50 men could be sent out on a variety of missions with adequate leadership. Squadrons could combine into increasingly larger mounted units, up to a total of 1,100 men, with a set chain of command that ensured adequate control in all situations. The rectangular squadron formation allowed the Boeotian horse a great deal of flexibility when forming for battle. If a narrow front was required, the Boeotians could present a formation that was only 17 yards across but 11 squadrons deep. This narrow and deep formation had the potential for a massed, weighted charge or an attack by successive squadrons. The Boeotian rectangular formations also could be deployed in the other extreme with an 11-squadron front, which easily covered 300 or 400 yards but had a depth of only 1 squadron, or 5 men. In this wide formation, the Boeotian cavalry could sweep forward against infantry and cavalry alike. Of course, a variety of formations between the two extremes could be deployed by arranging the squadron rectangles as desired. By far the biggest drawback to the rectangle was a difficulty in penetrating and breaking another solid formation, such as the phalanx.

At the time of Plataea, the Athenian cavalry was not up to the challenge of the Theban cavalry, let alone the Persian. In fact, there is disagreement as to the existence of an Athenian cavalry prior to the post–Persian War era. M. A. Martin believed that the creation of an Athenian mounted force was the result of the reforms of Solon. Service in the ranks of the cavalry was the obligation of the second highest class of Athenian citizens, and it may have been a sort of liturgy or obligation assumed for a period of time, perhaps one year.[25]

In contrast, Helbig argued that Athenian cavalry did not exist until after the Persian War. He based his argument largely on ceramic evidence: He believed the Archaic depictions of mounted warriors show either foreign cavalry (possibly Thessalian), mounted hoplites, or mounted hoplites accompanied by their squires.[26] Subsequently, other scholars have supported both Martin's and Helbig's conclusions. Snodgrass stated, "The most reasonable conclusion is that they [Athenian *hippeis*] used their horses only for transport to the actual battle ... they were armed as hoplites and, for the actual battle, dismounted and fought in the phalanx."[27] More recently, Greenhalgh argued that the Athenian mounted warrior did service as either a mounted hoplite, who dismounted to fight, or as a cavalryman. The mounted warrior served in alternative ways that depended on the situation.[28] And Bugh, after examining all the relevant literary evidence, the ceramic evidence, Solon's hippeis and the tradition of horses in Attica, and various other considerations which militated against an Athenian cavalry, was convinced that a force of Athenian horsemen did exist in the Archaic period.[29]

Martin and his supporters appear to be correct: There *was* an Athenian cavalry in the Archaic period. There are several pieces of evidence that, taken together, seem to be decisive. First, one of Solon's reforms was the establishment of four classes of citizens, the second of which was the hippeis.[30] It seems incredible that the term *hippeis*, meaning "knights" or "horsemen," would be applied to a class of citizens as a meaningless title. If this were the case, Solon could have just as easily labeled his second citizen class the *triacosiomedimnoi*, or "three-hundred-measure men," thereby maintaining the pattern he started with his first citizen class, the *pentacosiomedimnoi* or "five-hundred-measure men." The use of *hippeis* seems clearly to imply that these citizens provided horses and served as cavalrymen, whether dragoon or regular.[31]

The second piece or, rather, body of evidence is the Attic black-figure vases. From the time of Solon onward the mounted warrior and his actions were constantly depicted by the Athenian artists. They painted the mounted warrior in all the various aspects of cavalry: light cavalry (Figures 3.5, 3.6, and 3.12), heavy cavalry (Figures 3.8, 3.9, and 3.12), and dragoons (Figure 3.11). A recent historical work that surveyed much of the ceramic evidence recorded over one hundred surviving Archaic Athenian vase paintings which have cavalry motifs.[32] Further, it seems certain that the Athenian artists accurately painted figures from the real-life models they saw in the city daily.[33]

Finally, several ancient authors provided bits of evidence that strengthen the argument for an Archaic Athenian cavalry. Herodotus reported that Pisistratus' sons, Hippias and Hipparchus presumably, served as hippeis and pursued their father's routed Athenian opponents at the Battle of Pallene (546 B.C.).[34] Plutarch recorded that Cimon, the son of Miltiades, dedicated his bridle to Athena before Athens fell to the Persians, and borrowed a shield from the temple. This was obviously a necessary acquisition for a cavalryman intending to fight as a hoplite because mounted warriors rarely used shields; Cimon supposedly remarked that this was no time for equestrian skills.[35] Socrates, according to Plato, commented favorably on Themistocles teaching his sons equestrian skills; Paralos and Xanthippos were the foremost horsemen in Athens, and Cleophantus could ride standing on the horse's back and was proficient at throwing the javelin while mounted, a skill required of a cavalryman.[36] And Pollux, the lexicographer, in an explanation of *naucraria* (divisions of the Athenian citizen body for political, social, and religious purposes), wrote that each naucrary in Archaic Athens provided 2 horsemen and a ship for the service of the city.[37]

Considering that Archaic Athens had 48 naucraries, the Athenian cavalry numbered 96 men. Although this seems a small total, even by the standards of Archaic Greece, this was only the number of cavalrymen called to service for a given year. Cavalry duty at this time was rotated among selected members of Solon's second class of citizens on a yearly basis, as was the case with all liturgies.[38] Given there were 4 *phylai*, or tribes, at this time, the total strength of the Athenian cavalry was probably about 400 men.

The 96-man figure does provide the basis for a tentative reconstruction of the tactical organization of the Archaic Athenian cavalry. Because 4 naucraries made up a phratry, each phratry provided 8 hippeis. This may have been the basic unit of organization and control.[39] No doubt, there was an officer at this level who supervised the men of the phratry troop. Three phratries formed a *phyle*, or tribe, so a tribal squadron consisted of 24 men. The 4 *phylarchoi* commanded 1 cavalry squadron each.[40] A lesser officer probably had this duty much of the time because each *phylarchos* apparently was also the commander of his tribe's entire military unit. The senior phylarchos, a hipparchos, or another officer selected by the *polemarchos* (chief military officer of Athens) most likely commanded the regiment of Athenian cavalry.

The basic tactical unit of the Athenian cavalry must have been the 24-man squadron. This unit could deploy in several formations. If a narrow front was required, the squadron could form a rectangle with a 3-man front and a depth of 8 men. A formation with a 6-man front and 4 men deep would provide a slightly longer front and occupy a space 11 yards by 21 yards, if the distance between files was 1 horse's width and the interval between ranks was 1 horse's length. This formation could be made a square with 21 yards on a side by simply increasing the distance between files to the width of 3 horses. A 24-man squadron could also deploy in a formation with an 8-man front and a depth of 3 men. These squadron squares or rectangles could be used like building blocks to form various regimental formations.

By the time of the Persian Wars, the Athenian cavalry probably existed in a much reduced state or in name only. This was the result of political conditions in Athens, namely, the reign of the Pisistratids and the reforms of Cleisthenes. Aristotle clearly stated that Pisistratus disarmed the Athenians upon seizing control of the city.[41] Obviously, if this is true and if the condition lasted throughout the reign of the Pisistratids, the Athenian military ceased to exist for several decades. But this was probably not the case. Pisistratus was a popular leader and had a good deal of support among the middle class, or Solon's zeugitai, who were mainly hoplites. So this segment of Athens' population was probably not disarmed for long, if at all.

However, it was prudent for Pisistratus to disarm his chief opponents, the aristocratic and wealthy classes. His first bid for power was foiled by Lycurgus, head of the clan Eteobutadae and leader of the men of the plain or the large land-holders, and by Megacles, head of the Alcmeonidae and leader of the men of the coast. In 546 B.C., Pisistratus' opposition once again included the Eteobutads, the Alcmeonids, the Philaids, and other powerful aristocratic clans.[42] The members of these clans formed the pentacosiomedimnoi and the hippeis, and they were certainly disarmed. In addition, Pisistratus took hostages and exiled members of these groups.[43] The result was a weakened aristocratic opposition but also a much weakened pentacosiomedimnoi and hippeis from which the Athenian cavalry was selected. Although Hippias followed his father's policies initially, the assassination of Hipparchus led Hippias to resort to far harsher measures. More exiles and repression led to a further reduction in the strength of the aristocrats and in the cavalry recruiting base and finally to an armed clash between the forces of Hippias and the Alcmeonids.[44] Pisistratid policies certainly led to the termination of the Athenian cavalry by 510 B.C.—possibly much earlier. Hippias had to obtain the services of 1,000 Thessalian cavalry when he attempted to maintain his control of Athens in the face of the Spartan liberation of the city.[45]

Although the Athenian cavalry probably was reinstated with the fall of the Pisistratids, it seems unlikely that any attempt was made to bring it up to its pre-Pisistratid size and readiness, let alone to improve it. Athens was now concerned with the major political and social reforms of Cleisthenes. These were popular in nature, meant to dissolve the ties of clan and phratry, which were part of the Athenian aristocracy and cavalry. The city was divided into demes, the demes grouped into trittyes, and the trittyes combined into 10 tribes. All the citizens of Athens were registered in their demes. There was a functioning government by 507 B.C. when the new *boule*, or Council of Five Hundred, sat for the first time. Yet the reform process continued for a while. The 10 *strategoi* (generals elected by the citizens) did not take over command of the army until 501 B.C.; at that point, perhaps for the first time, the 10 tribes became responsible for the various contingents of the Athenian army and the ships of the navy.[46] In this atmosphere of political change and turmoil, little attention was given to the most insignificant part of the military, the cavalry.[47]

In fact, there were Athenian horsemen at the Battle of Plataea (479 B.C.), but their role was very limited. Herodotus reported that

the Athenian hippeis were used as messengers and couriers.[48] Ultimately, the Athenian cavalry was simply too small to face the Persian
horsemen.[49] The lack of an effective mounted force during the Persian Wars, particularly at the Battle of Plataea, was so keenly felt that
Aristides, one of the commanders of the Athenian forces at Plataea,
asked for 1,000 cavalrymen, along with 10,000 hoplites and 100 triremes, in his proposal to continue the war against the Persians.[50]
Though Athens would field a mounted force of 1,000 men as an im-
perial power, the buildup of the Athenian cavalry was a slow process,
taking place over the period of the *pentakontaetia* (the 50-year interval between the Persian War and the start of the Peloponnesian War).

Details of the early stages in the growth of the Athenian cavalry,
from 479 B.C. to 458 B.C., are unknown. Some historians believe
that by the Battle of Tanagra (458/457 B.C.), Athens possessed 300
horsemen.[51] It certainly had cavalry at this time, which took an active enough part in the fighting to sustain casualties. A grave stele
found in the Kerameikos recorded that Melanopus and Marcartatus,
Athenian hippeis, were killed while fighting the Boeotians and the
Lacedaemonians.[52] However, it seems unlikely that the Athenian
horse numbered 300. Athens had been concentrating on the Persian
threat and overseas naval engagements for much of this period, so
increasing the number and quality of the triremes and hoplites was
the essential policy of war. Large numbers of horsemen were not absolutely necessary, and the Athenian cavalry therefore received only
marginal attention. This was especially true because even if a large
mounted force became necessary, the Thessalians were Athenian
allies and could be called upon to provide these troops. This is exactly what happened at Tanagra, with unfortunate results for the
Athenians.

The Athenian army at Tanagra was composed of 14,000 men, including 1,000 Thessalian hippeis. As the initial fighting broke out,
the Thessalians deserted the Athenian cause and joined the
Lacedaemonians. Later that night, the Thessalian horsemen rode
around the Athenian army and attacked the supply train bringing
food to their former allies. When the Athenians responded to this attack and went to the aid of their supply train, the Lacedaemonian
army came to the support of the Thessalian cavalry, resulting in a

pitched battle. Thucydides said that this culminated in a clear Spartan victory.[53] Diodorus, on the other hand, reported that the battle was a draw, with both sides setting up victory trophies.[54] No matter who is correct, one thing is certain: The Athenians no longer could rely on the Thessalians to provide mounted units to augment Athens' infantry.

The defection of the Thessalian horse forced the Athenians to act decisively to improve their own cavalry. The size of the Athenian cavalry was increased to 300 men.[55] Presumably, this was accomplished by recruiting equally from each of the 10 tribes, so 30 men from each tribe now served in the cavalry. There certainly was a tribal officer (perhaps the phylarch) in charge of each 30-man troop. Exactly how these troops were grouped together into a larger unit or squadron is unclear. It is known that 3 hipparchoi were elected or selected at this time.[56] This leads to the conclusion that 3 squadrons were formed, each with a composition of 100 men and led by a hipparch.[57] The problem here is that 10 troops do not divide equally into 3 squadrons; 1 troop had to be broken up if each squadron was going to have an equal number of men. Yet it seems inconceivable that a tribal troop would be broken up because the men of a tribe always formed a single unit and fought together. Perhaps the squadrons were not of equal size; perhaps 2 squadrons were each composed of 3 troops or 90 men, while the last had 4 troops and 120 men. A third alternative, which seems the most likely, is that the troops were grouped into 2 squadrons of 150 men each. Thus, there were 3 command positions available; 1 hipparchos commanded the regiment of Athenian cavalry, while the other 2 each commanded 1 of the squadrons. All hipparchoi were apparently equal, so the commands were probably rotated at set intervals, perhaps daily.[58]

Although the 300-man regiment was obviously larger than any previous Athenian cavalry, it was inadequate to meet the needs of the Athenians. In 446 B.C., Athens' position in central Greece was weakened, and a new threat emerged. Tolimedes, an Athenian general, and his army suffered a total defeat at the hands of a combined force of exiles from Boeotia, Locris, and Euboea. The general and many of his men were killed, and the rest were captured. Consequently, Athens was compelled to evacuate Boeotia,[59] thus facing a resurgent and hostile Boeotian Confederacy with its sizable cavalry. A further blow to Athens occurred in the fall of the same year when Attica was invaded by a Spartan army commanded by Pleistoanax, one of the Spartan kings. The Spartans captured Eleusis and ravaged the plain of Thria before withdrawing.[60] The Athenian cavalry obviously was not strong enough to stop the destruction by the Spartans. More cavalry was needed to counter the Theban threat and to protect Attica.

To meet these new demands, Athens increased the size of its cavalry to 600 men over the next few years.[61] Each tribe provided 60 cavalrymen for service. Instead of forming a single 60-man unit, the tribal contingent was likely divided into 30-man troops. This would provide much needed control in the heat of battle and follow the Greek preference, typical of the times, for basic units of less than 50 men.[62] The 2 troops of a tribe formed a cavalry phyle, or tribe, that was the equivalent of a squadron. Each of the 10 phylai was commanded by a phylarchos. The phylarchoi, like the strategoi, were elected annually by the assembly. Two hipparchoi were also elected; each commanded a regiment of 5 phylai.[63]

The final step in the buildup of the Athenian cavalry, accomplished in the last decade before the Peloponnesian War, was to increase it to 1,200 men. This force had two elements: a 1,000-man citizen cavalry and 200 *hippotoxotai*, or mounted archers who were mercenaries.[64] With regard to the former, the 10 tribes provided the cavalrymen equally. The cavalry phyle was made up of 100 men, probably composed of 2 troops of 50 men each. Each phyle was still commanded by a phylarchos. There is virtually no information about the organization of the mounted archers. It is possible that their troops were composed of twenty men,[65] and though a troop of hippotoxotai could have been assigned to each phyle, more likely a five-troop squadron was assigned to each cavalry regiment. Thus, each hipparchos commanded 600 men in a combination of light and heavy cavalry.

Athens was able to increase its cavalry because the city subsidized the cavalrymen. This policy apparently began about the middle of the fifth century B.C., and its multiple funding measures proved Athens' intent to establish a powerful mounted force. Such measures were necessary to overcome the cost of acquiring and maintaining war-horses because Attica was not horse-breeding country.[66] The first financial assistance available to cavalrymen was the *katastasis*, a state loan to the cavalry recruit for the purchase of a war-horse. The new hippeus could receive as much as 1,200 drachmas.[67] Far from being an insufficient amount, this was enough to buy the finest horse in Athens; indeed, prized stallions and racehorses sold for this exact sum.[68] The katastasis limit may have been intentionally high to allow the new cavalryman to buy the best horse available and still have some funds left for the initial upkeep and/or trappings. Or perhaps the intent was to provide the recruit with sufficient funds to buy 2 mounts. The horseman was expected to repay this loan upon retirement from cavalry service.

Athens' second financial measure was aimed at helping the hippeis feed their horses, by providing the cavalrymen with *sitoi*, or grain allowances.[69] Xenophon recorded that the cavalry cost Athens 40 talents a year (240,000 drachmas). This figure almost surely represents the annual cost of the sitoi accurately because 40 talents gave each of the 1,000 hippeis a daily ration allowance of 4 obols.[70] The rations of the Athenian cavalry horses no doubt varied somewhat because each cavalryman was responsible for feeding his own horse, but the typical mount required about 20 pounds of feed daily to stay fit for service.[71] The horses were inspected at regular intervals at the *dokimasiai* to check on their condition and training, under the supervision of the Council of Five Hundred. Any horse showing poor conditioning and failing to perform to standard was rejected for service, and the cavalryman had to sell it and purchase another or possibly risk his status as a hippeus and be required to immediately repay the katastasis.[72]

Finally, Athens guaranteed to pay for the replacement of any horse killed or disabled in the service of the city. The mounts were inspected at the *timêsis*, or evaluation, conducted by each hipparchos, whose secretary recorded the owner's name, color of the horse, brand mark, and monetary value for the public records. Although these records were complete enough, they were very brief: "'Of Arkesos, black, with a snake, 700 drachmas'" or "'Of Konon, a chestnut, with a centaur, 700 drachmas.'"[73] The stated value was paid to the horse's owner if the animal was killed or disabled in the line of duty, allowing for rapid replacement.[74]

Obviously, these subsidies enabled Athens to recruit cavalrymen from a larger segment of the population than had previously been possible. Traditionally, the cavalry had been composed of members of Solon's pentacosiomedimnoi and hippeis—Athens' wealthy citizens. According to Solon's reforms, the former had a minimum yearly income or return from their property of 500 measures, wet or dry; while the latter's income was 300 measures, and they maintained war-horses. Pollux provided another indication of the wealth of the upper classes when he noted that the pentacosiomedimnoi spent a talent (6,000 drachmas) on the state, the hippeis 3,000 drachmas, the zeugitai 1,000 drachmas, and the *thetes* nothing.[75] Pollux's statement is obscure, and the exact meaning is uncertain, but he did show proportional wealth and/or spending ability.[76] Unfortunately, there is no census data available from fifth century B.C. Athens to indicate the size of the upper classes, but the pentacosiomedimnoi and the hippeis were only a very small percentage of the male Athenian citizen population.

Considering the performance of the liturgies and the liturgical class, it is possible to determine some approximate numbers for the two upper classes. It seems likely that the pentacosiomedimnoi made up the liturgical class, the group of citizens who performed the liturgies.[77] These entailed the financing of various public events, functions, and duties, including: the *choregia*, the production of a chorus; the *gymnasiarchia*, the employment of professional trainers for the city gymnasium; the *estasis*, providing a banquet for a tribe at festival time; and the *trierarchia*, maintaining a trireme for a year. The cost of performing a liturgy ranged from about 300 drachmas for a Panathenaic chorus to 6,000 drachmas or 1 talent for a trierarchy.[78] J. K. Davies argued convincingly that the liturgical class only had about 300 members.[79] Therefore, there were about 300 pentacosiomedimnoi. If the hippeis were three times more numerous than the top class, or numbered about 900, then the two upper classes of Athens that formed the traditional pool from which the cavalry was enlisted totaled only about 1,200 men, or less than 5 percent of the male Athenian citizen population.[80]

On the face of it, this number would seem to be sufficient to provide the necessary manpower for a 1,000-man cavalry force. But in the middle of the fifth century B.C., this traditional pool of recruits was reduced by two factors. The first was the performance of the trierarchy. This liturgy exempted the citizen from performing other military liturgies or duties for the trierarch not only financed the operation and maintenance of a trireme but also served as captain of the ship.[81] Obviously because the *hippotrophia*, or maintenance of a cavalry horse, was a military liturgy and duty, a trierarch would come from the cavalry pool. The ancient sources show the extent of these exemptions. Plutarch said that Pericles kept 60 triremes in commission for eight months each year.[82] Thus, 60 trierarchs were needed. Thucydides noted that in 431 B.C., the Athenians decided to maintain 100 triremes in commission every year, which meant the appointment of a like number of trierarchs.[83] And this same historian reported that, at the start of the Peloponnesian War, Athens had about 300 triremes.[84] Potentially, then, almost all of the pentacosiomedimnoi could be assigned a ship and excused from cavalry service.

The second factor diminishing the cavalry pool was age. Though male Athenian citizens were obligated to serve on active military duty from age twenty to fifty, cavalry duty was a young man's military assignment. Aristophanes, in the *Knights*, emphasized the youthfulness of the cavalrymen, and his Paphlagonian slave, the character representing the demagogue Cleon, spoke of the "young horsemen" who did him wrong.[85] Some years later, Xenophon wrote that the cavalry recruits had to come "from among those who are most highly qualified by wealth and bodily vigor" and that the cavalry commander should assure the parents and guardians that he would "put an end to their (sons') extravagance in buying expensive horses, and see that they soon make good riders."[86] Xenophon here was clearly commenting on youthful excess and inexperience. Of course, he himself was a member of the Athenian cavalry as a young man, as was Dexileos, who died in the fighting around Corinth in 394 B.C. at the age of twenty.[87] In a study of the hippeis who participated in the Pythaides at the end of the second century B.C., Bugh found that about 70 percent of the horsemen were less than forty years old, and about 30 percent were in their twenties.[88] Though one must use evidence from later centuries with caution, the numbers illustrate the youthfulness of the cavalrymen.

There is no way to know precisely how many members of Solon's pentacosiomedimnoi and hippeis were over forty and thus probably out of the cavalry personnel pool, but it certainly would have been more than 25 percent, or almost 400 men.[89] This means that, potentially, the trierarchy and age factors could have eliminated 45 percent of the eligible men from service in the cavalry. Actually, this percentage is too high because there would have been some overlap between the trierarchies and the over-forty group, but the pool was almost certainly reduced to less than 1,000.

The katastasis, sitoi, and timêsis provided the financial means and incentives for some of the upper level zeugitai to volunteer for cavalry service and buy and maintain war-horses. Once the new recruit was accepted and his horse purchased, his political-socioeconomic census class was no doubt changed to hippeis. In this way, the traditional classes were expanded until eventually, by 431 B.C., the pentacosiomedimnoi and the hippeis may have totaled as many as 4,000, a sufficient number to offset exemptions due to age, physical fitness, other liturgies, and casualties and deaths, with enough men remaining to form a battle-ready mounted force of 1,000.

Some of the tactics and tactical formations employed by the Athenian cavalry can be determined. Fortunately, the works of Xenophon, particularly the *Xenophontos Hipparchikos*, are available to enhance the meager sources of the late fifth century B.C. Although Xenophon wrote his works toward the middle of the fourth century B.C., little had changed in the Athenian cavalry. Moreover, he was proud of the exploits and traditions of the fifth century B.C. Athenian hippeis and sought to continue these through his writings.[90] His knowledge of Athens' mounted force is all the more valuable because it was firsthand knowledge: Xenophon himself served in the Athenian cavalry in the fifth century B.C. and his sons served in it in the fourth century B.C. Of course, due caution needs to be exercised when using a later source, particularly when the author has such far-ranging experiences in warfare, to discover any anachronistic and/or foreign elements.

The cavalry phyle was clearly the basic tactical unit in the Athenian cavalry.[91] The primary formation of the phyle was a square with 10 files of 10 men each (Figure 4.1). Each file had 3 officers: a *decadarchos,* or leader of 10, who led the file; the *pempadarchos,* or leader of 5, who was the sixth man in the file and led the second half or section; and the file closer. According to Xenophon, the positions of the *decadarchoi* called for men who were sturdy and bent on winning fame, and those of the file closers called for older, more sensible men who were capable of inspiring confidence in others in the charge and leading prudently in a retreat.[92] For every 100 men, there were 30 officers—enough officers in each phyle to ensure control and responsiveness to orders and to provide leadership, whether advancing or retreating. The 10-by-10 square covered an area 19 yards wide by 57 yards deep, if the distance between files was 1 horse's width and the interval between ranks was 1 horse's length. Obviously, this presented a fairly narrow front to the enemy, but the depth allowed for the placement of inexperienced or weak horsemen in the middle of the formation. This square was probably a good parade formation because the entire cavalry regiment of 5 phylai could form up in a space the size of a football field or the Athenian agora. Also, this formation was narrow enough that the cavalry could parade through the city on the major streets, such as the Panathenaic Way, in a column of phylai.[93]

The phyle was also capable of forming a rectangle with a front of 20 men and a depth of 5 without losing any of its integrity or cohesiveness.[94] The key to this was the file officers, specifically the pempadarchoi. To form this rectangle, the standard parade formation opened to the left and the pempadarchoi led their sections forward and to the left of the front sections, stopping when they reached the front rank. Each decad, or 10-man unit, then formed 2 files of 5, with the decadarchos leading the right one and the pempadarchos leading the left. The 20-by-5 rectangle occupied a space 37 yards across by 27 yards deep, with a distance of 1 horse's width between files and an interval of 1 horse's length between ranks. Of course, if the distance or interval or both were increased, the formation would occupy proportionally more space.

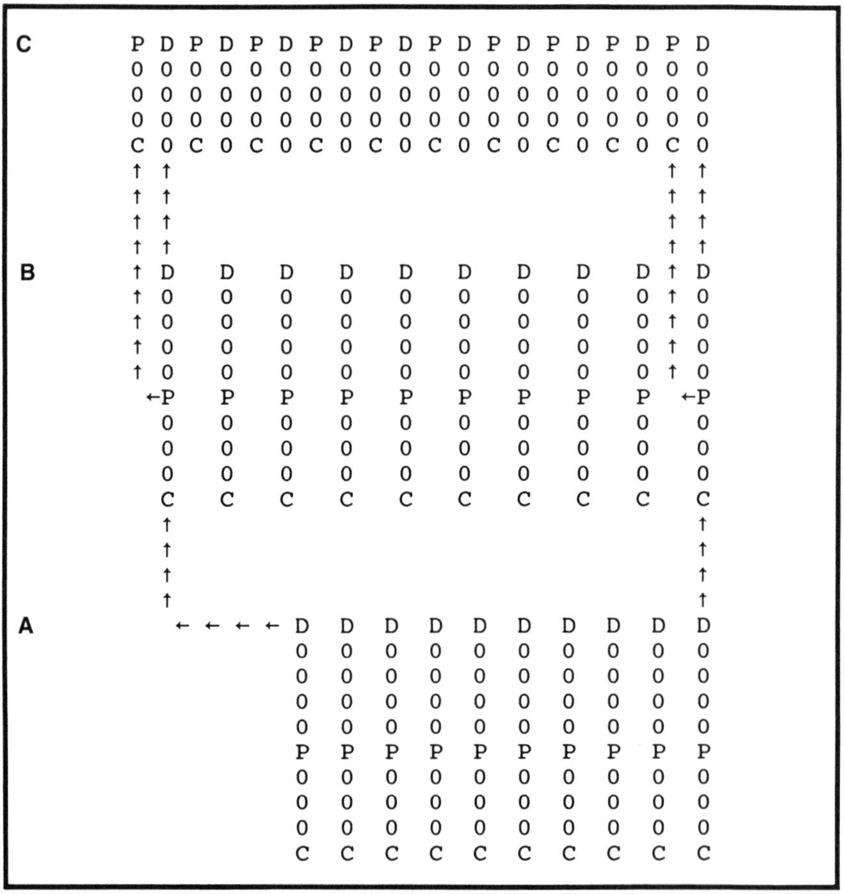

```
C    P D P D P D P D P D P D P D P D P D P D
     0 0 0 0 0 0 0 0 0 0 0 0 0 0 0 0 0 0 0 0
     0 0 0 0 0 0 0 0 0 0 0 0 0 0 0 0 0 0 0 0
     0 0 0 0 0 0 0 0 0 0 0 0 0 0 0 0 0 0 0 0
     C 0 C 0 C 0 C 0 C 0 C 0 C 0 C 0 C 0 C 0
     ↑ ↑                                 ↑ ↑
     ↑ ↑                                 ↑ ↑
     ↑ ↑                                 ↑ ↑
     ↑ ↑                                 ↑ ↑
B    ↑ D   D   D   D   D   D   D   D   D ↑ D
     ↑ 0   0   0   0   0   0   0   0   0 ↑ 0
     ↑ 0   0   0   0   0   0   0   0   0 ↑ 0
     ↑ 0   0   0   0   0   0   0   0   0 ↑ 0
     ↑ 0   0   0   0   0   0   0   0   0 ↑ 0
     ←P  P   P   P   P   P   P   P   P  ←P
       0   0   0   0   0   0   0   0   0   0
       0   0   0   0   0   0   0   0   0   0
       0   0   0   0   0   0   0   0   0   0
       C   C   C   C   C   C   C   C   C   C
       ↑                                   ↑
       ↑                                   ↑
       ↑                                   ↑
       ↑                                   ↑
A    ← ← ← ← D   D   D   D   D   D   D   D   D   D
             0   0   0   0   0   0   0   0   0   0
             0   0   0   0   0   0   0   0   0   0
             0   0   0   0   0   0   0   0   0   0
             0   0   0   0   0   0   0   0   0   0
             P   P   P   P   P   P   P   P   P   P
             0   0   0   0   0   0   0   0   0   0
             0   0   0   0   0   0   0   0   0   0
             0   0   0   0   0   0   0   0   0   0
             C   C   C   C   C   C   C   C   C   C
```

D Decadarchos
P Pempadarchos
C File Closer
0 Cavalry Troopers

Figure 4.1 *Athenian cavalry phyle formation. This diagram shows the evolution of an Athenian cavalry phyle from a 10-by-10 square to a 20-by-5 rectangle. The evolution begins in the standard parade formation (A), progresses to an extended, or open, formation (B), and is completed when the rear 5-man sections move left and forward (C). This evolution could have been performed while the phyle was either maintaining its position or advancing.*

It is likely that variations of the 20-by-5 rectangle with varying distance and/or interval were often employed in battle. The broad front allowed the horsemen to sweep forward without running afoul of one another. The shallow depth enabled orders to be passed more easily and accurately. And because the Athenian cavalry used javelins, a more open formation provided the necessary room for the horses and riders to maneuver.[95] Though horses can turn in a very short space if necessary—as can be seen in any rodeo barrel race—this is not a good idea in cavalry combat unless it is absolutely necessary since a fall or mistimed turn can be fatal. With a distance of several horses' widths between files and an interval of several horses' lengths between ranks, the entire phyle could advance toward an enemy, and as each successive rank came within range of the enemy, the horsemen could throw their javelins, turn their horses while maintaining their file organization, and retire to regroup for another attack.

The Athenian cavalry with its 2 regiments was certainly capable of deploying on both wings of a phalanx, but the preferred position apparently was a single formation on the left wing.[96] This deployment probably had two purposes. First, it obviously reinforced and strengthened the left wing—the weakest wing of the phalanx, in most cases, because it contained the inferior hoplites. Second, a strong cavalry presence on the left wing could prevent this wing from being enveloped. Although the horsemen might be pushed back by a concerted hoplite advance, any attempt to pivot in on the Athenian left would expose the backs of the enemy to an Athenian cavalry attack. This tactical deployment must have been developed to counter the Spartan threat for the Spartans had no mounted force and were notorious for enveloping their enemy's left wing.

Of course, for any military unit to perform well, training is a must. Considering that the hippeis were members of the upper classes, with myriad political, economic, social, and family responsibilities, finding time for the necessary training must have been difficult. Xenophon himself acknowledged this: "It is, perhaps, too much trouble to have them [the *hippeis*] out frequently when there is no war going on."[97] However, the city required the cavalrymen to train a certain amount of time. The Council of Five Hundred set this requirement and could change it when necessary.[98] While the exact amount of time spent on training is unknown, some training activities and lessons can be identified.

Xenophon recommended cavalry recruits learn to mount from the spring and thought this should be taught by a skilled instructor.[99] This activity apparently took place near the *Hipparcheion,* or office of the hipparchoi in the northwest corner of the Athenian agora.[100] The fourth-century comic poet Mnesimachos wrote, "Go forth, Manes, to the Agora, to the Herms, the place frequented by the phylarchs, and to their handsome pupils, whom Pheidon trains in mounting and dismounting."[101] Actually, the agora probably was the site of much of the cavalry training, having ample space for 2 or 3 tribes of cavalry to exercise simultaneously. In some Greek cities, the agora was called the *hippodrome.*[102]

Another training activity that could have taken place in the agora was mounted javelin-throwing. This practice was conducted by the individual phyle, rather than by a regiment or the entire Athenian cavalry.[103] Xenophon thought this drill should be conducted with each rider advancing to the front with his left shoulder aligned with the target. At the appropriate distance from the target, the rider should rise up slightly from the thighs and draw back his weapon in his right hand and then throw the javelin with the point slightly raised.[104] From this description, it is clear that the rider's target was either straight in front of the horse or to the horse's left, requiring the rider to throw across the neck of his mount. An Attic red-figure crater clearly shows the hippeis practicing the javelin throw as Xenophon described (Figure 4.2). Here, the horsemen used hoplite shields suspended from poles as targets for their weapons.[105] It is interesting to note that the riders pass by the targets on either side, indicating that the horsemen were practicing a form of attack that would carry them past or through the enemy. Almost certainly, the javelins were thrown at very close range with this tactic, probably less than 5 yards from the target, to impart a maximum amount of force. Clearly, there were two possible aim points and goals—either to drive the javelin into the shield, thus rendering it useless to the hoplite, or to hit the post below the shield, thereby simulating a hit on the legs of the hoplite or on a fallen opponent[106] (Figure 4.3). Of

Figure 4.2 *Athenian cavalrymen practice throwing javelins at suspended shields (fourth century B.C. Attic red-figure crater). Courtesy of the Musée du Louvre, Paris. Copyright R.M.N.*

course, the cavalrymen also had to practice throwing their weapons from a greater distance, between 10 and 20 yards from the target.[107] The javelin would need a curved trajectory for the greater range, and the target would not be as precise. This tactic was more suitable for confronting a massed infantry formation or phalanx.

The cavalry also had to practice formation riding and tactics, drills probably not conducted in the agora. The hippodrome or one

Figure 4.3 *Light cavalryman throwing his javelin (not shown) at a fallen hoplite. Stele of Dexileos (fourth century B.C.). Photograph by the author.*

of the Attic plains was obviously more suitable for this type of active training exercise and better able to accommodate either a regiment or the entire Athenian mounted force.[108] The horsemen had to be able to march in column, extend the front, and form a battleline expeditiously and without losing cohesion. Also, all of these formations and evolutions had to be done at various gaits. Finally, the hippeis had to practice the advance and attack, shock tactics or the charge, and regrouping for another charge or a withdrawal.

To ensure that the cavalry was battle ready, a series of parades and demonstrations were performed for the public and city officials, apparently three times each year. At the Lyceum, the cavalry paraded by regiment in their line of battle, exhibited equestrian skills, and demonstrated the art of javelin-throwing.[109] The Academy display emphasized formation riding, finishing with a charge.[110] Finally, the *anthippasis*, or mock battle, was performed during the Olympieia and the Great Panathenaia at the Hippodrome. First, the entire cavalry formed a single formation with a front that stretched across the Hippodrome and swept forward, driving the people out of the riding area. Then, the cavalry regiments opposed each other and simulated attacks, pursuits, and withdrawals. The finale was a series of charges; the regiments faced each other and, on a given signal, charged, passed through the opposing formation, and regrouped for another charge. This was done three times, and the pace of the charge was increased each time. The phyle showing the best skills was awarded a prize.[111]

As the Peloponnesian War drew near, the Athenian cavalry was among the best in Greece and appeared ready to meet the challenge as a result of almost fifty years of effort. Indeed, the Athenian mounted force was stronger, at 1,200 men, than any other cavalry except the Thessalian. This strength was the product of a policy specifically designed to create a strong detachment of Athenian horsemen. The katastasis, sitoi, and timêsis lightened the financial burden of owning and maintaining a horse for public service so that more citizens could afford to serve as cavalrymen. Moreover, the strength of the Athenian cavalry was further enhanced by the employment of 200 mercenary horsemen as mounted archers. The Athenians expected their subsidized mounted force to be battle ready. The organization of the Athenian cavalry was such that the men fought alongside friends and neighbors in a phyle controlled by numerous officers. Training was mandated by the Council of Five Hundred, and well-honed skills were displayed at various parades and reviews. In part, this Athenian cavalry buildup was a response to the threat of the Boeotian horse. The Boeotian cavalry had a long tradition, and the federal military organization of the Boeotian Confederation provided an extremely powerful mounted force: The 11 districts each provided 100 cavalrymen, for a total of 1,100 horsemen. Ultimately, these 2 mounted forces would clash repeatedly during the Peloponnesian War.

5

Greek Cavalry in the Peloponnesian War

The Peloponnesian War (431–404 B.C.) has often been described as the war of the elephant versus the whale. Sparta, its Peloponnesian League, and their Boeotian Confederacy allies had a huge army—an elephant. Athens and its allies or empire commanded the sea with the largest navy in the Mediterranean—a whale. And yet, the role played by mounted forces, or the horse should not be overlooked or forgotten in a study of this war. Cavalry fought on both sides, in all theaters of war, and in a variety of roles. Although it was not the decisive element for either side, cavalry was vital for success in many operations. It was the first line of defense against invasions or incursions, so much so that Sparta organized a mounted force for the first time in almost two centuries to counter offensive activities. On the battlefield, cavalry created a victory for the Thebans at Delium, saved the Athenian infantry from annihilation at Mantinea, and denied victory to the Athenians at Syracuse.

Cavalry was actually very prominent in the initial fighting between Athens and Sparta. In 431 B.C., the Spartan king Archidamus led an army across the Isthmus of Corinth and into Attica. After an unsuccessful attempt to capture the fortified town of Oenoe, Archidamus marched into the territory of Eleusis and the Thriasian plain. Near the Rheiti streams, the Athenian cavalry attacked, possibly as the leading elements of the Spartan army began to cross.

Though Thucydides said the Athenians were routed, this was no more than the opening skirmish of the war, and casualties were probably light on both sides.[1] The failure of the Athenian hippeis to stop the advance of Archidamus only meant that 1,200 horsemen were no match for the advanced guard or possibly a good portion of a large Spartan army.[2]

Archidamus led his army through the Thriasian plain to Acharnae, where the Lacedaemonians and their allies encamped. Then, the Spartan king sent out detachments to ravage this largest Attic deme, hoping the Athenians would come out from behind the walls of the city and fight a major, decisive battle. Pericles' response to Archidamus' tactic was to continually send units of the Athenian cavalry to harass and attack the raiding parties from the Spartan army.[3] Though Thucydides, our principal source for the Peloponnesian War, did not describe the harassing tactics employed by the Athenian horsemen, Xenophon, writing in the mid–fourth century B.C., provided a vivid account of Syracusan hippeis employing similar tactics against a Theban army:

> But the horsemen sent by Dionysius, few though they were, scattering themselves here and there, would ride along the enemy's line, charge upon them and throw javelins at them, and when the enemy began to move forth against them, would retreat, and then turn round and throw javelins again. And while pursuing these tactics they would dismount from their horses and rest. But if anyone charged upon them while they were dismounted, they would leap easily upon their horses and retreat. On the other hand, if any pursued them far from the Theban army, they would press upon these men when they were retiring, and by throwing javelins work havoc with them, and thus they compelled the entire army, according to their own will, either to advance or to fall back.[4]

This type of action by the Athenian cavalry seriously impeded the ability of the invaders to ravage the Attic countryside and destroy significant amounts of property. All raiding parties had to be protected from mounted attack by large numbers of hoplites; small formations of heavy infantry were an insufficient deterrent and could be surrounded and possibly destroyed, and light-armed troops, or peltasts, could be ridden down.[5] Yet large formations had to move slowly to maintain proper order and integrity and to ensure there were no gaps or other opportunities for the ever-vigilant mounted defenders of Attica to exploit. Their slow pace was reduced even further by frequent harassment and attack. The efforts of the Athenian hippeis and their allies were largely successful because the Spartans were prevented from venturing into central and southern Attica, and little permanent damage was done.[6] The people of Athens apparently recognized the success of Pericles' policy for they elected him strategos again the next year.[7]

Although Archidamus apparently had a sufficient cavalry to counter the Athenian mounted threat, his cavalry assets were not sufficient to oppose a combined force of Athenian and Thessalian horse. Accompanying the invading Spartan army were units of Theban, Phocian, and Locrian horsemen.[8] Given that Thucydides recorded that every Spartan ally had to send two-thirds of its total military assets with Archidamus, the Theban mounted force consisted of 7 regiments or 700 men.[9] The numbers for the Phocians and the Locrians are unknown, but it seems likely the two poleis could have furnished a total of at least 100 horsemen or possibly as many as 100 each. Thus, Archidamus' mounted force consisted of between 800 and 900 men. Of course, even without reinforcements from allies, the Athenian cavalry was stronger, with 1,200 men. But Athens' hippeis were reinforced by units of Thessalian cavalry; Larisaean, Pharsalian, Crannonian, Pyrasian, Gyrtonian, and Pheraean horsemen came to Athens' aid.[10] Though no figures are recorded, if each of the Thessalian political entities listed dispatched a single squadron of 4 troops, or 160 men, this increased Athens' mounted strength by 960 riders. Then, the mounted defenders of Attica numbered more than 2,000. This meant Pericles had sufficient horsemen to confront Archidamus' cavalry and still have ample mounted units available to harass the ravagers and raiders.

With this numerical superiority, it seems likely that Athenian mounted units constantly remained near and watched the Spartan camp. This occasionally led to the interception of and conflict with not only enemy raiders but also enemy horsemen as they attempted to leave. This seems to have been the case, for example, when elements of the two opposing mounted forces clashed at Phrygia. As Thucydides reported:

> There was a cavalry skirmish at Phrygia between a company of Athenian horsemen, assisted by some Thessalians, and the Boeotian cavalry, in which the Athenians and Thessalians fully held their own, until their heavy infantry came to the support of the Boeotians, when they were routed. A few of the Thessalians and Athenians were killed, but their bodies were recovered the same day without a truce.[11]

Thucydides seemed to imply that the full Boeotian mounted contingent engaged in battle with several units of the Athenian cavalry, supported by some Thessalian mounted units. The exact number of the Athenian cavalry involved in this engagement is uncertain. Thucydides used the term *telos,* which simply means a unit.[12] Probably, the Athenian telos was composed of several phylai, or several hundred men. If the Thessalians were equal in strength, the defenders numbered about 600, enough to separate and pursue several groups of raiders or to safely contest a large enemy mounted force, such as Archidamus' Boeotian cavalry. The rapid arrival of heavy infantry to support the routed Boeotians placed this battle near the Spartan camp. Thus, the Athenians and Thessalians were assigned to observe and, where possible, confront enemy units.

Although no further cavalry actions were reported by Thucydides, this does not mean that none took place. In fact, the author himself told us that he only recorded the unusual or notable. So as cavalry engagements became a daily occurrence, he naturally stopped reporting them.[13] Further, Thucydides did not indicate that Pericles changed his defensive policy, which means that units of Athenian and Thessalian horse sallied forth daily from the city to confront, harass, attack, and confound the Spartans and their allies. As this continued until the invaders left Attica, the defenders were active for another month or so, for the Spartans attempted to ravage some of the area between Mt. Parnes and Mt. Brilessus. However, Archidamus remained in Attica only as long as his supplies allowed, no doubt because the activity of his foragers was also adversely affected by the Athenian and Thessalian horsemen. At that point, the Lacedaemonian army marched out of Attica and into Boeotia.[14]

Attica was invaded again in 430, 428, 427, and 425 B.C. The evidence suggests that the Athenian cavalry bore the brunt of the fighting in 428 B.C., but there is no indication of the Athenian reactions to the other invasions. About 428 B.C., Thucydides said, "And sallies were made as usual by the Athenian cavalry wherever opportunity offered, which prevented the great mass of the enemy's light-armed troops from going beyond their watch-posts and laying waste the districts near the city."[15] The tone of this statement implies that this was the routine response to a Spartan invasion. It therefore can be safely concluded that all such invasions met the same response and were challenged by the Athenian hippeis, and that Thucydides, as was his practice, ignored the routine and commonplace.

The Athenians took the offensive by sending out naval raids against the Peloponnesus and other places beginning in the first year of the war. As Archidamus was attempting to ravage Attica in 431 B.C., Pericles dispatched 100 ships with 1,000 hoplites and 400 archers to sail around the Peloponnesus and raid its coastal towns. The Athenian fleet was reinforced by 50 Corcyran ships. Methone in Laconia was attacked, but it was saved by the timely and bold intervention of Brasidas and a small guard detachment. Other towns were less fortunate. Pheia in Elis was taken and the countryside ravaged for several days.[16] In 430 B.C., as the Lacedaemonian army again invaded Attica, Pericles himself led a naval expedition against the land of Pelops. This force consisted of 100 ships, 4,000 hoplites, and 300 cavalry. Additional ships for this expedition were provided by the Chians and the Lesbians. The raiders landed near Epidaurus and ravaged the land around the city. The Athenian army assaulted the city walls with no success. Later, Troizen, Hallieis, and Hermione were also raided. Pericles' expedition met its greatest success with the capture and sacking of Prasiae in Laconia.[17]

The Athenian cavalry that Pericles took on this expedition was used for rapid, far-reaching raids and reconnaissance duties. These horsemen had virtually free rein for the Spartans possessed no mounted force to impede them. This overseas deployment marked a first for the Athenians: For the first time in history, their hippeis and mounts sailed on horse-transports. These vessels were old, converted triremes.[18] Each transport accommodated 30 cavalrymen, their horses and equipment, and the necessary grooms and servants. The trireme was propelled by about 170 rowers; the horse-transport used 60 rowers. The upper deck, which was once occupied by banks of rowers, now was used for the horses. The animals were placed between the bow and the quarter-deck, standing sideways to the ship's centerline with their rumps against the boards of the stanchions and their chests against rails set up for the purpose. Half the animals were installed forward of the mast, and half aft.[19] From this time on, cavalry contingents were part of a number of Athenian overseas expeditions.

These Athenian naval raids occurred every year in which the Lacedaemonians invaded Attica, and they hurt the Peloponnesians who lived on or near the coast. Sparta's only way to counter the Athenian activity was to send out roving guard patrols, raise local levies, or recall the army from Attica. Whatever the response, the relief force had to march to the location of the raid in time to foil the Athenians.[20] But foot soldiers—even the professional soldiers of Sparta—marched too slowly for effective response. Even with a march rate of 50 miles per day, it was a three-day forced march from Attica to Sparta.[21] And because the Spartans had no cavalry, there was no option for a more rapid deployment.

In 425 B.C., the situation for Sparta worsened. The Athenians established a fort at Pylos in Messenia. This was garrisoned by Athenian and Messenian hoplites, with most of the latter having recently served at Naupactus. Units from this garrison raided and ravaged the countryside and encouraged the Messenian helots to join the Athenian cause.[22] Considering the Spartan phobia about helot revolts, this must have been a major concern to them. The next year, the Athenians captured the island of Cythera off the Laconian coast, and using this base, they raided the nearby coastal towns of Laconia.[23] With this operations site within easy striking range of the Peloponnesus, naval raids could now be launched more frequently and rapidly into the heart of the Spartan homeland for Athenian ships no longer had to sail from the Piraeus every time.

To counter this dual threat, the Spartans devised a dual response. First, they established garrisons at a number of key locations,[24] probably in southern Laconia. This area, the most threatened by the Athenian ships at Cythera, contained a number of towns important to the Spartans, but it was small enough that neighboring garrisons could support one another rapidly. Second, the Spartans organized a force of 400 cavalrymen and archers.[25] This new cavalry, raised in haste to meet the pressing Athenian threat, was probably as large as possible and contained all the horses suitable for cavalry duty in Laconia. The horsemen may have been aristocrats, but it is more likely that the aristocrats only furnished the horses for others to ride. Considering the traditional contempt for and disinterest in mounted units in Sparta, it is possible the *hypomeiones,* or subordinate citizens of Sparta, were assigned that duty.[26] This cavalry was apparently meant to have a twofold role. First, it was a quick-reaction force that could rapidly ride to an area threatened by the Athenians. Given the Spartans' lack of training in mounted combat at this time, it seems likely that, initially at least, the horsemen only used their mounts for combat mobility and dismounted to engage the Athenians. However, if the same horsemen were assigned to the cavalry for any length of time and if training and combat were fairly frequent, this situation undoubtedly changed fairly rapidly and the horsemen probably became proficient with their mounts and mounted combat. Second, this force was a countermeasure to the Athenian-Messenian activity around the fort at Pylos. Mounted units could observe the comings and goings, harass raiding parties, patrol Messenia and increase the Spartan presence, and run down escaping helots.

Unfortunately, little is known of the organization of the new Spartan cavalry. If the Lacedaemonians showed the same concern for organization and control with this new mounted force as they did with their infantry, the Spartan cavalry must have been highly organized. The organization which the Spartans knew best and could most readily adapt to meet their needs was that of their infantry, and so it is likely this model was used. Thus, the basic tactical unit was the cavalry *mora,* or regiment of 100 men. Each mora was commanded by a *hipparmostes.*[27] When the new cavalry was organized in

424 B.C., there were 4 morai. In less than a decade, there were 6, which meant the size of the Spartan mounted force was 600 men.[28] No doubt, the mora was broken down into two *pentecostyes,* or 50-man squadrons. Each *pentecostys* was commanded by a *penteconter.* Finally, each pentecostys contained 2 25-man *enomotiai,* or troops. The leader of each *enomotia* was the *enomotarchos.*[29]

If the infantry model was faithfully followed by the Spartans, the basic formation of the cavalry mora was a rectangle with a 12-man front and a depth of 8 men (Figure 5.1). This was formed by having each enomotia parade in a formation with a 3-man front and a depth of 8 men. The enomotarchos led the right file and was part of the front rank. The *ouragos,* or rear leader, rode behind the last rank as the twenty-fifth man.[30] The 12-by-8 rectangle occupied a space 23 yards across the front and 45 yards deep, if 1 horse's width separated the files and 1 horse's length separated the ranks. If a broader front was needed, the 12-by-8 rectangle could easily be expanded by adding distance between files or become a 24-by-4 rectangle by opening the formation and having the rear 4-man section in each file move forward. With standard distance and interval, the 24-by-4 rectangle occupied an area 47 yards across the front and 21 yards deep.

The northern Greeks also used cavalry as a means of defense against invasions and incursions. In 429 B.C., the Athenian general Xenophon, the son of Euripides, along with two of his colleagues, departed Potidaea with a force of 2,000 hoplites and 200 cavalry. This force marched north, skirting Olynthus to the city of Spartulos. En route, the Athenians were joined by a few peltasts from Crousis. The Athenians believed Spartulos would be betrayed to them, but this was a vain hope for the city was garrisoned by Olynthian and mercenary hoplites, Chalcidian light-armed infantry, and Chalcidian cavalry.[31] Although the exact numbers are not known, it seems likely the number of hoplites on both sides was about equal, but the Chalcidians definitely had the advantage in light infantry and horsemen.

The cavalry available to the Chalcidians was considerable. The Olynthian horse alone numbered about 500 men.[32] This could be supplemented by an additional 500 troopers, for a total of 1,000, if the full strength of the Chalcidian League was employed.[33] The Olynthian horse was commanded by 2 hipparchoi.[34] With a force of

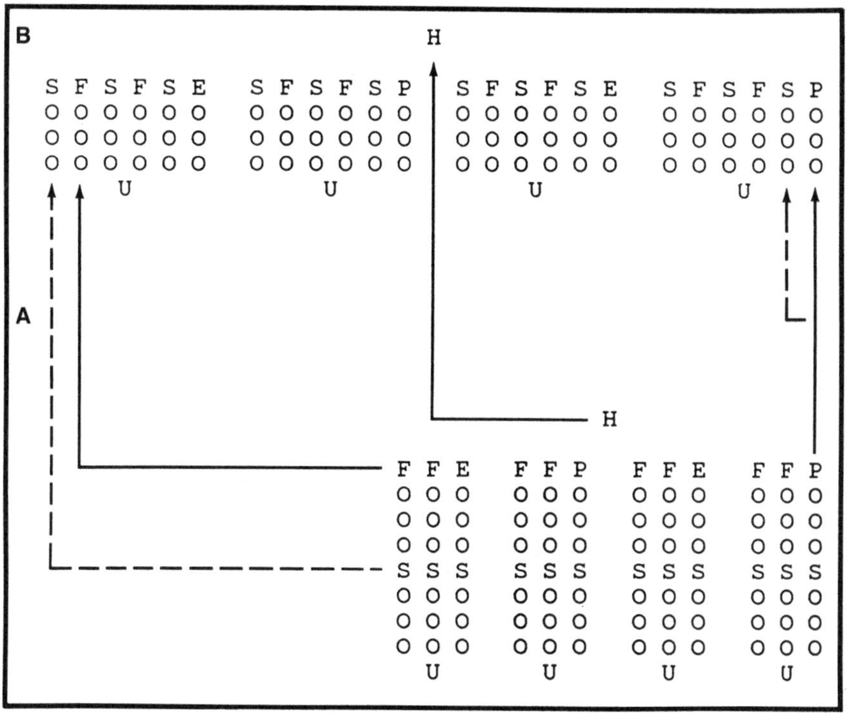

```
B                        H
 S F S F S E    S F S F S P │ S F S F S E    S F S F S P
 O O O O O O    O O O O O O │ O O O O O O    O O O O O O
 O O O O O O    O O O O O O │ O O O O O O    O O O O O O
 O O O O O O    O O O O O O │ O O O O O O    O O O O O O
 ↑ ↑ U            U         ↑   U              U    ↑ ↑
 │ │                        │                       │ │
 │ │                                                │ │
 │ │                                              ┌─┘ │
A│ │                                              L    │
 │ │                                                   │
 │ │                             ┌──────────── H        │
 │ │                             │                       │
 │ └─────────────────────── F F E    F F P    F F E    F F P
 │                          O O O    O O O    O O O    O O O
 │                          O O O    O O O    O O O    O O O
 │                          O O O    O O O    O O O    O O O
 └ ─ ─ ─ ─ ─ ─ ─ ─ ─ ─ ─ ─  S S S    S S S    S S S    S S S
                            O O O    O O O    O O O    O O O
                            O O O    O O O    O O O    O O O
                            O O O    O O O    O O O    O O O
                              U        U        U        U
```

H Hipparmostes
P Pentecostys
E Enomotachos
F File Leader
S Section Leader
U Uragos
O Cavalry Troopers

Figure 5.1 *Spartan cavalry mora formations. This diagram shows a Spartan cavalry mora in formation: (A) is the standard 12-by-8 rectangle, and (B) is the 24-by-4 rectangle. Here, for clarity, the enomotiai and pentecostyes are shown separated. In actuality, no such separation existed.*

500 men and 2 commanders, it is logical to conclude that the Olynthian cavalry was divided into 2 regiments of 250 men each. Thus, the Chalcidian League cavalry as a whole contained 4 regiments and 4 hipparchoi. Each regiment was composed of 5 50-man squadrons; every squadron had a commander, or ilarch, and was the basic tactical unit. The easiest formation for this size unit was a rectangle with a 10-man front and a depth of 5 men.

At the approach of the Athenians, the Chalcidians sallied forth from Spartulos, no doubt led by the cavalry and light-armed troops, which formed a screen while the hoplites deployed. A battle ensued close to the walls of the city. Because the Athenians were not surprised by the actions of the Chalcidians, Xenophon must either have had his army in a battle formation, rather than in a marching column, or have deployed his forces as rapidly as the Chalcidians. The Athenian hoplites defeated the opposing heavy infantrymen, who retreated into the city. However, as the battle continued between the Chalcidian horsemen and light-armed soldiers, covering the retreat of their hoplites, and the Athenian cavalry and the light-armed troops from Crousis, pursuing the withdrawing foe, the tide of battle turned in favor of the defenders of Spartolus. The pursuing cavalrymen and light infantry were defeated and apparently driven from the battlefield for their presence is not mentioned again by Thucydides.[35] As the two sides disengaged, another contingent of peltasts arrived from Olynthus.

These fresh troops inspired the Chalcidians to resume the conflict. The reinforced peltasts, supported by the Chalcidian cavalry, attacked the Athenian heavy infantry and drove it back to its baggage train. The Athenians were then subjected to a rain of javelins. When their hoplites advanced against the peltasts, the light-armed troops gave ground. The weight of the hoplite panoply made it impossible for the heavy infantrymen to catch their lightly armed foes. As the hoplites attempted to return to their formation, the peltasts reversed and again attacked with javelins.

The Chalcidian cavalry delivered the decisive blows to the Athenian army. According to Thucydides, "Then the Chalcidian cavalry riding up, kept charging the Athenians wherever opportunity offered, and by throwing them into complete panic routed them and pursued them a great distance."[36] From this, it is clear that, besides falling on and riding down any stragglers and small groups, the horsemen charged a number of times, presumably at gaps, and disorganized and confused units. These repeated attacks finally caused panic and fear among the hoplites. As the Athenians broke and fled, the Chalcidian horsemen rode down and slew many of the fleeing soldiers. The Athenians lost 330 men and all their generals in this engagement; most of these casualties can be attributed to the action of the Chalcidian light-armed infantry and cavalry.[37]

Although the Athenian hoplites had seemingly won the day with their defeat of the Chalcidian heavy infantry, the victory was turned into a defeat by cavalry and light-armed forces acting together. Thanks, in part, to superior numbers, the Chalcidian horsemen and peltasts not only defeated their Athenian counterparts but, more importantly, also drove them from the field. Without this support, the Athenian hoplites were vulnerable to the mobile, skirmishing tactics of the cavalry and light infantry, which caused casualties, frustration, and anxiety for the opposing heavy infantrymen. The final element in the Chalcidian victory was the repeated charges of the cavalry, delivering blow after blow until the Athenians broke and fled. The battle was climaxed by the pursuit of the Chalcidian horsemen and the slaughter of the fleeing soldiers.[38]

Clearly, cavalry was important for defense. But it also demonstrated its worth on the battlefield. In 424 B.C., at Delium, the Athenians were once again defeated by a mounted force: This time, the Boeotian cavalry was the decisive element. Several days before the battle, the Athenians had marched an army into southern Boeotia and captured Delium, a temple site that was then fortified with a ditch, wall, and wooden towers. The Athenians intended to use this fortified site as a base of operations for raids and incursions into Boeotia. On the fifth day after leaving Attica, with the work on the fortifications near completion, the Athenian army (except for a garrison) and workers departed for home. The commander, Hippocrates, remained behind to ensure that the guard was properly posted and the work completed. The army marched 10 *stadia* (approximately 2,000 yards), at which point the Athenian hoplites and the cavalry halted while the light-armed soldiers and workers continued on toward Athens.[39]

In response to the invasion, the Boeotians gathered their forces at Tanagra. When it was learned the invaders were returning to Attica, most of the Boeotarchs wanted to disband the army and let the soldiers return to their cities. But Pagondas, apparently having debated unsuccessfully with his colleagues, appealed directly to the soldiers and persuaded them to attack the retiring Athenians. Even though it was late in the day, the Boeotians broke camp and marched out to intercept the enemy. After marching for several hours, when Pagondas was sure his army was close to his foes, he halted at a place where a hill intervened between the two armies so that neither could see the other. He then deployed the Boeotians for battle.[40]

Although Thucydides did not mention any scouts, the Boeotians must have used their cavalry in this capacity.[41] They knew the Athenian army had left Delium, and this information was received quickly enough for Pagondas to act upon it. The distance between Tanagra and Delium was approximately 6 miles.[42] While it is possible that runners were used, and a good runner could have covered this distance in about an hour or so, runners were vulnerable to Athenian cavalry patrols.[43] More likely, Boeotian mounted units, possibly one of the cavalry regiments, kept track of the Athenian activity at Delium. At set intervals and/or at times of special activity, messengers were dispatched to update the Boeotarchs at Tanagra.[44] This would explain not only the Boeotarchs' knowledge of the Athenian departure from Delium but also Pagondas' exact knowledge of the location of the halted Athenian army, which allowed him to stop and deploy just out of sight of his enemy.

Apparently, the Athenians were also using cavalry units as scouts. Hippocrates was notified of the Boeotian army's movements and subsequently sent orders to the Athenian army to form for battle. He left 300 Athenian horsemen at Delium to supplement the garrison, with orders to protect the fort and, if possible, to attack the Boeotian army. Hippocrates then joined his command. Pagondas countered the Athenian commander's planned cavalry attack by sending a detachment to watch the fort at Delium and its garrison.[45] Then, he moved his battle formation up the slope on his side of the intervening hill and onto the ridgeline that looked down upon the Athenian army. Pagondas had 7,000 hoplites in a phalanx, with the Thebans on the right some 25 shields deep. The center was held by the Haliartians, Coronaeans, Copaeans, and other peoples from around Lake Copias. Thespians, Tanagraeans, and Orchomenians held the left. The hoplites forming both the center and the left were probably not as deep as the Thebans. Ten thousand light-armed troops, 500 peltasts, and 1,000 cavalry were divided and placed on both wings.[46]

The Athenian phalanx also contained 7,000 hoplites, who were drawn up in a uniform depth of 8 men. The Athenian cavalry, which probably had less than 500 men, was divided between the two wings.[47] There were only a few allied light-armed troops for most had accompanied the workers marching to Athens. Hippocrates exhorted the Athenians to fight well because a victory would mean that the Peloponnesians would be deprived of Boeotian support and the Boeotian cavalry.[48]

Before Hippocrates had finished his speech, the Boeotians raised the paean, or victory song, and began to advance downhill. The Athenians likewise began to advance but at a run, in an apparent attempt to negate the advantage of a downhill attack. While the hoplite phalanxes met and a fierce struggle ensued with shield pressed against shield at times, the wings of both armies were kept apart by rushing streams and ravines. The Athenian hoplites on the right drove back the Boeotian left. The Thespians suffered the worst casualties because they stood firm and thus found themselves surrounded. Some Athenians were even killed by fellow Athenians in this confused combat. The Thebans on the right of the Boeotian phalanx forced back the Athenians opposite them, step by step.[49]

Pagondas, upon realizing that his left was in trouble, ordered 2 cavalry tele from the right wing, probably 2 regiments of 100 men each, to ride around a hill and fall upon the rear of the Athenian right.[50] This was far from an easy task. First, because the streams prevented the cavalry of either army from advancing, the 2 tele had to move backward while maintaining their formations. Next, they had to turn outward, away from their own rear, for cavalry riding behind the Boeotian line could very well be taken for the enemy or seen as retreating—and in either case was likely to cause a panic among the infantry soldiers. Then, the Boeotian horsemen had to ride around the hill and completely behind the Athenian left and center without attracting too much attention or getting involved in a fight. Finally, the 2 tele had to attack the rear of the Athenian right.

The cavalry tele overcame the difficulties and reached the Athenian right in time to save the day. Thucydides reported that the sight of the cloud of dust raised by the approaching horsemen was enough to cause some of the Athenians to flee. When the Boeotian horsemen suddenly appeared and charged, the Athenian right broke, and the hoplites fled. The Athenian left, hard pressed by the Theban infantry, followed suit. A general rout of the Athenian army followed. The Boeotian cavalry and the newly arrived Locrian cavalry pursued and slew the fleeing soldiers until night halted their activity.[51] Only the arrival of darkness allowed the fleeing Athenians to escape without further losses. According to Thucydides, the Athenian casualties included Hippocrates, about 1,000 hoplites, and numerous light-armed and support personnel. The inclusion of the latter seems to indicate that the Theban horse caught up to the Athenian light-armed troops and workers.[52]

The Boeotian cavalry performed well at Delium. When information was the most important commodity, the cavalry scouts provided accurate intelligence data. Pagondas and the other Boeotarchs knew when the Athenian army left Delium and the route it took. Pagondas was so well informed about the movements of the enemy that he did not blunder about the countryside looking for them; in fact, he was able to march to within a short distance of his opponents, halt out of their sight, form his battleline, and gain the advantage of the terrain unchallenged. During the battle, the Boeotian horsemen were the decisive element in the victory. They accomplished the difficult task of pulling out of an ongoing battle, wheeling out and riding around both a hill and the enemy formation, and falling on the enemy rear with complete surprise and devastating results. When the Athenian army broke and fled, the Boeotian cavalry delivered the last blows of the battle in its pursuit. Pagondas' use of his cavalry was innovative, and tactically brilliant, and it showed a coordination that would become the hallmark of Philip II and Alexander III of Macedon.[53]

The Athenian cavalry proved its worth in a losing cause at Mantinea in 418 B.C. when it prevented the annihilation of 1,000 Athenian hoplites. On the day of the battle, the Mantineans and their allies, including the Athenians, deployed for battle on the plain south of the city. The Mantineans held the right wing of the phalanx. Next to them were their Arcadian allies, then the Argive elite battalion composed of 1,000 specially chosen hoplites, followed by the remainder of the Argive contingent, the Cleonaeans, and the Orneates. One thousand Athenian hoplites formed the left wing of the phalanx, supported by 300 Athenian cavalry on their left. Thucydides did not record the strength of each contingent or the total strength of the army, but the Mantineans and their allies probably had about 10,000 hoplites.[54]

The Lacedaemonian army, commanded by King Agis, marched north after ravaging the territory south of the city of Mantinea and was unexpectedly confronted by the Mantinean army. Although there was some cavalry with Agis' army, the Spartan king obviously was not using his horsemen as scouts. Upon seeing the Mantineans and their allies, Agis immediately deployed his army from a line-of-column into a battleline, possibly with his cavalry acting as a screen. The Spartan phalanx had the Tegeates and a few Spartans on the right. If the Spartan king commanded the right of the phalanx, then the few Spartans on the right could well have been the 300 hippeis or the king's foot-guard. The Maenalians and the Heraeans of Arcadia were positioned next. The main body of the Lacedaemonians formed the center, with a unit of *neodamodeis* (newly enfranchised helots) and a unit of veterans who had served with Brasidas in Thrace on their left. Finally, the left wing of the phalanx was held by the Sciritae. Agis placed cavalry units on both wings. Thucydides did not identify this mounted force or give its size, but given that all 6 Spartan infantry battalions were present, Agis' horse probably was composed of the 6 morai of the Spartan cavalry plus some miscellaneous horsemen from the other poleis. Thus, the mounted contingent numbered slightly more than 600 men. Thucydides did say that the Lacedaemonian army appeared larger than its opponent, and if this is accurate, Agis commanded more than 10,000 hoplites.[55]

When the two armies began advancing, the Mantineans, the Argives, and the other allies moved forward impetuously, with haste and disorder. In contrast, the Lacedaemonians and their allies marched slowly and orderly, to the music of flute players. As usual, both armies drifted to their right: The men in the extreme right-hand files moved rightward to protect their exposed right side, and the other files conformed to this movement. Agis, fearing his left would be encircled by the overlapping enemy right, ordered the Sciritae and the Brasideans to extend the line to the left. To fill the gap created by this maneuver, the Spartan king ordered 2 of the

Lacedaemonian battalions from the right center to move into the vacated hole. Although the Sciritae and the Brasideans obeyed the order, the polemarchs commanding the two Lacedaemonian battalions, Hipponoides and Aristocles, refused to move their troops.
Before the gap in the Spartan battleline could be closed by maneuvering all the units back into their original positions, the Mantineans, the Arcadians, and the 1,000 picked Argives attacked and
routed the Sciritae and the Brasideans and presumably the Spartan
cavalry on the left wing. They rushed into the vacant position and
started to envelop the Lacedaemonians on the left center.[56]

The Lacedaemonian right center and the right wing of the phalanx pressed forward to engage the main body of the Argives, the
Cleonaeans, the Orneates, and the Athenians. Some of these troops
did not wait for the Spartans' first blows before they began to give
ground. The Athenians who stood firm in the face of the Spartans
and the Tegeates found themselves in danger of being surrounded
for some of the Argives and others on their right had pulled back and
the right wing of the Lacedaemonian phalanx was beginning to encircle the Athenian left.[57] Fortunately for the Athenian hoplites,
their cavalry came to their aid. As Thucydides wrote, "They [the
Athenian infantry] would have suffered more than any part of the
whole army if their cavalry had not been present and proved helpful
to them."[58]

Although the exact tactics used by the Athenian cavalry are not
known, some conclusions can be drawn. First, the Athenian
horsemen did not abandon their position and flee the battlefield in
the face of the Spartan advance. If they had, they could not possibly
have regrouped and returned in time to help their fellow Athenians.
Second, the Athenian cavalry apparently prevented any envelopment of the flank or rear of their hoplites by the Spartan horsemen
on Agis' right wing. The Athenian hippeis may have skirmished with
their Spartan counterparts and driven them off. Or, perhaps, the
mere presence of the Athenian horsemen had been enough to deter
any attempt at maneuver by the less experienced Spartan horsemen,
including any attempt at a flank or rear attack on the Athenian hoplites. Because Thucydides made no mention of any Spartan cavalry
activity and the Athenian hoplites were able to withdraw unmo-

lested later, the Spartan horsemen obviously were mere spectators on this day. Finally, Thucydides implied by his use of the words *proved helpful* that the Athenian cavalry prevented an envelopment of the Athenian left. This must have been accomplished by means of a mounted attack on the Tegeate-Spartan infantry. Considering that the Athenians used javelins, a series of attacks was probably launched: Phyle after phyle charged, rode as close to the enemy as possible, threw their javelins, and retired to regroup for another attack. With the Tegeates and Spartans turning in toward the Athenian hoplites, the right or unprotected side of the phalanx was exposed and certainly became the object of the attacks.[59] Whatever the tactics, the Athenian horsemen were so effective that the encirclement was prevented from closing around the Athenian left before the hoplites were able to withdraw.

Agis, finding his left was in dire trouble, pivoted some portion of his right and marched against the Mantineans, Arcadians, and the 1,000 picked Argives. The Athenians and others on the Mantinean left did not fall upon the exposed flank of this maneuvering element; therefore, either they had completely withdrawn from the battlefield or Agis had left some troops, possibly the Tegeates, facing them to prevent any such possibility. Agis advanced, and the Mantineans and their allies broke and fled when they saw the approaching Lacedaemonians. Agis had won his victory.[60] The Lacedaemonians suffered about 300 casualties, but their opponents lost at least 1,100 men, with the Athenians losing 200.[61]

Although the Mantineans and their allies lost the battle, the Athenian cavalrymen had saved their hoplites from a devastating loss. The Athenians lost 200 men or about 15 percent of their complement at this battle. Yet if the encirclement of the Athenian left had taken place, the casualties would have been much greater. To put this in perspective, consider that the Persians were enveloped at Marathon (490 B.C.) and lost 6,400 men out of a force of about 23,000—a casualty rate of 32 percent.[62] Similarly, when the Romans at the Battle of Cannae were encircled, their losses showed the potential magnitude of the disaster that can befall an army in such a position: They lost 70,000 men out of an army of about 80,000,[63] for a casualty rate of 88 percent.Using these percentages and remembering that the Athenian contingent totaled 1,300 cavalry and infantry, Athenian losses could have been between 400 and 1,150 men if the encirclement had been accomplished.[64] Only the courage and the proficiency of the Athenian hippeis prevented this kind of disaster.

Unfortunately for the Athenians, both cavalry numbers and proficiency were on the side of the Syracusans when the Athenian Sicilian Expedition attempted to capture Syracuse. The Syracusan horsemen performed all the roles expected of cavalry, ancient or otherwise: They acted as scouts, provided screens during retreat, harassed the enemy workers and foragers, attacked disorganized units, fought the enemy cavalry, and pursued the retreating foe. In short, the Syracusan cavalry was a definite factor in the successful defense of the city and the defeat of the Athenians.

The Athenian general Nicias was well aware of the size and quality of the Syracusan cavalry even before the Sicilian Expedition sailed from the Piraeus. In the *ecclesia*, the Athenian assembly, he expressed his fear that the expeditionary force would "be shut out from the land by their [the Syracusans'] numerous cavalry."[65] In fact, the Syracusan cavalry had 1,200 men.[66] The basic tactical unit of this mounted force was probably the 80-man squadron.[67] However, considering that the Greeks liked units of 50 men or less for control purposes, each squadron was no doubt composed of 2 40-man troops and had at least 3 officers, 2 troop leaders, and 1 squadron commander. This organization allowed for easy mustering and better control in combat. Five squadrons formed a cavalry regiment of 400 men; so with 15 squadrons, Syracuse had 3 mounted regiments. The regiment may actually have been called a *triton*,[68] and it seems likely that each was commanded by a high-ranking officer. A single officer or hipparchos commanded the entire cavalry.[69]

If the Syracusans followed the normal Greek practice, the basic formation of its cavalry was a square or rectangle. An 80-man squadron could form with 8 files of 10 men, 10 files of 8 men, 16 files of 5 men, or 20 files of 4 men. Probably the first of these was used as a parade formation (Figure 5.2), allowing the cavalry to parade in a column of squadrons on streets that were only 15 yards wide, if the files were separated by 1 horse's width. Even narrower streets could have

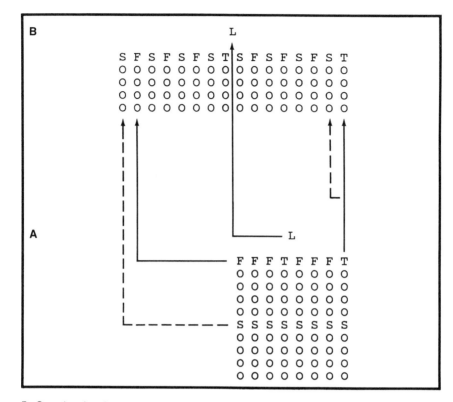

L Squadron Leader
F File Leader
S Section Leader
O Cavalry Troopers
T Troop Leader

Figure 5.2 *Syracusan cavalry squadron in formation. (A) is the 8-by-10 rectangle, and (B) is the 16-by-5 rectangle.*

been used if the cavalry rode in a column of troops. Further, the 8-by-10 rectangle allowed each triton to occupy a space only 75 yards across by 57 yards deep, if the distance between files was 1 horse's width and the interval between ranks was 1 horse's length. This meant the entire Syracusan cavalry could have mustered in the agora. For battle, the Syracusan cavalry squadron must have altered its formation between the 8-by-10 and the 16-by-5 rectangles, depending upon the tactical situation. Though the former provided a narrower front and greater depth, the latter (which was a modification of the 8-by-10 rectangle formed by having the rear 5-man section in each file move left and forward) provided a broader front with less depth. If the standard distance and interval were used, the 16-by-5 occupied an area 31 yards across by 27 yards deep; thus 5 squadrons, or a triton, in a line of squadrons had a front of 155 yards and a depth of 27 yards.

To counter the threat of the Syracusan cavalry, Nicias asked the Athenian assembly for "hoplites in large numbers, both of our own and of our allies, and from our subjects, as well as any from the Peloponnesus that we can attract by pay or persuasion; many bowmen, and also slingers, so that they may withstand the cavalry of the enemy."[70] The Athenian assembly voted the generals full power to muster whatever forces they thought necessary. With this mandate, Nicias, Alcibiades, and Lamachus sailed from Athens with 134 triremes (of which 100 were Athenian), 2 50-oared Rhodian galleys, 5,100 hoplites (including 1,500 Athenians), 480 archers, 700 slingers, 120 light-armed Megarian exiles, and 1 horse-transport with 30 cavalrymen, their equipment, and their mounts.[71]

It is curious that the Athenians did not include more cavalry in this expedition, particularly because Nicias made a special point of acknowledging the threat of the Syracusan mounted force. Several explanations for this have been offered. J. MacInnes believed that the Athenian *demos* (voting public) was indignant about the conduct of the hippeis at Amphipolis several years earlier. On this occasion, Cleon was attempting to recover the city from the Spartan general Brasidas and had marched part of his force to Amphipolis. When Cleon ordered the army to withdraw, according to MacInnes, the Athenian left, including the cavalry, failed to move expeditiously because of their dislike of their general. To hasten the withdrawal, Cleon wheeled the right into column and began to march past the city, at which point Brasidas sallied forth and attacked the Athenians. In the ensuing battle, Cleon was killed, as were the chances of recovering the city. The Athenian left, including the cavalry, fled rather than turn about and assist their general. The cavalry had shown cowardice and unreliability. Thus, the Athenian assembly avoided sending the hippeis on campaigns away from Attica.[72]

Bugh concluded that the small number of Athenian cavalrymen sent on the Sicilian Expedition testified to the fact that the Athenians believed that various Sicilian cities would provide horsemen for their cause. After all, a number of the cities in Sicily were hostile to Syracuse, and the presence of a large Athenian army provided them with an opportunity to retaliate against their larger, more powerful neighbor. The 30 Athenian hippeis that were sent were not meant to form a cavalry unit and confront their Syracusan counterparts but to act as scouts and messengers only.[73] Other scholars have argued that it was not possible to ship enough cavalrymen and their mounts overseas: There were too few horse-transports to send even half the Athenian horsemen and their mounts to Sicily. This was insufficient to make a difference.[74]

This last argument definitely seems to be at least one part of the answer. Athens apparently had only 10 horse-transports at this time, and at no point during the Archidamian War was there any indication that Athens ever transported more than 300 cavalrymen by ship.[75] Moreover, it is clear that Nicias, Alcibiades, and Lamachus did not think 300 horsemen would make a difference. In his speech to the assembly, Nicias did not ask for Athenian cavalry to counter the Syracusan horsemen but rather requested large numbers of archers and slingers.[76] Also, the Athenian assembly voted the expedition commanders full power to make up the expeditionary force as they saw fit.[77] Consequently, Nicias and his colleagues could have included 300 hippeis had they thought it essential. In fact, only 30 horsemen were included.

The second part of the answer probably had to do with the defense of Attica. Athens had lost some cavalrymen due to the Archidamian War. Thucydides reported that 300 hippeis died as a result of the plague,[78] and other casualties occurred as a result of the fighting. Though no record of the number of casualties due to combat exists, it should be remembered that the Athenian cavalry had defended Attica from five Lacedaemonian invasions and taken part in campaigns in various places, including the Chalcidice, the Peloponnesus, and the Isthmus area. So, by the end of the Archidamian War, the Athenian cavalry may have had only about 600 men.[79] At less than full strength—in fact, only about one-half its prewar size— the cavalry would not have been able to compensate for the deployment of 300 horsemen overseas. Even if it was at full strength at the time of the Sicilian Expedition, the Athenian strategoi, including Nicias, Alcibiades, and Lamachus, no doubt were very reluctant to ship 300 horsemen to Sicily. They must have known that war could break out again at any time, particularly as a result of an expedition against Syracuse, a Spartan ally, and that Attica could be invaded again. A cavalry force depleted by the loss of 300 men meant that Athens' primary defense against incursions and invasions was weak, possibly too weak to properly resist.

Whatever reason or reasons the Athenians had for not sending a sizable mounted force with the Sicilian Expedition, the Syracusan cavalry quickly demonstrated its importance. The first hostile move that the Athenians made against Syracuse was a naval raid in the territory south of the city. Syracusan mounted units responded quickly enough to overtake, attack, and kill some of the light-armed troops as they returned to the ships.[80] Although the Athenians remained inactive for a time, Syracusan cavalry units constantly scouted the Athenian army in its camp at Catana. Syracusan horsemen frequently rode right up to the Athenians to shout insults at them. Among other things, they asked "if the Athenians had come to share the home of the Catanians or to restore the Leontines to their old homes."[81] The Syracusans were, in fact, calling the Athenians cowards for remaining idly at Catana and not venturing forth. Plutarch reported that this constant haranguing caused sufficient unrest among the Athenians to force Nicias to act.[82]

Amid the growing discontent, the two Athenian generals successfully completed a daring movement of their army from Catana to a site near the Olympieium, a temple south and west of the city of Syracuse (Figure 5.3). This movement was accomplished by ship at night. At the same time, as the Syracusan army marched north to confront their enemy, the two forces unknowingly crossed paths in the darkness. When the Syracusan cavalry scouts found the Athenian army gone from its camp and reported this to their commanders, the Syracusan army turned around and marched back to the city, only to find the Athenians encamped near the Olympieium and protected by field fortifications.[83]

On the following day, both sides prepared for battle. In the Athenian battleline, the Argives and Mantineans were on the right. The

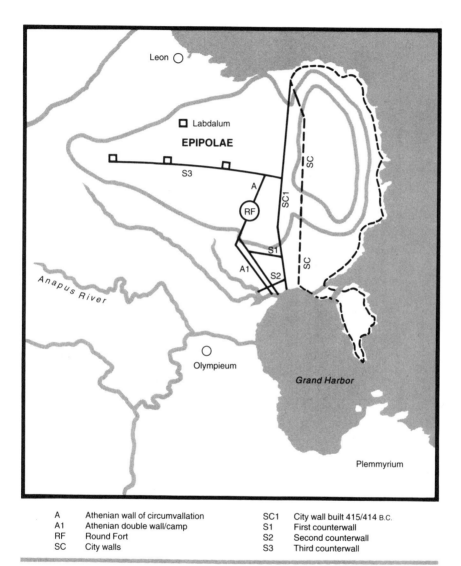

A	Athenian wall of circumvallation	SC1	City wall built 415/414 B.C.
A1	Athenian double wall/camp	S1	First counterwall
RF	Round Fort	S2	Second counterwall
SC	City walls	S3	Third counterwall

Figure 5.3 *Siege of Syracuse.*

Athenians formed the center of the phalanx, with allied hoplites on the left. The Athenian phalanx had a uniform depth of 8 shields. However, Nicias and Lamachus deployed only one-half their strength in the battleline; the other half of their army formed a hollow square around the Athenian camp. In contrast, the Syracusan phalanx was 16 hoplites deep. It was probably the same length as the Athenian line, so the Syracusan phalanx contained twice the number of hoplites as the opposition battleline, but the total strength of both armies was about the same. The Syracusan phalanx also had some allied troops, notably some Selinuntian infantry, 200 Geloan cavalry, 20 Camarinaean horsemen, and 50 Camarinaean bowmen. These allies were probably positioned on the Syracusan left. The 1,200 Syracusan cavalrymen were concentrated on the right wing.[84]

The advance of the Athenian phalanx caught the Syracusans by surprise. Some of the Syracusan soldiers had actually broken ranks and gone into the city. This could indicate that the battlelines were formed early in the morning but that the Athenians did not advance until later in the day (possibly around the time for the midday meal) or that the Syracusan hoplites were undisciplined or both. As the Syracusans raced back to their positions in the ranks, the light-armed troops of both armies skirmished in the gradually narrowing space between the two hostile forces. Belatedly but with spirit, the Syracusan phalanx moved forward. The ensuing struggle lasted for some time, during which a storm erupted over the battlefield; the thunder and lightning caused considerable apprehension among some of the soldiers on both sides. The Argives were the first to gain an advantage over their opponents, which resulted in the Syracusan left being driven back. Subsequently, the Syracusan center and right succumbed to the pressure of the Athenians. The Syracusan infantry broke and fled toward the city and safety.[85]

Though the Athenians had the opportunity to crush the Syracusans and win the city at this time, they were unable to successfully pursue and exploit their victory because of the presence of the Syracusan cavalry. Ecphantus, the commander of the Syracusan cavalry, used his 1,200 men, who had no mounted opposition and were undefeated and unbroken, to effectively screen the retreating hoplites from any pursuit.[86] Rather than staying in a concentrated force, the horsemen must have deployed by tritons or possibly even squadrons across the battlefield between the Athenians and the fleeing infantry. Individual hoplites and small groups from the Athenian army that tried to advance rapidly were attacked and driven back or killed. Large units were able to advance only slowly because of the need to constantly maintain their formation and integrity and because of the harassing tactics of the enemy horsemen. Instead of being slaughtered, almost all of the fleeing Syracusans reached safety due to the efforts of the cavalry. (Thucydides reported that only 260 Syracusans were killed or captured.[87]) This was so dissatisfying to Nicias and Lamachus that they refrained from any further action that year and sent a special request by trireme to Athens for money and cavalry.[88]

In response to that request, the Athenians sent 250 hippeis, 30 hippotoxotai, and 300 talents of silver to Sicily in the spring of 414 B.C. Although the cavalrymen and the mounted archers brought their equipment, they did not bring their horses—they had remained in Attica for it was expected that horses could be obtained in Sicily with the 300 talents.[89] Nicias and Lamachus had also worked over the winter to acquire allies who could supply both horsemen and horses. Overtures were made to the various tribes of the Sicels, and Egesta was urged to send as many mounts as possible. Ships with ambassadors were sent to Carthage and Tyrrhenia with offers of friendship.[90] This activity resulted in the arrival of 300 Egestan horsemen, between 100 and 250 other horsemen (including Naxians and Sicels), and enough horses to mount the Athenian hippeis and hippotoxotai. By spring 414 B.C., the Athenian Sicilian Expedition had a mounted force of between 650 to 800 men.[91]

The fighting resumed that spring, with the Athenians moving quickly and seizing the Epipolae. At the time, the Syracusan army was only 25 stades away, conducting a review in a meadow. The timing of this attack seems to indicate that the Athenian generals either knew that the Syracusans would be busy elsewhere, possibly because of informers inside the city or the use of cavalry scouts, or that they were simply lucky in their timing. Obviously, the Syracusans were not scouting the Athenians. When news of the enemy move reached the Syracusan army, it broke off its parade and moved uphill as fast as possible. Upon reaching the Epipolae, the Syracusans immediately attacked. The disorganized and doubtless winded soldiers were defeated in short order and withdrew to the city. A day or so later, the Syracusan generals marched the army out of the city, with the intention of engaging the Athenians and halting the construction of the Round Fort at Syce. But the Syracusan hoplites did not maintain their formation and were so disordered that the generals led them back to Syracuse without giving battle.[92]

However, the defense of Syracusan soil was not abandoned. Units of the Syracusan cavalry were left on the Epipolae, ordered to harass the Athenian workers collecting stone and other building materials for the fortifications. The construction must have been substantially slowed by this force for unarmed workers, whether individually or in groups, would have been afraid to venture forth in search of the necessary materials, and sending escorts with every party of workers would have been very time consuming. At some point, to counter this mounted threat, the Athenian generals sent 1 tribe of hoplites and all their cavalry against the units of Syracusan horsemen; the latter were defeated.[93] This time, Nicias and Lamachus had the necessary forces to counter the mounted threat, and as a result, the Athenians were able to complete the Round Fort.

For a while, the campaign around Syracuse became a wall-building contest between the Athenians trying to erect walls to encircle and isolate the city and the Syracusans attempting to construct a series of counterwalls. Skirmishes and battles around the construction sites were frequent, as each side sought to disrupt or stop the other's work. In one of these fights around the second counterwall, the Syracusan cavalry saved part of their own army and killed the Athenian general Lamachus. This battle most likely occurred somewhere between the end of the second counterwall and the Anapus River. The Syracusan army was apparently drawn up facing north and about even with the end of the wall. The Syracusan right was toward the city, the left was near the river, and most of the cavalry was on the left wing. The Athenians formed the right half of their phalanx with their allies on the left, unsupported by any cavalry. Possibly, the Athenian and allied horsemen were being kept busy elsewhere by part of the Syracusan cavalry not on the battlefield. As usual the Athenian hoplites were superior to their counterparts. The Syracusan infantry broke and fled; the soldiers on the right moved toward the city, behind the second counterwall, and those on the left raced along the Anapus River.[94]

Three hundred picked Athenians advanced on the run to keep the Syracusan soldiers on the left from crossing a bridge over the Anapus River and reaching safety. The Syracusan cavalry, with some infantry support, attacked and drove the picked hoplites back. The horsemen continued forward and charged the Athenian right, and the sudden rain of javelins halted the advancing Athenians and came close to causing widespread panic. Lamachus, seeing his right weakening, led a contingent of Argive hoplites and some bowmen to the stricken Athenian right. Perhaps attempting to rally the Athenian hoplites and lead them forward, Lamachus and a few followers crossed a ditch that was part of the defense of the counterwall. The Syracusan cavalry isolated this group and killed all of its members, including Lamachus. (In fact, Plutarch recorded that Lamachus and Callicrates, a Syracusan horseman, fought and killed each other.) The body of the dead Athenian general was carried off to the city. Eventually, the Athenians recovered, advanced, and forced the Syracusans to retire to the city. Victory was gained, but at the cost of a general.[95]

Thus, although the Athenians won the day, the Syracusan horsemen made this a Pyrrhic victory by killing Lamachus. For some time, possibly since the beginning of the spring campaign, Lamachus had been the officer pushing forward the Athenian effort. Nicias was ill, suffering from a kidney disease that sometimes left him almost totally incapacitated. This illness continued to plague him and must have sapped his strength and energy until he actually asked to be relieved of his command.[96] Further, Nicias had been against the Sicilian Expedition from the start and was elected as one of its commanders against his own wishes. In a speech before the Athenian assembly, he argued that Athens should not send ships and men to Sicily and become involved in a war that was none of its business. He warned that Athens' enemies would take advantage of the absence of much of the city's military to reopen hostilities and that Athens itself was still recovering from the effects of the plague and recent war.[97] Thus, the death of Lamachus left in sole command a general who was not only sick but also a reluctant participant and who did not believe in the cause. By eliminating Lamachus, the Syracusan cavalry guaranteed that the energy needed to complete the Athenian campaign successfully was absent.[98]

Of course, almost all the citizens of Syracuse failed to realize the true implications of the death of Lamachus at the time. They saw only the Athenian army in control of the Epipolae; the continued, although too leisurely, work on the wall of circumvallation; the Athenian fleet in the Grand Harbor; and the arrival of Sicel and Italian reinforcements for the invaders. For those in the city, the Syracusan army had been defeated repeatedly, and it seemed only a matter of time before the city fell or was surrendered to the Athenians.

The arrival of the Spartan general Gylippus changed the mood in the city almost immediately. In part, this was due to the influx of reinforcements who accompanied him. These included 700 seamen and marines from Gylippus' ships who were now equipped as hoplites, 100 Himeraean hoplites, 100 Himeraean cavalrymen, 1,000 Sicels, probably cavalry and light-armed troops, and some Geloan and Selinuntian cavalry and light-armed infantry.[99] Further, Gylippus was able to promise more help because Corinthian ships were on the way.[100] Syracuse was not alone after all.

Yet more than anything, the new Syracusan outlook was the result of Gylippus' own attitude and his active approach to the defense of the city. This Spartan general did not wait but quickly seized the initiative and reversed the course of the war. Gylippus marched the Syracusan army out to face the Athenians. As the army was forming, he sent a herald to the invaders to say that if they agreed to leave in five days, he would make a truce. And though the herald was treated badly and the Athenians formed for battle, Nicias did not lead his army against the Syracusans even when they became disordered and Gylippus was forced to withdraw.[101] This was a victory by default for Gylippus and the Syracusans, and the initiative was now on the side of the defenders. A day later, Gylippus took advantage of the Athenian hesitancy and captured the fort at Labdalum, allowing the Syracusans to start a third counterwall.[102] The Athenians would now have to deal with the Syracusan fort and garrison at Labdalum and another counterwall in order to complete their circumvallation of the city.

Gylippus' only mistake in the first days of command was to discount the effectiveness of the Syracusan cavalry in battle. As the third counterwall was being built, he daily led the Syracusan army out in front of it and drew up for battle. The Athenians responded by forming for battle themselves. On one of these occasions, Gylippus thought the moment right and advanced. A battle was fought in the area between the walls, delineated on the north by the third counterwall, on the south by the first counterwall, on the east by the wall of the city built during the winter of 415/414 B.C., and on the west by part of the Athenian wall of circumvallation. Gylippus had chosen a battlefield that was too restricted for the Syracusan cavalry to operate, so the Syracusan hoplites had to fight unsupported. The result was a victory for their Athenian counterparts.[103]

Later at an army assembly, Gylippus acknowledged to the Syracusan soldiers that the defeat was his fault because he had arranged the battleline between the walls, depriving the army of cavalry and light-armed support.[104] This surely improved the morale and fighting spirit of the Syracusan soldiers: Not only had the general admitted the defeat was his fault, he had also recognized his mistake and was unlikely to repeat it. The Syracusan hoplites could count on being properly supported by their cavalry and light infantry at the next battle.

The next time Gylippus led the army out, he was more careful in his selection of a battlefield. The Spartan general formed his army with its left wing overlapping the end of the third counterwall; the rest of the phalanx stretched out onto the Epipolae. Syracusan and allied horsemen, numbering 1,000, were posted on the right wing. The Athenian army formed opposite the Syracusans. None of our sources mentioned the presence of cavalry with the Athenian phalanx, but some units of Nicias' horse may have been on the left wing facing the Syracusan cavalry. When the battle began, the Syracusan mounted units attacked the Athenian left, drove it back, and routed it.[105] According to Thucydides, "Because of this the rest of the army was defeated by the Syracusans and driven headlong within the fortifications."[106] The Syracusan cavalry was the decisive element in this victory, a victory that allowed the Syracusans to extend their third counterwall beyond the wall of circumvallation the next night.[107] The Athenian chances of completing the circumvallation now were very small.

Simultaneously, in another part of Syracusan territory, a detachment of Syracusan cavalry was in the process of decreasing the efficiency of Nicias' naval units. Nicias had fortified a headland called the Plemmyrium, which jutted into the entrance of the Grand Harbor opposite the city, and he sent his supplies, ships, and crews there. From this vantage point, the Athenian trierarchs could keep a better watch on the Syracusan ships and put to sea faster. However, the Plemmyrium offered scant forage and firewood and had no water, and the sailors had to go beyond the fortifications to acquire these necessities. The Syracusans responded to Nicias' move by placing a triton, or one-third of their cavalry, at a hamlet near the Olympieium. The Syracusan horsemen patrolled constantly and attacked all Athenian foragers, resulting in the loss of some experienced rowers and sailors who could not be replaced locally and the physical deterioration of others due to a lack of water and other important necessities.[108] As Thucydides concluded, "It was especially as a result of this that the condition of the crews then began to decline."[109] Nicias' fear, expressed months earlier at the Athenian assembly—that the Syracusan cavalry would shut the expedition off from the land—was coming true.

Nicias was forced to acknowledge the untenable position of the Athenian Sicilian Expedition in a letter to the Athenian demos in the fall of 414 B.C. He stated that although the Athenians had won most of the battles, this success was negated by the arrival of Gylippus and reinforcements. This had forced the cessation of work on the wall of circumvallation. Further, the Athenians were now the besieged because "we cannot go far into the country because of their [the Syracusans'] cavalry."[110] He also commented on the diminishing capacity of his ships and crews; both were worn out from constant use—the ships waterlogged and the crews tired and depleted. "And our crews have been and still are wasted, because our sailors, forced to go out a distance for wood, forage, and water, are constantly killed by the cavalry."[111] Nicias lamented the fact that desertions were high, particularly among the servants and mercenaries. In fact, this may explain what happened to the horsemen from the various cities and tribes who had joined the Athenians in the spring; they had simply gone home, reducing Nicias' mounted contingent once again to almost nothing. In the end, Nicias asked to be relieved of his command.[112]

Although the Athenians voted to send a relief force to Sicily, the Sicilian Expedition's circumstances deteriorated still further before it arrived. Gylippus and the Syracusans launched a coordinated sea-land attack to capture the Plemmyrium. Thirty-five Syracusan triremes sailed from their harbor to attack the Athenian ships, only to be met by 60 hastily manned Athenian triremes. A large naval battle took place at the entrance of the Grand Harbor. As many of the Athenian troops on the Plemmyrium watched the ships engage one another, Gylippus attacked and captured the Athenian forts in the vicinity. This netted him most of the Athenian supplies, the rigging for 40 ships, and 3 triremes. Further and most importantly, the Syracusans held both sides of the entrance of the Grand Harbor and could hinder the flow of ships and supplies to the Athenians. Though the Athenian triremes sank 11 Syracusan ships and won the naval engagement, this was a costly victory.[113]

With this success, the Syracusans were full of confidence and initiated a series of skirmishes and battles. Most of these actions took place in the Grand Harbor as fleet met fleet, but the Syracusan army also took the field, lined up before the walls protecting the Athenians, and skirmished and probed the defenses. This forced the Athenians to man their walls and prevented them from concentrating their strength.[114] Of course, the cavalry of both sides had only minor roles in this type of fighting.

At this point, the Athenian generals Demosthenes and Eurymedon arrived with reinforcements. Their force consisted of 73 ships, more than 5,000 hoplites, and many light-armed infantry. The Athenians sent no additional cavalry, probably because Attica was on the verge of being invaded and the horsemen were needed at home. Demosthenes was resolved to act quickly and decisively to regain the initiative and achieve victory. To do this, he realized the key was completing the wall of circumvallation. He thus collected most of the Athenian soldiers and all the workers and made a night march up onto the Epipolae. Here, the Athenians captured the Syracusan fort by surprising the garrison. However, some members of the garrison escaped in the dark and warned the Syracusans and their allies of the Athenian presence.[115]

The abruptly aroused Syracusans rushed toward the fort. As the two armies collided in the darkness, a very confused battle ensued. For some time, the Athenians had the advantage and managed to push their foes back. In trying to drive the Syracusans away, keep them from rallying, and gain a victory, the Athenians advanced rapidly but quickly lost their order and cohesion in the dark. A contingent of Boeotians, recently arrived from Greece, charged part of the confused Athenian army and routed it. Now, the battle degenerated into a series of minor clashes over much of the Epipolae, waged between units of the contending armies. More confusion was added by the arrival of fresh Athenian troops who did not know friend from foe in the dark. Disorder, darkness, fear, and surroundings that were unfamiliar to many of the newly arrived soldiers eventually caused panic and flight among the Athenians.[116]

With the Syracusans and their allies in pursuit, many Athenians dashed for any apparent avenue of escape. Some found their way off the Epipolae. Many died. Some plunged off cliffs and bluffs. Some ran into enemy soldiers and were killed. Some ran into fellow Athenians but were mistaken for the enemy and slain. A large number who were unfamiliar with the country got lost and wandered around in the dark. As night gave way to day, the Syracusan cavalry sallied forth, scattered across the Epipolae, and rode down and killed all the stragglers they could find.[117]

For Demosthenes, this defeat proved that the campaign was hopeless. Although he eventually convinced Nicias that the Athenians should pack up, board their ships, and sail home, they were prevented from departing by the eclipse of the moon on August 23, 413 B.C.: According to the soothsayers, the Athenians could not depart for another twenty-seven days. Subsequently, the Syracusans initiated confrontations on land and sea almost daily.[118] On one such occasion, the Syracusan ships sailed forth, while part of their army assaulted the Athenian walls. When the Athenians sent out some hoplites and cavalry to fall upon the attackers, these defenders were cut off, attacked, and routed. The Syracusans pursued vigorously, in part because the Athenian horsemen did not effectively screen the retreat but rather joined in the flight. As a result, all the retreating infantry and cavalry tried to get through a single gate at the same time, and the gate was soon jammed with milling, frantic men. To facilitate their escape, the Athenian horsemen dismounted, abandoned their horses, and joined the press of humanity. The Syracusans killed some of the soldiers at the gate and captured 70 horses.[119] Because this was the last time Thucydides mentioned it with the Sicilian Expedition, the cavalry apparently ceased to exist after the loss of these horses.

On another occasion, the Syracusans blocked the entrance of the Grand Harbor. When an Athenian attack on the ships at the entrance proved unsuccessful, there was only one possible avenue of escape—an overland march to some friendly town or city.[120] The Athenians were preparing for an immediate night retreat, but this was delayed by a Syracusan trick. Syracusan horsemen, posing as friends, rode up to the Athenian lines, and told the guards the enemy army was blocking the roads, and suggested it would be better if they did not march out until daylight. Nicias, cautious as ever, delayed the Athenian departure for about 36 hours, giving the Syracusans ample time to send out parties to watch all the roads, fords, and bridges.[121] The Athenians now had no chance to sneak away but had to withdraw in the face of the Syracusan and allied cavalry.

The Athenian retreat began with the army split into 2 divisions. Nicias commanded the leading division, and Demosthenes led the rear. The army deployed for the march in a hollow square, with the baggage and supplies in the protected center. The Athenians marched almost due west, away from their camp and the city of Syracuse. At a crossing of the Anapus River, they were confronted by a guard detachment that was easily pushed aside, and the march continued. However, the Syracusan cavalry and light-armed troops began to harass the Athenians. Javelins rained down on the men in the rear and on the flanks of the retreating formation. The first day of the retreat ended with the Athenians having marched 40 stadia, or about 5 miles.[122]

The second day's march was relatively uneventful. Obviously, the Athenians were kept under observation by the Syracusans, but no attacks were made. The marching men stopped after only 20 stadia to forage for food in an area with some houses and to collect water from the streams.[123] In fact, the respite of the second day was due to the Syracusans' effort to collect their forces; on the third day, as the Athenians began their march, a large force of cavalry and light-armed soldiers attacked. Thucydides described the ensuing clash:

> [As] the Athenians went forward, the cavalry and javelin-men of the Syracusans and their allies, being in considerable force, sought to impede their march on either side by hurling javelins and riding alongside. For a long time the Athenians kept up the fight, but at length returned to the camp of the day preceding. And they no longer had provisions as before, for by reason of the enemy's cavalry it was no longer possible to leave the main body.[124]

Thucydides' description is clear. Javelin-men ran at and alongside the retiring army, threw their weapons, and withdrew, a sequence that was repeated often. The Syracusan cavalry rode parallel to the formation, waited for an opportunity, dashed in, and then withdrew to wait for another chance. This harassment was so fierce that the Athenians were forced to return to their previous camp, having made no progress. To add to their misery, the Syracusan horsemen stayed close, preventing foraging by the hungry soldiers.

The next morning, the Athenians began the march very early. Although the harassment continued, the retreating army was able to push its way into the hills. This eliminated the mounted threat, but the Athenians found their way blocked by a wall built across the road in the hill pass and defended by Syracusan infantry. An assault on the wall was repulsed by its defenders, and the Athenians were forced back onto the plain for the night.[125] When they began their march on the fifth day, the Syracusan cavalry and light-armed troops reappeared and attacked all sides of the Athenian formation. Thucydides reported:

> The Syracusans surrounded them [the Athenians] and attacked on every side, wounding many; if the Athenians attacked they retreated, but if they retreated they would charge, falling chiefly upon the rearmost in the hope that by routing them a few at a time they might put the whole army in a panic.[126]

Obviously, the entire Athenian army was sometimes surrounded by a combination of light infantry and horsemen. Although the Athenians tried to fight back, to stop the light-armed soldiers from throwing their javelins by advancing against them at the run, the Syracusan light infantrymen were faster and fell back until the Athenians turned to rejoin their formation. Then, the javelin-men fell upon the beleaguered soldiers with a vengeance, particularly on those in the rear. This was not only an effort to kill as many as possible but also an attempt to inspire panic and fear that would spread to the entire Athenian army. In the face of this harassment, the Athenians advanced no more than 6 stadia.[127]

Nicias and Demosthenes felt it was imperative to break away from the pursuing and harassing Syracusans. They decided to have the soldiers build a lot of campfires, giving the impression that the army was camping for the night, and then to sneak away under the cover of darkness. This ruse was successful: The Athenian army was able to leave its camp undetected and march some distance. Unfortunately, the two halves of the retreating army marched at different rates; the leading division under Nicias marched rapidly and stayed in formation, while Demosthenes' rear division moved more slowly and became confused and disordered. When the Athenian camp was found to be empty at daybreak, the Syracusan cavalry set off in hot pursuit, followed by the light infantry. The Syracusan horsemen attacked Demosthenes' division the minute they caught up to it. Mounted units assaulted the Athenians on all sides, drove them together, and stopped all forward progress. The attacks were so effective that Demosthenes and his men broke formation and took refuge in an olive grove surrounded by a low wall. Though the wall and the trees kept the horsemen at bay, they did not impede the Syracusan light-armed troops, who shortly appeared on the scene. Javelins rained on the men scattered among the trees. After the Athenians endured this for much of the day, Gylippus proclaimed to the surrounded soldiers that if the islanders would come forward, they would go free. Although few of the allies deserted the Athenians, their position was hopeless. Later in the day, Demosthenes and his 6,000 men surrendered to Gylippus.[128]

Meanwhile, Nicias continued to lead his division onward. The day after Demosthenes' surrender, the seventh day of the retreat, the Syracusans caught up to Nicias and informed him of the fate of his counterpart and the other Athenians. The two sides exchanged proposals; Gylippus and the Syracusans asked Nicias to surrender, but he countered by offering to pay reparations in exchange for the freedom of his men. When each side refused the other's offer, the Syracusans attacked and surrounded the Athenians. Once again, the tactic was to destroy the Athenians with missiles rather than by close combat, and the rain of missiles only stopped when night fell. The next day, Nicias managed to push his soldiers as far as the Assinarus River, even though his army was attacked constantly by Syracusan horsemen and light-armed soldiers. At the river's edge, the Athenians, due to thirst and a desire to escape the deadly rain, broke and rushed into the water. The Syracusans closed in on three sides of the disorderly, frantic mass and continued their grim work. Many Athenians died: Some were killed by the enemy weapons, but others drowned or were trampled to death. The Syracusan cavalry crossed the river and formed to prevent any Athenians from escaping. As those who did manage to survive the watery ordeal were pursued and cut down by the horsemen, Nicias finally surrendered to Gylippus to stop the slaughter.[129]

Throughout the Sicilian Expedition, the lack of cavalry hurt the Athenians, while the Syracusan cavalry performed all the functions expected of mounted units at the time and played a prominent role in the victory. The Syracusan horse countered the first naval raids and scouted the enemy camp at Catana. Although the Athenians won the first battle, they were unable to make it a decisive victory and possibly end the campaign right then because their opponent's cavalry effectively screened the fleeing infantry. The Syracusan horsemen harassed the workers building the Athenian wall of circumvallation, and in one of the battles around the walls, they killed the Athenian general Lamachus—the one man who had the energy to carry on an active campaign. Even the arrival of Athenian and allied cavalry did not alter the superior position of the Syracusan cavalry on the battlefield. And in the end, this cavalry made it possible to defeat and capture the retreating Athenians by scouting, harassing, and running to ground the divisions of Demosthenes and Nicias.

Although the fighting was finished in and around Syracuse, combat had resumed in Attica. As the Athenian relief force sailed for Sicily in the spring of 413 B.C., an army of Lacedaemonians and their allies, under the command of the Spartan king, Agis, invaded Attica. After ravaging the countryside, Agis fortified Decelaea for use as a permanent, year-round camp from which raiding parties could be sent.[130] Thucydides stated that this was "one of the chief circumstances that brought ruin to their [the Athenian] cause."[131] Enemy activity around this fort deprived Athens of its most fertile area, forced all the citizens off the land and into the city, and provided a haven for runaway slaves. Apparently, 20,000 slaves escaped to the Lacedaemonians in the first year alone.[132]

The Athenian response to this was to send their cavalry to observe the enemy at Decelaea and attack the raiding parties. However, because this required the constant use of men and horses over a prolonged period of time, it quickly began to take a toll on both. Horses went lame on the rocky Attic ground. Men and horses were wounded in the constant skirmishing, and neither had any time to rest and recover for the Spartans manned their fort throughout the year. Thus, the strain on the cavalrymen was so great, in fact, that they alone were excused from standing guard on the walls of the city at night. This at least allowed them a night's sleep before the next day's riding and fighting.[133]

The true cost of this type of warfare on the Athenian cavalry can be clearly seen in the records of the cavalry sitos for the year 410/409 B.C. The Athenian cavalry at full strength had 1,000 men. If about 300 cavalrymen were in Sicily, the cavalry left to defend Attica was composed of some 700 men. In the first prytany (Athenian month) of 410/409 B.C., the number of effective horsemen in Athens totaled 609. This number gradually dropped during the next several months to 484 effective hippeis in the fifth and sixth prytanies. In the seventh prytany, the cavalry size jumped to 666 but gradually fell again in the remainder of the year. Thus, the Athenian cavalry had only about 450 men at the end of the year.[134]

Nevertheless, the Athenian horsemen, fighting with great intensity and inspiration, performed well on several occasions. In the spring or early summer of 410 B.C., King Agis advanced close to the walls of Athens with a large force. He hoped to capture the Long Walls by assault because these were unguarded due to the political turmoil in the city. As Agis' force drew near, Athenian cavalry, peltasts, bowmen, and some hoplites emerged from the city and attacked, killing a number of Agis' troops with missiles. The Athenian heavy infantry probably formed a battleline a short distance from the city gate. This formation acted as a protective shield for and gave confidence to the other troops. The light-armed soldiers rushed forward to throw their javelins and shoot their arrows, knowing they could retreat safely behind their own hoplites if necessary. The Athenian horsemen's primary role, no doubt, was to keep the enemy cavalry busy and away from the Athenian light-armed soldiers. As a secondary mission, elements of the Athenian cavalry probably attacked the rear and far flanks of Agis' formation if they got the opportunity. In the face of this unexpected opposition, Agis retreated and later sent his extra troops home.[135]

Though cavalry skirmishes must have been frequent in the years 410–409 B.C., the next major mounted engagement involving the Athenian cavalry that our sources mention occurred in 408 B.C. Once again, Agis mustered a large army, consisting of 12,000 hoplites, 12,000 light-armed soldiers, and 1,200 cavalry, including 900 Boeotian horsemen. He made a night advance toward Athens, hoping to catch the defenders when they were weak. The Spartan king certainly was aware that Alcibiades had recently sailed with a sizable army. Agis' soldiers surprised the Athenian outposts and killed some of the pickets, but a few escaped and raised the alarm in the city. The walls of Athens were immediately manned. As daylight dawned, the Athenians saw the Spartan army drawn up for battle, and the Athenian generals sent out their cavalry. Although Diodorus said the Athenian horse was about equal to Agis' cavalry, this is probably an overestimate.[136] Even considering that the Athenians had used every means available, it does not seem possible that Athens could have re-built its mounted force to its full strength of 1,000 men. The city had been virtually under siege since 413 B.C. Every commodity had to be brought in by ship from places around the Aegean or even more re-mote locations, including horses for cavalry mounts and the neces-sary grain to feed them. Probably, the Athenian cavalry consisted, at most, of 600 to 700 men.[137]

The horsemen of the two sides fought before the walls of Athens. The Boeotian horsemen had been superior at Delium, but on this day, the Athenian hippeis defeated their opponents. In explaining the Athenians' victory, Diodorus noted that the Athenian horsemen were fighting in front of their families and friends, who lined the walls to view the battle. With this audience, they were determined to win—or die in the attempt.[138] Though this is surely true, it should also be remembered that desperate men fight with unbelievable courage and skill. The horsemen of Athens fought with the skill, bravery, and tenacity of men fighting a battle they dared not lose. Unfortunately for them, final victory or defeat did not rest with the Athenian hippeis but rather with the fleet. And when this fleet was caught on the beach and destroyed at Aegospotami, the Peloponne-sian War ended as an Athenian defeat and a Lacedaemonian victory.

Cavalry performed in all theaters of this war, from the northern Aegean to the island of Sicily. As expected, cavalrymen proved effec-tive in scouting, screening, and harassing. They also were effective as the first line of defense for territory—so much so that the Spartans had to organize and field a mounted force for the first time in two centuries to defend Laconia and Messenia. And yet, in certain cir-cumstances and with far-reaching consequences, cavalry was some-times the decisive element on the battlefield. The Chalcidian cav-alry, with some support, broke the Athenian hoplites. Theban horsemen got into the rear of the Athenians at Delium, caused panic, and broke the Athenian phalanx, which provided the Theban cause with a resounding victory. At Mantinea, the Athenian cavalry prevented the Spartans from enveloping the Athenian hoplites and thus prevented a disaster. And finally, the Syracusan horsemen turned a potentially decisive Athenian victory in Sicily into a minor one, killed the most effective and active Athenian general, rolled up the Athenian phalanx, and prevented the Athenian army from retreating to safety. Greek horsemen were now proficient at the second stage of cavalry development, wherein the horse was used as a fighting platform. Greek hippeis were finally ready to play an even more prominent role on the battlefield as the third stage of cavalry development evolved.

6

Greek Cavalry in the Fourth Century B.C.

The fourth century B.C. has justifiably been recognized as a period of great change in infantry warfare. Iphicrates, Epaminondas, Pelopidas, and Philip II all won renown and are known today for innovative infantry tactics. And yet, even more far-reaching and generally less well-recognized changes occurred at this same time in the role of cavalry on the battlefield. First, a sizable and proficient mounted force was not only desirable but also, at times, essential for a successful campaign, particularly in Asia, where the Persian horsemen were numerous. Second, a new coordination between cavalry and infantry began to appear. No longer were the cavalry roles and duties restricted to the beginnings and ends of battles—to scouting, screening, and skirmishing before and to screening, harassing, and pursuing after. Cavalry became an integral part of the battle plan, whose maneuvers were timed to aid the infantry and achieve victory. And finally, the cavalry charge, ending in shock, became important as a means of projecting force in battle.

At the beginning of the century, the Ten Thousand, while attempting to march out of Asia, keenly felt the consequences of having inadequate cavalry when facing the Persians. This group of Greek mercenaries, who actually numbered about 10,500 hoplites and 2,500 peltasts, had been part of Cyrus' army and were involved in the attempt to put that Persian on the throne.[1] Before the Battle

123

of Cunaxa, the Greeks had not been concerned about cavalry support because Cyrus' army totaled between 40,000 and 80,000 men, including at least 3,000 horsemen.[2] However, after the battle, with the death of Cyrus and the dissolution of his army, the Greek infantrymen found themselves alone and without any mounted support, deep inside Persian territory. The Ten Thousand faced the same prospects as the Athenians retiring from Syracuse.

Clearchus, the Lacedaemonian exile commanding the Greeks, recognized this deficiency in horsemen.[3] Yet he did not have to face this problem in battle, nor did he make any attempt to rectify it for the Persians initially did not try to interfere with the passage of the Greeks. In part, this policy was the easiest way for the Persian king to get the Greeks away from Babylon and out of the center of his empire. When Clearchus and the other generals were tricked, captured, and later executed, the Greek mercenaries elected new commanders, one of whom was Xenophon. These new generals soon came to realize the need for a cavalry force.

At first, Xenophon downplayed the strength of the Persian mounted threat for his men. He told the Greeks:

> But if any of you is down hearted because we are without horsemen while the enemy have plenty close by, let him reflect that your ten thousand horsemen are nothing more than ten thousand men, because nobody ever lost his life in battle from the bite or kick of a horse, but it is men who do whatever is done in battle.[4]

This must have been an attempt on Xenophon's part to encourage his men—an effort to lift their spirits in the face of seemingly hopeless odds. As a former Athenian hippeus with experience in the closing years of the Peloponnesian War, he must have known about the effectiveness of the Athenian cavalry in the first years of the war, as well as the story of the retreating Athenian army at Syracuse, and he surely had seen the effect he and his companions had on the invaders of Attica. Clearly, he was aware of the power of horsemen to harass and inflict injury upon marching infantry.

These lessons were reinforced and the truth revealed to everyone on the next day's march, particularly to Xenophon, who commanded the rear guard. The march began with the hoplites in a hollow square formation. The center of this square contained the baggage animals, with the supplies and the camp followers. As the Greek mercenaries progressed, Mithradates, a Persian nobleman, arrived with 200 mounted archers and 400 foot-archers and slingers. Mithradates had been one of Cyrus' followers and had visited the Greeks before, so he and his force were allowed to approach the Greek formation unchallenged and unimpeded. When they were close to the Greeks, the Persians let loose with their missiles at the rear guard. Within a short time, this began to take its toll, all the more so because the Greeks could not strike back: The range was too great for the javelins of the Greek peltasts, and the arrows of the Cretan archers also fell short. The latter situation was the result of two factors. First, the Cretan archers were unarmored and stayed inside the rear-guard formation for protection. Second, the Cretan weapons had a shorter range because they used shorter arrows than the Persian weapons did. This allowed for a shorter draw of the bow and consequently less propulsion force on the arrow.[5]

As the attacks of the Persians continued, the rear guard, on orders from Xenophon, attempted to close with their harassers. This resulted in the Persian light-armed forces giving way before the advancing hoplites and peltasts, who nevertheless suffered casualties as the withdrawing horsemen employed the "Parthian-shot" technique. Further, the Greeks of the rear guard could pursue only a short distance, for going too far from the main body left the unit unprotected and exposed the rear guard soldiers to extreme danger. If the two segments of the Greek mercenary army became separated and isolated, they could be attacked individually and destroyed piecemeal. Yet even a short pursuit required a fighting withdrawal or return to the main body. Once the rear guard broke off the pursuit and turned, the Persians fell upon the retiring soldiers. This harassment prevented a rapid march, and, in fact, on the first day, the Greek mercenaries traveled only 25 stadia, or about 3 miles.[6]

That evening, Xenophon proposed to his fellow generals some changes to counter the Persian tactics. He suggested that a unit of slingers should be organized from among the Rhodians and any others who knew how to use a sling. So these men would be eager to serve in this capacity, they were to be paid for their slings and receive special privileges. Next, he said, a cavalry unit should be formed. All the horses, both private and baggage animals, were to be inspected, and those found suitable used. Riders were to be sought from among the hoplites. These proposals were implemented, and the next day, the Ten Thousand had 200 slingers and 50 cavalrymen.[7]

Two days later, Xenophon's organizational changes bore fruit. The Greeks had just crossed a ravine when Mithradates appeared at the head of 1,000 horsemen and 4,000 light-armed troops, in this case archers and slingers. When the Greeks were about 8 stadia from the ravine crossing, the Persians moved through the terrain obstacle, advanced quickly, closed the Greek formation, and began to shower the mercenaries with missiles. Anticipating the return of the enemy and their tactics, Xenophon had already given orders to the Greek rear guard: All elements—hoplites, peltasts, and cavalry—were to charge the Persians and support one another. The cavalry in particular was to charge with abandon.[8]

Just as the first missiles began to find the range and hit their targets and at the appropriate signal, the Greek rear guard executed its orders. It turned about, the horsemen charged at full speed, and the peltasts and hoplites advanced as rapidly as good order allowed. The fact that the Persian sling stones and arrows were falling among the mercenaries indicated two things. First, the distance separating the two forces at the time was probably only 100 to 300 yards, or something less than the extreme ranges of bow and sling. And second, the archers and slingers were most likely in front of the Persian horsemen for shooting over the heads of mounted riders would have been very difficult.[9] The Persian light infantry, without a doubt, did not wait to receive the charge of the Greek horsemen but rather turned and fled, probably running into their own horsemen in the process. As the soldiers attempted to make their way between the horses, this caused confusion in the ranks of the Persian cavalry. All the Persians subsequently fled toward the ravine crossing and safety. The confused mass was struggling to cross when the Greek horsemen and then the Greek foot soldiers arrived and attacked the backs of the fleeing foe. Many Persian infantrymen were killed, and 18 Persian horsemen were captured.[10]

Although small, Xenophon's improvised cavalry force was largely responsible for this victory. It was the charge of the horsemen that panicked the Persian light-armed soldiers and drove them back. The Persian archers and slingers could have easily evaded the advance of the Greek peltasts and hoplites; indeed, they had done exactly that several days before. The mercenary cavalry was the new element on the battlefield. It provided an element of speed—enough speed to cover the 100 to 300 yards and catch the archers and slingers. The Greek horsemen also provided psychological shock. Archers and slingers could not stand up to a cavalry charge. The sight of the rapidly advancing horsemen riding in formation with lowered spears had to send terror into the hearts of the lightly clad and armed Persians. Once the rout was on, it was impossible for the Persian horsemen to deploy and dangerous for them to delay in a confused mass and face the oncoming Greek heavy infantry. Naturally, the Persian horsemen won the race to the ravine, and most got safely across. The Persian light infantry suffered a different fate.

Another casualty of this engagement was Mithradates' confidence. This Persian nobleman was so shaken by the presence of the mercenary horsemen and the near disaster they had caused that in subsequent encounters, he refrained from closing with the Greek formation. Instead, Mithradates consistently kept his cavalry and light infantry at extreme missile range, and arrows and stones alone were used to slow the Greeks' march. These were easily countered by the Greek slingers (who outdistanced their counterparts because they used lead bullets) and the Cretan archers (who now were using the longer Persian arrows for greater range).[11] Thus, the Ten Thousand escaped the fate of the Athenians at Syracuse and passed off the plains of Iraq and into the foothills. Although more threats and dangers awaited them, they would not come from cavalry.

Several years later, another Greek commander learned the importance of having good cavalry in Asia. In 396 B.C., the Spartan king, Agesilaus, departed Greece and went to Asia Minor to pursue the war, begun in 400 B.C., to free the Ionian Greek cities from Persian domination. He took with him a force of 8,000 infantry, composed of 2,000 emancipated helots and 6,000 allies, and a staff of 30

Spartiates.[12] This force was combined with a Greek army in Asia Minor, composed mostly of the remnants of the Greek force that had fought for Cyrus—the famous Ten Thousand. These mercenaries had been in Spartan employment since Thibron recruited them at the start of the war. They now numbered about 4,000 men and were commanded by Xenophon.[13] Agesilaus' only cavalry was a small force of about 400 men, probably drawn from the citizens of several Ionian Greek cities.[14] Although Agesilaus had adequate infantry, his mounted assets were far too modest to be of much use against the Persians in battle because those opponents always employed large cavalry forces, considered the best element of the Persian army. Also, the Ionian cavalry was far inferior in weapons and training, a fact that Agesilaus learned almost immediately.

The poor quality of the Ionian Greek horse was revealed in a small skirmish that took place while Agesilaus was campaigning in Phrygia. The Spartan king's advanced cavalry screen, which probably included at least half and maybe all of his horsemen, came face to face with a Persian mounted force of about equal size. Both units crested the same hill simultaneously. This encounter surprised both Greeks and Persians alike, and for a short time, neither made a move. The Greek cavalry was drawn up in a phalanx-like formation, with a depth of 4 horsemen and a width of between 50 and 100, depending upon the actual number in the advance screen. In contrast, the Persian formation was much deeper, probably between 15 and 20 riders and with a front of only 12. After the initial surprise and confusion wore off, the Persians charged first, with the Greeks following suit almost immediately. When the two forces met and the fighting became hand to hand, the Greeks found themselves at a distinct disadvantage. Their spears were weak; the shafts of the Ionian spears broke when they made contact with the body-armor of the Persians. The Persians' cornel-wood javelins, on the other hand, were more elastic, durable, and deadly. Twelve Ionians and 2 horses were killed very quickly. Better weapons, combined with a deep formation, allowed the Persians to break the Greek line. In response, the Greeks turned and fled. The rout was short lived as Agesilaus arrived with the main body and the Persians were forced to withdraw in the face of a vastly superior force. Agesilaus now realized the poor quality of his cavalry and knew that to continue to operate in Asia Minor, he needed an effective mounted force. He halted his advance and campaign, turned his army around, and marched back to Ephesus, where he spent the winter recruiting and training. In particular, he sought horsemen, especially mercenary horsemen.[15]

The Ionian Greek poleis probably had only limited mounted assets at this time. Traditionally, a city-state drew its cavalrymen from the upper-class citizens, who could afford to furnish themselves with the necessary arms and armor and buy and maintain one or more war-horses—a very expensive undertaking. At its height at the start of the Peloponnesian War, when its citizen population exceeded 40,000 and contained a high proportion of wealthy citizens for a Greek polis, Athens had only 1,000 cavalrymen, and these were subsidized.[16] Thus, it was unlikely that a large number of Ionian citizen cavalry could be found, particularly in light of political activity in the area in preceding years. Since the middle of the fifth century B.C., most of the Ionian Greek poleis had been members of the Delian League and Athenian Empire. The Athenians encouraged democracies and popular activities and discouraged aristocracies and elitist activities. Naval warfare and hoplites—democratic in nature—were fostered in place of cavalry. And with the return of the Ionian cities to Persian control, all military activity was no doubt discouraged. Moreover, the effectiveness of citizen cavalry was sometimes limited. Citizen horsemen had the disadvantage of being involved with the affairs of family and city: Farms, businesses, politics, civic duties, and family obligations all took up their time and effort. Consequently, citizen cavalrymen did not adequately practice the skills necessary for mounted warfare, nor could they usually remain on campaign for any extended period of time. Nevertheless, Agesilaus needed men who could ride, fight mounted, and be drilled to the point where they were the equal of the Persians. So the Spartan king concentrated on recruiting mercenaries for his mounted force.

Though Greek mercenary soldiers had apparently always been available, they were particularly common and numerous at this moment in history.[17] In large part, this was the result of the Peloponnesian War, which created a pool of available and trained military men. Before the war, most city-states provided adequate employment for

all their citizens. And because most men were farmers, their employment was on the land. Even the marginal land in much of Greece
provided a living from, among other things, olive trees and vines. Of
course, every polis had its blacksmith, carpenters, potters, painters,
laborers, and so forth. Several of the largest cities, notably Athens
and Corinth, were centers of trade and industry, where many Greeks
and even foreigners found employment. But the war changed this;
Athens was now in economic ruin, with its population decimated by
the plague and war casualties. The olive groves had been cut down.
The slaves had run away, and the mines were closed.[18] Although Athens suffered most severely, this story was repeated in various areas
throughout the Greek world. The men who came back from the war
found centuries of work destroyed and decades of work ahead before
some sort of normal, prosperous life would return. Unfortunately,
not all men wanted or could afford to wait that long. Xenophon reported that some of Cyrus' Greek mercenaries "abandoned fathers
and mothers, or had left children behind with the idea of obtaining
money to bring back to them."[19] Isocrates gave an even bleaker assessment when he said that "many [are] compelled through a lack of
bread to serve as mercenaries."[20]

Besides depriving men of the opportunity and ability to make a
peaceful living, the Peloponnesian War also was the school of Greece
for many. There, they learned the trade of war. Because the conflict
lasted for twenty-seven years, several generations grew up knowing
only war and fighting. The last ten years of the war, in particular, saw
many Athenians, Spartans, Boeotians, Corinthians, Arcadians, and
other Greeks continuously in military service. This was the period
when Attica was garrisoned by invaders and Athens was besieged;
Athenian and Spartan fleets contended for control of the Aegean
(with Athenian allies being attacked or breaking away), and Greek armies were everywhere. Xenophon's own life and experiences may
well have been typical for the men who grew up in this period. Born
at the beginning of the Peloponnesian War, he heard at an early age
stories of the invasions of Attica in the initial stages of the conflict,
and the Athenian military successes were, of course, great entertain-
ment. The Peace of Nicias was celebrated in the city, but the continuation of the fighting and the departure of ships and men to various

parts of the Greek world were exciting events—events a boy of ten or twelve would have watched eagerly. In his early teens, he no doubt witnessed the departure of the Sicilian Expedition and experienced the pain and suffering its defeat brought to the city. As he began his own military training, there was a new intensity and concentration as he realized that Spartans had a permanent fort in Attica, that his family's lands and property were being destroyed, and that his city was in danger. Finally, his early manhood was dominated by the rigors and dangers of the incessant and demanding cavalry warfare of the last years of the war. Apart from the fact that most men served as hoplites, his was probably a common background.[21]

Although mercenaries were common in the Greek world and could be found in numerous cities, Agesilaus adopted a rather unique recruiting method. He drafted the wealthiest citizens in the Ionian cities allied with Sparta as cavalrymen. However, he offered them a way to evade the obligation: Anyone who supplied a horse, suitable arms and armor, and a qualified rider to fight in his place was exempted from personal service. This alternative was so attractive to the Ionian upper class that every draftee supplied a fully equipped horseman to fight in his stead. Agesilaus also directly recruited all available horsemen willing to serve for pay. He soon had a large number of willing mercenaries ready and eager to serve and fight as cavalrymen.[22]

Mercenaries are looked down upon in contemporary times because they fight for money instead of their country or patriotism. But in the fourth century B.C., Greek mercenaries were highly professional soldiers who were sought by both city-states and foreign monarchs alike. In acquiring mercenaries, Agesilaus acquired soldiers whose fighting abilities, training, and bravery were superior to those of citizen levies, in part because their physical condition and discipline were much greater. To fight effectively, possibly for long periods of time, a soldier in the ancient world (or the modern world, for that matter) had to be in good physical shape if he expected to survive, let alone be victorious. The best examples of professional soldiers who followed this doctrine were the Spartans. From the age of seven until fifty, every Spartan soldier exercised regularly. At home, these citizens ran, jumped, threw the javelin, wrestled, and practiced with the various arms and armor of their profession almost daily. Not even a campaign stopped the conditioning process for the Lycurgan Law required all Spartiates to exercise and practice gymnastics while on campaign.[23] Agesilaus was more aware of and knowledgeable about the positive military benefits of this hard program than most Spartan kings because he had undergone the standard training of a Spartan citizen as he grew up. (Normally, the heirs to the dual monarchy were exempt from this toil.[24]) He knew the value of physically fit soldiers and preferred to have mercenaries whose fitness was closer to his ideal, rather than the young men from the wealthy families of Ionia who did not train their bodies for the rigors of combat. A few years later, Jason of Pherae expressed what must have been Agesilaus' feelings when he said, "In each city very few men train their bodies, but among my mercenaries no one serves unless he is able to endure the same hard toil as I."[25] That Agesilaus thought such conditioning important is clear from the fact that he led by example; the Spartan king regularly went to the gymnasium at Ephesus and exercised with the soldiers of his army.[26]

Of course, the best physical condition was absolutely useless if proper discipline was not maintained, particularly when fighting against superior numbers—a situation Agesilaus constantly faced in Asia Minor. Traditionally, citizen soldiers were subject to civilian discipline, enforced by a civilian court. Because they were elected officials, generals usually found it easier and safer to note offenses, await the end of the campaign, and then bring the offender or offenders to trial before the appropriate court. Even the legendary Spartan discipline was more a matter of habit and training, which began at the age of seven for males, than of enforcement in the field by the king. In contrast, mercenaries were subjected to strict, harsh discipline set forth and enforced by their generals.

Although the methods used by Agesilaus are unknown, some can be logically deduced from the practices of all armies, and others can be found in the practices of his contemporaries. Obviously, minor offenses could draw some sort of extra duty, such as added guard duty or a supervised work detail. More serious offenses may have resulted in the loss of pay or some sort of corporal punishment. Lysander, for example, was reported to have flogged a soldier for breaking ranks during a march.[27] Of course, flagrant and serious crimes, such as theft, desertion, or dereliction of duty, drew extremely harsh measures.[28] Concerning desertion, Frontinus reported, "The Spartan general Clearchus used to tell his troops that their commander ought to be feared more than the enemy, meaning that the death they feared in battle was doubtful, but that execution for desertion was certain."[29] For dereliction of duty, Iphicrates apparently killed a sentry he found sleeping at his post, commenting, "I left him as I found him."[30] In fact, the purpose of this discipline was to turn an assorted group of individuals from various parts of the Greek world into a well-organized, well-ordered, and well-disciplined fighting force.

As mercenaries were much more accustomed to obedience than citizen soldiers, they likewise could be drilled and trained for combat to a higher degree.[31] Nepos gave us a picture of the goal of all mercenary commanders in his description of Iphicrates' army:

> At Corinth [during the Corinthian War], he commanded his army with such strictness that no soldiers in Greece were more practiced or obedient to their general, and he introduced them to the habit, that when the general gave the order for battle, they formed themselves without their leader's intervention, and stood in such a formation, that they appeared to have been individually stationed by an expert commander.[32]

Some sort of discipline and maintenance of formation had always been recognized as essential to the integrity of the hoplite phalanx, and most poleis took care to ensure this through training. In the case of his infantry, Agesilaus and his commanders simply had to improve this training. However, many city-states neglected to devise a similar program for their cavalry. Agesilaus' horsemen, in contrast, drilled and trained constantly throughout the winter. During the entire season, the hippodrome at Ephesus was full of riders exercising and training their mounts, and units also used this facility to practice the various cavalry formations. In the more open fields of the city, cavalrymen underwent weapons training, throwing javelins at targets that may have been shields suspended from poles. Mounted combat was also on the training program, including mock battles.

The Spartan king encouraged the progress of the various units by holding contests: Prizes were awarded to the units with the best horsemanship and the greatest proficiency with the javelin.[33]

Yet one question arises: Who trained and commanded the mercenary cavalry that Agesilaus was creating for his army? It seems unlikely that this was an Ionian Greek. Though the Ionians had had excellent cavalry in the Archaic period, the long concentration on naval warfare with the Delian League and the Athenian Empire probably meant that mounted warfare was neglected for some time. This tendency would only have been increased by Athens' support of democracies and the demos at the expense of aristocracies and aristocrats, the traditional cavalry class. With their renewed domination, the Persians, in certain places, encouraged the aristocrats as a means of political control but probably not as a military force. In fact, the extent of the deterioration of the Ionian hippeis is clearly evident from their performance in 396 B.C.; the cavalry that took the field with Agesilaus was not up to the challenge of the Persian horsemen.

Agesilaus' cavalry expert was certainly not a Spartan. The Spartans had no tradition of mounted warfare and apparently thought it of little value, except under certain conditions. Indeed, the first Spartan cavalry since the seventh century B.C. was created only thirty years before Agesilaus went to Asia. In 424 B.C., during the Peloponnesian War, a force of 400 horsemen was established as a quick reaction force to counter Athenian naval raids.[34] But this force had a very limited function, and the view that cavalry had only a restricted role did not change with time. In 418 B.C. at the Battle of Mantinea, the Spartan cavalry, though present on the field, apparently took no part in the combat; the Athenian horsemen operated unmolested throughout the conflict.[35] At the Battle of Coronea (394 B.C.), Agesilaus did not employ the excellent cavalry he brought from Asia at all but chose a costly series of direct infantry assaults against the Thebans and their allies.[36] And at the Battle of Leuctra (371 B.C.), the Spartans once again showed their disregard for mounted units; the Spartan cavalry was composed of those men who were physically the weakest and of dubious courage. As a result, this force was quickly overwhelmed.[37]

Where, then, did Agesilaus obtain the expertise to develop a cavalry force in 396 B.C. capable of successfully confronting the Persians? The obvious answer is that there was an experienced, able cavalryman among the Spartan king's officers. Although the sources do not identify the majority of his officers, the name of one of them was repeatedly mentioned in association with mercenaries, cavalry, and horses—Xenophon.

Xenophon had been a member of the Athenian cavalry in the last years of the Peloponnesian War. He had joined the expedition of Cyrus and was present at the Battle of Cunaxa (400 B.C.). When the Greek commanders of the mercenaries were captured and killed by the Persians, he was one of the men elected general by the desperate mercenaries. During the march to the Black Sea, Xenophon commanded the rear guard and had ample opportunity to study the Persian cavalry firsthand, through daily combat. (If one survived the experience, constant confrontation was one of the best ways of learning about an opponent.) In fact, Lycurgus, whose laws had turned the Spartans into the finest infantry in Greece, had been so concerned by this that one of his laws forbade his people from making frequent campaigns against the same foes "in order that these not learn how to make war."[38]

The Greek mercenaries' judgment of Xenophon proved correct, and he showed himself to be a skilled tactician and innovator. To counter the harassing tactics of the Persian archers, slingers, and cavalry, he collected all the Rhodians and others skillful with the sling and organized them into units of slingers whose bullets carried farther than the Persian sling stones. He requisitioned all the suitable horses and riders and formed a small cavalry unit for use against the Persian horsemen.[39] These allowed the mercenary army to negate the harassment. When the retreating Ten Thousand found themselves in mountainous terrain and facing a hostile infantry force, Xenophon suggested tactics more suitable to the conditions than the normal phalanx. The enemy was routed, and the march continued.[40] Finally, Xenophon devised a night-march formation designed to retain the integrity of the army by keeping the slower-moving infantry from being outdistanced by the faster cavalry: The horsemen rode behind the hoplites and thus had to maintain the same pace as the foot soldiers.[41] Consequently, the units of the mercenary army did not become separated, which could have led to the same disastrous results as those that befell the retreating Athenians at Syracuse.

Agesilaus probably became acquainted with Xenophon almost immediately upon his arrival in Asia. Xenophon was the commander of the Cyreans—the 4,000 Greek mercenaries, formerly part of Cyrus' army, who had been employed by Agesilaus' predecessors Thibron and Derkylidas. This force made up one-third of the heavy infantry in Agesilaus' army. It is inconceivable that an intelligent and able commander like Agesilaus would allow an unknown subordinate to retain command of so high a percentage of his army. Rather, Agesilaus would have gotten reports on all the unit commanders from the outgoing general, Derkylidas, and a series of officer conferences and gatherings would have been held to detail and plan the campaign of 396 B.C. These apparently were sufficient to convince the young Spartan king of the ability of the Athenian mercenary commander for Xenophon commanded the Cyreans during that campaign.[42] Equally, once the deficiency in mounted assets was known, it is inconceivable that this same able and intelligent king would not use to his advantage the experience and knowledge of a subordinate of Xenophon's caliber.

Therefore, considering Agesilaus' lack of knowledge of cavalry and Xenophon's competence in both cavalry and Persian tactics and weapons, it seems almost certain that Xenophon played a major role in the organization and training of the mounted units for Agesilaus' army.[43] While the sources that deal directly with Agesilaus' Asian campaign give only a few details concerning his horsemen, it is possible to obtain a fairly accurate picture of the organization, training, and weaponry of the Greek mercenary cavalry. Later in his life, Xenophon wrote two works that dealt with the development of skilled riders and a capable cavalry force.[44] Although these works were written for an Athenian audience, the Asian and Persian influence is readily apparent, and the works obviously incorporated the techniques of mercenary cavalry for the enlightenment of the citizen cavalry trooper or officer.

Xenophon did not specify the size of a file, but because he called the file leaders decadarchoi, or leaders of 10, it appears that he thought a file should be composed of 10 men. He believed that the file leaders should be the strongest, most aggressive, and bravest of the troopers. The file closers should be the oldest, most stable, and most sensible men—those who could give confidence in the advance and lead well in the retreat. No doubt Xenophon thought the section leader, the leader of the second 5 men, should be almost as able as the file leader. To determine the file order, the cavalry commander should choose the file officers, but from then on, each rider should choose the man who rode behind him. Thus, the file leader chose the number 2 man in the file, the number 2 man chose the number 3 man, and so forth. In this way, each trooper had someone behind him whom he knew and trusted.[45]

Xenophon's basic formation was the rectangle. This was common among the Greeks, but Xenophon certainly knew of at least one other formation in use at the time: The Thessalians had been allies of the Athenians, and so he was aware that they used a rhomboid or diamond formation. It is uncertain if he knew about the Scythian wedge, even though Athenian soldiers stationed in and around Thrace and the Chersonses must have seen and reported it. For whatever reason, he did not recommend or discuss the diamond formation of the Thessalians or the wedge of the Scythians. Although the actual size and shape of the rectangle he employed could change depending upon the nature of the terrain and other conditions, Xenophon must have felt that the rectangle should be at least 5 men deep for a battle. A well-drilled cavalry should be able to go from a column to a narrow front to a broader front and finally into a battleline without stopping and without confusion. To ease this transition, Xenophon believed that the number of files in the parade formation, the one used to muster the troopers, should have an even number, making it far easier to double or halve the number of files and the frontal area of the formation.[46]

If he followed the Athenian model, as seems likely, Xenophon's basic combat unit was the 100-man squadron, which was composed of 2 50-man troops. This followed his criterion of even files exactly. A squadron in parade formation had 10 files of 10 men each. To narrow the front, the number of files could be halved down to 5 by having 1 troop form behind the other. To broaden the front, the number of files could be increased to 20 by having the rear section of each file move left and forward, thus creating a 20-by-5 rectangle. Regardless of the formation, discipline had to ensure that the horsemen at all times retained their order and followed the file leaders. This was essential to ensure that orders were passed effectively, formations were changed without confusion and loss of cohesion, and attacks and withdrawals were made professionally and with as few casualties as possible.[47]

Another factor of importance to the integrity of the formation was the behavior of the horses. The animals had to behave properly and be thoroughly trained. Those that showed any signs of bad behavior, such as biting, kicking, or simply having too much spirit, would be excluded from the formation since they could be disruptive among so many horses and men packed close together. Xenophon also emphasized the need to train and condition a horse so that it would be able to endure the hardships encountered by the cavalry and not become tired to the point where the rider was endangered or had to drop from the formation. The distances over which the ancient Greek horsemen practiced are unknown, but later cavalry corps expected their mounts to be able to begin a charge from a mile or so away from the enemy, gradually increase the speed of the advance, reach a full gallop within several hundred yards of the enemy line, and hit the line with maximum force. Then, the horses were expected to have enough energy left to carry the rider in mounted combat for a time and advance or withdraw as necessary.[48] It was the duty of the cavalry commander to ensure that the horse of every man in his command received enough food, exercise, and training. This, in part, could be determined quite easily by leading the various squadrons in drills and maneuvers and observing the conduct of both riders and horses. Of course, the maneuvers had to be conducted over the various types of terrain and obstacles that the horses and riders would encounter and be expected to overcome, including walls, ditches, ravines, hills, and rivers. The cavalry commander also encouraged excellence by having the various units and individuals compete in field trials and by awarding prizes to the best.[49]

Xenophon thought the cavalry should be armed in the Persian fashion. Instead of using a spear, as the Ionian Greeks apparently did, each man should carry two cornel-wood javelins, which he should be able to throw accurately while mounted or use as thrusting weapons. For close combat, Xenophon thought the *kopis* or *machaira*, the single-edged, curved slashing sword, was the best weapon for horsemen. For his personal protection, each cavalryman should wear the Boeotian helmet, a breastplate with a neck piece, armor on the left hand and arm (the exposed arm and hand that held the horse's reins), and high boots to protect the feet and lower part of the legs. Likewise, the horse should be protected by quilted armor, especially on its chest and stomach.[50] In this panoply, the horse and rider were far better protected and equipped than in the traditional Greek armor and arms. Combined with the organization and training recommended by Xenophon, this equipment made the Greek cavalry of Agesilaus an effective mounted force for countering the Persian horsemen.

The effectiveness of the cavalry that was created for Agesilaus' army was demonstrated at the Battle of Sardis (395 B.C.). Early in the spring, Agesilaus made his last two moves with regard to his army. First, because a new group of officers had arrived from Sparta as replacements, the king utilized some of these in his command structure. Xenophon was officially relieved of the command of the Cyreans and replaced by Herippides, Scythas was made commander of the helot hoplites, and Mygdon became commander of the allied infantry. Agesilaus appointed Xenocles and another, almost certainly Xenophon, to command the cavalry.[51] This joint command was necessary because of the duality of the cavalry and its role: It was composed of both allied citizen and mercenary horsemen, so it would seem Agesilaus thought it best to have a Spartiate command the citizen horsemen and a mercenary command the mercenaries. Furthermore, the cavalry was split up a great deal of the time, half on one wing and half on the other for battle or half as an advanced guard and half as a rear guard. Thus, two commanders were necessary.[52] Agesilaus' second move in regard to the army was his attempt to increase the confidence of his soldiers by showing them the weakness of the enemy. When the Spartan king had the Persian prisoners of war stripped and sold as slaves in the presence of his own troops, the whiteness and softness of the Persians was clearly evident to all the Greeks.[53]

When the campaign began, Agesilaus and his army advanced from Ephesus to the area around Sardis unmolested. His army probably had about 15,000 infantry and more than 2,000 cavalry.[54] As the Greeks approached the city, the camp followers of the Greek army, who had scattered to plunder and forage, were attacked by units of the Persian satrap Tissaphernes' horse, which had just arrived. Even though the Persian horsemen probably outnumbered his own by 2 to 1, Agesilaus ordered his cavalry to intercept the Persians and protect the foragers. The appearance of Agesilaus' horse caused the Persians to form a battleline, with the Pactolus River at their backs. The Greek cavalry held the Persians in check and kept them from withdrawing across the river. Agesilaus brought up the main body of the army and, seeing that the Persians were without infantry support, decided to attack. He drew up his army for battle and then offered prayers and sacrifices to the gods.[55]

Agesilaus now made a coordinated infantry-cavalry attack upon the Persians. Xenophon reported:

> Therefore, after offering sacrifices, he at once led his phalanx against the opposing line of horsemen, ordering the first ten year-classes of the hoplites to run to close quarters with the enemy, and bidding peltasts lead the way at a double-quick. He also sent word to his cavalry to attack, in the assurance that he and the whole army were following them. Now the Persians met the attack of the cavalry; but when the whole formidable array together was upon them, they gave way, and some of them were struck down at once in crossing the river, while the rest fled on.[56]

Xenophon was clear in his description. First, Agesilaus ordered his cavalry to charge and occupy the attention of the enemy horsemen. While this was proceeding, the Greek peltasts advanced at the run to support their cavalry, and Agesilaus himself led the youngest of the hoplites forward as rapidly as possible, while still maintaining good order, to deliver the final blow. The Persian cavalry withstood the Greek horsemen but were kept busy defending themselves. With the arrival of the peltasts and, shortly thereafter, the hoplites, the Persians broke and fled. The retreating horsemen were pursued into the Pactolus River by both Greek cavalry and peltasts. About 600 of the enemy were killed either in the water or on the banks of the river. This battle ended with the sack of the Persian camp by the soldiers of Agesilaus' army.[57]

Though the sources do not give all the details one could want, it is clear that the Greek cavalry, Agesilaus' big weakness the year before, showed great skill and courage against a numerically superior Persian mounted force. The Greek horsemen had met the Persians, exhibited good order and discipline, forced them into a position where there was little room to maneuver with a river at their backs, and held them there. The largely mercenary mounted force had wheeled, circled, attacked, and regrouped so effectively that Agesilaus had time to advance his entire army, give orders, array the infantry for battle, and sacrifice to the gods while the Persians remained threatened and unable to withdraw to safety. Finally, Agesilaus' horse had led a combined infantry-cavalry attack that resulted in victory.

Later in the fourth century B.C., the ideas of coordinating cavalry and infantry and making the most of cavalry on the battlefield were taken further by the Theban commander Epaminondas. At the Battle of Leuctra (371 B.C.), Thebes and Sparta faced each other to determine which city would be dominant in Greece. Cleombrotus, one of the Spartan kings, arrived ahead of the Thebans with an army composed of about 10,000 hoplites, an unknown number of peltasts, and 1,000 cavalry. Four of the 6 Lacedaemonian infantry morai were present, numbering approximately 2,300 men, of which 700 were Spartiates. Spartan allies contributed the rest of the hoplites. The light-armed forces consisted of Phocian and mercenary peltasts. The cavalry was furnished by Phlius, Heraclea, and Sparta. Considering that Cleombrotus had 1,000 horsemen, a fairly large number for a Spartan army, and was facing the threat of the Boeotian cavalry, the Spartans probably recruited as many horsemen as possible from their allies and sent all 6 morai of the Spartan cavalry.[58]

The army that Epaminondas led onto the field was slightly smaller than that of the enemy. The Theban general likely had between 6,000 and 7,000 hoplites, and about 800 cavalrymen. The Thebans had contributed approximately one-half of both the heavy infantry and the cavalry, or about 3,500 hoplites and 400 horsemen. The remainder of the soldiers came from the Boeotian allies.[59] These must have included some light-armed infantry, even though the ancient sources did not mention any on the Theban side.

On the morning of the battle, as the two sides were arming and preparing to fight, the hostilities opened with an unusual occurrence. Epaminondas apparently gave orders that the noncombatants and any others who felt apprehensive about being on the Theban side should depart the camp and return home. As a result, those who had brought supplies, some members of the baggage train, and the men of Thespies left the camp. The Spartans responded to this by detaching the mercenaries of Heiron, the Phocian peltasts, and the cavalry of Heraclea and Phlius from the left wing of the assembling army to pursue the withdrawing Boeotians. These light-armed infantrymen and horsemen rapidly overtook the departing individuals, fell upon them, and drove them back to Epaminondas' camp.[60]

As the two armies deployed for battle, Cleombrotus placed the Lacedaemonian morai on the right of the phalanx, with the allied hoplites holding the center and left (Figure 6.1A). Cleombrotus' phalanx had a uniform depth of 12 shields. The left wing contained Heiron's mercenaries, the Phocian peltasts, and the Heraclean and Phliasian horsemen. The Spartan cavalry was placed in front of the Lacedaemonian infantry morai. Xenophon criticized the poor quality of the Spartan horsemen since they lacked training and experience. This was because the wealthy citizens, who owned the horses, only provided the cavalry mounts to the troopers when the army was called out. Consequently, the troopers were denied adequate opportunity to ride and train with the horses. Further, those chosen to serve as cavalrymen were the weakest physically and the least ambitious and courageous. Thus, at Leuctra, the Spartan cavalry was composed of inexperienced and unmotivated horsemen.[61]

In response to Cleombrotus' formation, Epaminondas massed the Theban hoplites 50 shields deep on the left of his phalanx, di-

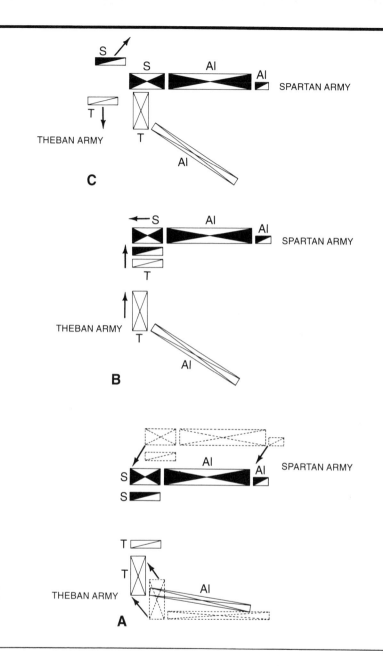

C

SPARTAN ARMY

THEBAN ARMY

B

SPARTAN ARMY

THEBAN ARMY

SPARTAN ARMY

THEBAN ARMY

A

THEBAN ARMY		SPARTAN ARMY	
Theban Hoplites	3,500	Spartan Hoplites	2,300
Allied Hoplites	3,500	Allied Hoplites	7,700
Theban Cavalry	400	Spartan Cavalry	600
Allied Cavalry	400	Allied Cavalry	400

Infantry   T = Theban   Infantry   S = Spartan

Cavalry   Al = Allied   Cavalry   Al = Allied

Figure 6.1 *Battle of Leuctra (371 B.C.).*

rectly opposite the Lacedaemonian morai. The Boeotian allies formed the center and right, employing a less than normal depth of no more than 5 shields for they had to stretch out to match the length of the enemy line. The Boeotian cavalry was positioned in front of the Theban infantry. In contrast to his assessment of the Spartan cavalry, Xenophon praised the Boeotian horsemen for being well trained and ready. Besides a long tradition as cavalrymen, maintained by constant riding and mounted training, the readiness of the Boeotian horse was at a peak due to a recent war with the Orchomenians and the Thespians.[62]

The battle opened with the advance of both armies. The Lacedaemonians drifted to the right, as was customary, with the intent of overlapping the enemy. Epaminondas chose to advance with his left, moving obliquely across the field with his right refused. To hasten the overlap and subsequent envelopment, Cleombrotus, using his cavalry as a screen, began to extend his line to the right, probably by turning the 4 morai into a column and marching to the right as quickly as possible (Figure 6.1B). Cleombrotus wanted to get outside the Theban left flank and then turn his column into a line and wheel into the Theban left. At this point, Epaminondas' cavalry charged across the space between the 2 armies and hit the Spartan horsemen. This shock drove the Spartan mounted troops back into their own infantry and caused a great deal of confusion as horses, riders, and hoplites were all mixed together.[63]

As the Boeotian horse disengaged and the Spartan cavalry fled the field, Pelopidas led the Sacred Band forward on the double and attacked the Lacedaemonian phalanx at the point of confusion, near where Cleombrotus stood between the first and second morai (Figure 6.1C). The remainder of the Theban hoplites followed suit. It appears that only the right 2 morai were heavily engaged.[64] Although Cleombrotus fell in the early stages of the fighting, the Spartans were able to assist their mortally wounded king from the field, and they continued to fight as they attempted to regroup. Plutarch praised the professionalism of the Spartans for not breaking because of the confusion and loss of their king.[65] And Xenophon noted approvingly that the Spartans held their ground and got their king off the field.[66]

However, as the losses continued to mount, particularly among the Spartiates, things changed. With the deaths of the polemarch Deinon, Sphodrias, a tent-companion of the king, and Cleonymus, Sphodrias' son, the right fell back slightly. Supposedly, Epaminondas then asked his Thebans for "one step forward to please me." This resulted in the whole Spartan right being pushed back one step and giving way, after which the rest of the army followed suit.[67] The Lacedaemonians lost 1,000 men, including 400 Spartiates, and their hegemony over Greece.[68]

The cavalry of both sides had important roles, and though the Spartan cavalry failed, the Boeotian horsemen were very effective. Cleombrotus tried to use his cavalry to mask or hide the movement of his 4 morai to the right: The Spartan king apparently thought the horses and riders and the dust they raised would conceal and protect the extending Spartan right until it was ready to turn on the Theban left. Any mounted force was expected to screen for its deploying army, which usually meant going forward and skirmishing with light-armed troops and other cavalry until the phalanx was formed. Then it returned to the wings to await pursuit or withdrawal. But Cleombrotus tried to have his horsemen do more by actually screening for a maneuvering phalanx. This was tactically a good plan, but the horsemen had to be able to fight well enough to hold their position against attack. The Spartan cavalrymen were not that good.[69]

By contrast, Epaminondas knew he had good cavalry and used it for the opening move in the battle. The Boeotian horsemen projected force by using the charge against their counterparts. This drove the Spartan horsemen back into their infantry, created a point of confusion and weakness that could be exploited, and exposed the Spartan morai to attack. Epaminondas may not have planned it quite that way, but at the very least knowing his cavalry was superior to and could defeat its opponent, he planned to have his infantry attack behind his mounted units—coming out of the dust and horses and falling suddenly upon an unsuspecting formation. This was a coordinated cavalry-infantry attack with the former leading the way, and it showed some of the same ideas and abilities associated with the later Macedonian leaders Philip II and Alexander III.[70]

In 362 B.C. at Mantinea, where the Thebans once again faced the Spartans, Epaminondas sought to create another opportunity by placing even more emphasis and reliance on his cavalry. The clash between the opposing forces actually began very early in the morning on the day of battle. As he was approaching the city, the Theban commander detached his cavalry, which consisted of some 3,000 Boeotian and Thessalian horsemen, and sent it toward the city ahead of the army. This deployment apparently had two purposes. First, it was one way to screen for the army and gather intelligence. The cavalry would run into any opposition as it closed on the city, which would be reported to Epaminondas. Clearly, the Theban general was not going to march blindly into the enemy, as Agis had done in this very region in 418 B.C. Second, the Theban and Thessalian horsemen were on a large raid. Epaminondas hoped his fast-moving mounted units would capture enough Mantinean citizens and livestock to force the city to capitulate. Before they left, he told his horsemen "that probably all the cattle of the Mantineans were outside the city and also all the people, particularly as it was harvest time."[71]

Unfortunately for Epaminondas' plan, the Athenian cavalry, allies of the Mantineans, arrived in the city before the Theban and Thessalian horsemen. At the appearance of the latter, the Mantineans appealed for help to the tired and hungry Athenians, who had just completed the journey from Eleusis via the Isthmus of Corinth. The Athenian horsemen mounted and sallied forth to meet their more numerous foe. As soon as they came upon the enemy, they charged and crashed into Epaminondas' cavalry. The Thebans and Thessalians must have been taken by surprise by the suddenness of the attack, possibly because they had broken formation to chase livestock and ravage the countryside. Ultimately, the action of the Athenian hippeis allowed the Mantineans to get inside the city and deprived Epaminondas of an easy victory.[72]

Later in the day, the two armies formed for battle in the plain south of the city (Figure 6.2). The Mantineans and their allies took a defensive position at a point where the plain narrowed to about 1 mile and foothills protected the flanks of the phalanx. The Mantineans and Spartans held the right of the phalanx, with the

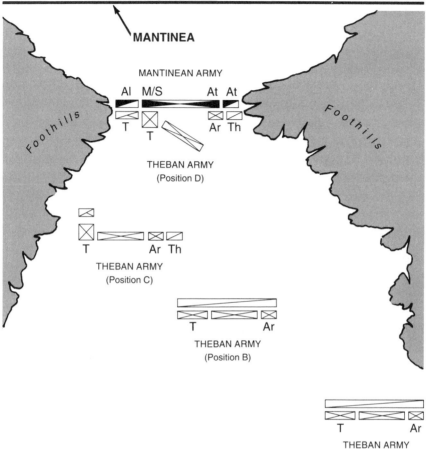

Figure 6.2 *Battle of Mantinea (362 B.C.).*

Eleans and Achaeans in the center. The Athenian hoplites formed on the left. This phalanx contained about 20,000 hoplites with a depth of about 12 shields. The 2,000 cavalrymen were divided and placed on both wings. Presumably, the Athenian horsemen, numbering less than 1,000 at this time, were on the left with their own hoplites, while slightly more than 1,000 Elean and allied cavalry deployed on the right. The right-wing horsemen were formed in a rectangle, with a depth of 6 horses.[73]

Epaminondas marshaled his phalanx south of the Mantinean formation and on the east side of the plain (Figure 6.2—Position A). His phalanx had the Thebans on the left, the Boeotians next, and the other allies in the center. The Argive hoplites held the right. Epaminondas had about 30,000 hoplites, and at this time, the phalanx had a uniform depth. Around noon, Epaminondas began to move his army northwest across the plain. The Theban commander had his 3,000 horsemen maneuvering in front of his army in order to raise clouds of dust and prevent the enemy from clearly seeing his movements (Figure 6.2—Position B). Upon reaching the west side of the plain, Epaminondas halted and grounded arms, giving the impression that he did not intend to launch an immediate attack. As a result, the Mantineans and their allies relaxed; some of the cavalrymen even dismounted, removed their breastplates, and unbridled their horses.[74]

While the Theban and Thessalian cavalry still milled about and obstructed the Mantinean view, Epaminondas began to mass hoplites on his left by moving unit after unit behind his own infantry line. He continued this until all the Thebans and Boeotians were in a deep formation on the left (Figure 6.2—Position C). Although no source stated the depth of this portion of the phalanx, it seems likely that Epaminondas had some 7,000 hoplites 50 shields deep and 140 shields across. The cavalry was divided about equally; one half took a position in front of the Theban-Boeotian left, while the other formed on the right wing. Light-armed infantry supported both cavalry formations.[75] Xenophon recorded Epaminondas' intent:

> For he was preparing to make the contest with the strongest part of
> his force, and the weakest part he had stationed far back, knowing

that if defeated it would cause discouragement to the troops who were with him and give courage to the enemy. Again, while the enemy had formed their horsemen like a phalanx of hoplites,—six deep and without intermingled foot soldiers,—Epaminondas on the other hand had made a strong column of his cavalry, also, and mingled foot soldiers among them, believing that when he cut through the enemy's cavalry, he would have defeated the entire opposing army; for it is very hard to find men who will stand firm when they see any of their own side in flight.[76]

In short, Epaminondas was going to engage the enemy, right and left, with his best soldiers—the Boeotians and the Argives—while the inferior hoplites in his center were kept out of the fighting. The key to his plan lay in defeating and breaking the enemy cavalry on the Mantinean right for when the cavalry broke and fled, it would be hard for the infantry to stand firm.

Once his army was ready, the Theban general quickly had his soldiers take up their arms, then he ordered the advance. The Mantineans and their allies scrambled to reestablish their formation when the advance of the Theban army was perceived. The cavalry was in particular disarray as grooms and riders attempted to bridle horses and horsemen frantically reequipped and rearmed themselves. As the advance continued, Epaminondas detached from his right wing the light-armed peltasts, Argive hoplites and mounted units, probably the Thessalians, and sent them across the plain toward the Athenians on the Mantinean left. After moving very rapidly in a diagonal path away from the Theban line and toward the enemy left, the horsemen and light infantry skirmished with the Athenians, occupying their attention and posing a constant threat. The Athenian cavalry was so disrupted by the attack of the Thessalian horse that it needed help. A unit of Elean horsemen was sent from the Mantinean right to aid the Athenian hippeis. Meanwhile, the Argive hoplites took up a position in the foothills, facing the flank of the Athenians. This prevented the Athenian hoplites from advancing or maneuvering to aid the Mantinean right.[77]

When his army had advanced the appropriate distance, with its center refused, Epaminondas' Theban cavalry charged the cavalry on the Mantinean right wing. The Theban horsemen were supported by light-armed infantry, which moved as rapidly as the cavalry. Shortly thereafter, the Theban and Boeotian hoplites assaulted the Mantineans and Spartans. After the cavalrymen threw their first javelin, the second must have been used as a thrusting spear. Indeed, the combat was probably so close for a short time that the principal weapons of the attacking horsemen were their swords. The allied horsemen, who were from various poleis and not used to fighting together, were overwhelmed, forced back by the shock, and broken. Attempting to get away from the attackers and the slaughter occurring in the confused mass, allied horsemen fled north toward the city of Mantinea and safety (Figure 6.2—Position D).

Those in the rear of the formation got away easily, but those in the front had to continue the struggle until the formation loosened enough for them to escape. The Theban cavalry and its light-armed troops continued to press forward against the remnants until they were even with the rear of the Mantinean phalanx. At this point, Epaminondas' Theban horse began to turn to the right, behind the Mantinean and Spartan hoplites. This threat, combined with the pressure of the Boeotian heavy infantry, broke the entire right wing of the Mantinean army. As the Theban cavalry and light-armed soldiers continued the envelopment, word of the death of Epaminondas reached them. The Boeotian horsemen immediately began to disengage and withdraw. The Boeotian light infantry continuing on toward the Mantinean left actually reached the area of the Athenian hoplites. But because the latter were withdrawing in an orderly fashion and still maintained a formation, this was a costly continuance. In close quarters, light-armed infantry was never able to contend with hoplites, and this was no exception. The Athenian hoplites killed a number of the Theban light-armed soldiers before the latter withdrew.[78] Ultimately, although the Theban army won the battle, the death of its general made this an expensive victory and one that could not be exploited.

The Mantineans and their allies used their cavalry in a very traditional way, but Epaminondas assigned his horsemen several important tasks and a major role in the battle. First, he attempted to gain an easy victory by sending them on a large-scale raid. Had the Theban and Thessalian mounted units been able to capture a large number of citizens and numerous head of livestock, the city probably would have surrendered without a fight. Unfortunately for Epaminondas, Mantinea had been reinforced by the Athenian cavalry, which came to the aid of its ally and sallied out to meet the threat. The Athenians fought well and deprived the Thebans and Thessalians of success.

Second, Epaminondas employed his cavalry as a means of screening and concealing his movements and deployments. As he moved his army west across the plain, closer to the enemy line, he exposed its flank. To prevent a surprise attack and hide his maneuvers, Epaminondas ordered his horsemen to ride between the two forces. Their presence ensured that no attack would be launched and that the dust raised by several thousand horses would hide the Theban army. As Epaminondas redeployed before his attack, his cavalry continued its activity and prevented the Mantineans and their allies from seeing the preparations and the massed formation. This was so effective the Mantineans were initially caught off guard by the Theban advance.

Finally, Epaminondas counted on his cavalry to be the key to victory, giving it the principal roles in the battle. Initially, the Thessalian horsemen were to occupy and pin down the Athenians so they could not attack the weakest elements of the Theban army and/or aid the Mantinean right wing when it came under attack. Then, the Theban cavalry was to attack the allied mounted units on the Mantinean right and break them by shock. Once this was done, Epaminondas knew that seeing their horsemen flee would create a morale problem for the infantry soldiers in the Mantinean army: They would be reluctant to hold their position and maintain the battleline. Further, with the defeat of the Mantinean cavalry, the right flank of the phalanx would be exposed. The fast-moving units, cavalry and light-armed, would be able to move past the phalanx, turn in, and attack the exposed and vulnerable rear. In fact, the shock of the Theban charge accomplished Epaminondas' goals. Only his death prevented an envelopment and a decisive victory.

Epaminondas' use of his cavalry was the culmination of a half century of attention and development. In the first part of the fourth century B.C., a new emphasis was placed on cavalry in Greek warfare. For campaigns in Asia, the Greek commanders found that an effective cavalry was a necessity in order to counter the horsemen of the Persians. Xenophon's small, improvised mounted force was the principal reason why the Ten Thousand did not suffer the same fate as the Athenian Sicilian Expedition. A strong, disciplined, well-trained cavalry also was the element that Agesilaus needed for a successful campaign in Ionia. In addition, Agesilaus combined cavalry and light infantry in a coordinated attack that defeated a large Persian mounted force. It was on the battlefields of Greece that the cavalry charge as a means of projecting force appeared. And Epaminondas used both the cavalry charge and coordinated tactics at Leuctra and Mantinea to good effect. It only remained for cavalry to be used as the decisive element of the battle, as the "hammer" of the Macedonian army, for cavalry to reach its peak.

7

The Cavalry of Philip II and Alexander III

During the reigns of Philip II and Alexander III of Macedon, the role of Greek cavalry on the battlefield reached its apex—in fact, the high point for cavalry warfare in Europe until well into the modern era.[1] Although these Macedonian kings employed horsemen in all the traditional ways, Philip and Alexander perfected the coordinated infantry-cavalry attack and used their cavalry as the means of dominating the battlefield. The charge of the Macedonian cavalry, whether against cavalry or infantry, was meant to project force, defeat and break the enemy at the point of contact, and gain victory. The Macedonian cavalry was the "hammer" that beat the enemy on the "anvil" of the Macedonian phalanx. This period truly saw the third and final stage of Greek cavalry development, in which the cavalry charge, using the weight and speed of the horse as an element of force, decided the battles.

Philip came to the throne of Macedon in 359 B.C. as the result of a military defeat and disaster. Perdiccas III, Philip's brother and the king of Macedon, was defeated in battle by the Illyrian king, Bardylis. Four thousand Macedonians, including the king, died on the battlefield. This defeat was avenged a year later when Philip led an army against Bardylis. Both sides had about 10,000 infantrymen, many of whom were probably peltasts. The Illyrian king had 500 cavalry troops, and Philip had 600.

Bardylis deployed his infantry in a line, with his best men in the front ranks, while likely placing his cavalry on both wings. Philip also deployed an infantry line but concentrated his best infantrymen on his right and positioned all his cavalry on his right wing. As Philip advanced, he ordered his horsemen to ride past the Illyrians' left flank and attack their rear. The Illyrian cavalry was either ridden down by the Macedonians, or, more likely, it fled in the face of the advancing horsemen. In either case, it left the field of battle for none of our sources mentioned any action or even the presence of the Illyrian horsemen after the battle began. The movement of the Macedonian cavalry was so decisive that Bardylis was forced to redeploy his infantry into a defensive square. Philip's infantry then attacked the left front corner of the square, and at the same time, the Macedonian horsemen attacked the rear and flank. Eventually, under the pressure of the Macedonian infantry, a gap appeared in the square that the Macedonian cavalry charged. The Illyrians broke. As the enemy soldiers fled, Philip's horsemen pursued, killing many of the fleeing Illyrians. Bardylis lost 7,000 men as a result of this defeat.[2]

Philip's cavalry, although small, had played a vital role in this battle. The Macedonian cavalry's aggressive charge not only eliminated the Illyrian horsemen but also made the Illyrian king take the defensive. The square formation did not allow for offensive movement and maneuvers: After going on the defensive, Bardylis' only hope of victory was that his square would hold and that Philip's forces would destroy themselves on the spears of his men. However, this did not happen. Instead, the combined attack of the Macedonian infantry and cavalry created a weakness that the latter exploited, causing the enemy to break and flee. The battle climaxed with the Macedonian cavalry delivering the last blows in the pursuit of the Illyrians.

Over the next twenty years, Philip built the finest army in the world. A major part of this buildup was the development of a large, powerful, and efficient cavalry force. One thing in Philip's favor was the Macedonian tradition of mounted warfare. Alexander I served as a reluctant ally of the Persians at the Battle of Plataea (479 B.C.), probably using both cavalry and light infantry.[3] Perdiccas II attempted to defeat the invasion of Macedonia (429 B.C.) by Sitacles, the Thracian king, with horsemen only.[4] And Amyntas, while attempting to regain control of his land from the Olynthians in the early fourth century B.C., had an ample supply of horsemen but sought the help of the Spartans because he needed heavy infantry.[5]

Yet Philip did not rely solely upon tradition for his cavalry. He adopted a deliberate policy to increase the size of his mounted force, a policy with two elements. First, Philip subsidized his cavalrymen. Unlike Athens, which gave various types of payments to the hippeis, the Macedonian king gave his horsemen land in return for service in the cavalry. As Philip expanded his kingdom, more and more land was available for allotment, and more and more horsemen became available for the army. This was how he disposed of captured territories around Methone, Amphipolis, and Olynthus.[6] And second, Philip did not restrict service in his cavalry to Macedonians only. He enrolled Greeks, Thessalians, Cretans, and others.[7] Apparently, loyalty and performance were the characteristics Philip rewarded.

The results of this program were striking. In 358 B.C., Philip had 600 horsemen in his battle with King Bardylis.[8] Six years later in a confrontation with Onomarchus, Philip commanded 3,000 cavalrymen, of whom 1,500 to 2,000 were Macedonian.[9] At Chaeronea (338 B.C.), Philip's Macedonian horsemen numbered 2,000, but this probably represented only two-thirds of the total strength of the Macedonian cavalry.[10] Finally, at the time of Alexander's invasion of Asia, the Macedonian mounted assets totaled 3,300 heavy cavalry troops, known as the Companion Cavalry, and 400 light cavalrymen, called the *prodromoi* or *sarissophoroi*.[11]

The Companion Cavalry was composed of about 14 territorial ilai, or squadrons, and the *agema*, or royal squadron. The territorial squadrons were recruited from and organized by districts and towns of the Macedonian kingdom.[12] Each territorial squadron had a complement of about 200 horsemen and was commanded by an ilarch or squadron commander. Though the squadron was the basic tactical unit, each squadron was divided into troops, perhaps 4 50-man troops, for better control. The territorial organization apparently was also kept when regiments of cavalry were formed. The 14 squadrons made up 2 regiments, the cavalries of Upper and Lower Macedonia. Each regiment had its own commander.[13]

In contrast to the territorial squadrons, the agema was composed of 300 men.[14] Although there was a squadron commander, the agema was often led by the Macedonian king himself. This was natural because the royal squadron was a special unit whose members were handpicked by the king, and the principal function of the royal squadron was to protect him and fight at his side.[15]

The Companion Cavalry was heavy cavalry, so the cavalrymen wore armor for protection. The standard equipment was a metal helmet and breastplate, although the latter was sometimes replaced by a multilayered or quilted cloth corslet.[16] The principal weapon of the Companion horsemen was the cavalry *sarissa*. This weapon, designed specifically for use by the cavalry, was a light, cornel-wood spear that weighed about 4 pounds and had an overall length of about 9 feet. On the front end of the spear was a double-edged, flaring blade about 11 inches long; the rear end had a similar blade that was slightly longer. The cavalry sarissa was thus long enough to reach the enemy but short enough for easy movement. The light weight allowed the rider to wield the weapon without undue fatigue or to throw it like a javelin, if necessary. The dual blade arrangement permitted the horsemen to thrust the weapon using either the overhand or the underhand grip or to strike downward with the rear end without having to shift the spear in his hand. It also gave the cavalryman an emergency, single-bladed weapon if the shaft of the spear broke.[17] Of course, as a backup weapon, all the Companion cavalrymen carried the kopis, the curved, single-edged slashing sword.[18]

As light horsemen, the prodromoi wore little or no body armor, probably only a metal helmet with a leather or cloth corslet. This light armor was consistent with their mission as scouts for the army.[19] However, as their second name, *sarissophoroi*, tells us, these scouts were armed with a rather unusual weapon during battle, the long infantry sarissa.[20] This spear was 15 to 18 feet in length, tipped with a double-edged blade about 20 inches long, and had a counterbalance butt-spike. Depending upon its length, the sarissa weighed between 12 and 14 pounds.[21] With 8 to 11 feet of spear projecting in front of the horse when the weapon was leveled, the sarissa gave the sarissophoroi a much longer reach than any of their opponents, whether infantry or cavalry. This allowed the Macedonian light cavalry to be used as a shock unit in battle.[22] The prodromoi were organized into 4 squadrons of 100 horsemen each.[23] These squadrons formed a regiment, with a single commander.[24]

The squadrons of the Macedonian cavalry deployed in wedge-shaped formations for battle. Apparently, the wedge originated with the Scythians and was adopted by Philip II for his mounted units.[25] At least one Macedonian scholar believed that Philip introduced the wedge as early as the first year of his reign and that this formation allowed the Macedonian cavalry to break Bardylis' square.[26] Of course, there were two important advantages to the wedge. First, the front was narrow and gradually widened, allowing for easy penetration of an enemy line or formation. And second, the squadron leader was at the apex or tip of the wedge, and thus, all the other horsemen followed him like a "flight of cranes."[27]

If the ranks of the wedge adhered to the progression of 1, 3, 5, 7, 9, 11, and so on, then each 100-man squadron of the prodromoi formed a wedge of 10 ranks with a gradually increasing width, the first rank having 1 horseman and the last having 19 (Figure 7.1A). If the interval between ranks was 1 horse's length and the distance between files was 1 horse's width, a prodromoi squadron wedge made a triangle with a depth of 57 yards and a base of 37 yards. Obviously, each territorial squadron of the Companion Cavalry with a complement of 200 men formed a larger wedge. The territorial squadron wedge had 14 ranks, with a maximum width of 29 horsemen (Figure 7.1B). The largest squadron wedge was formed by the royal squadron. Its complement of 300 riders deployed a wedge with 17 ranks and a base of 35 horsemen.

Of course, simply increasing the number of horsemen and adopting a special formation was not sufficient to develop an efficient and formidable cavalry. Discipline and training were also necessary and were key parts of Philip's program. Unfortunately, our sources in this area are less than adequate, and it is impossible to discern the training of the Macedonian cavalry. Yet there is a clear impression that the discipline was strict and the training hard and constant for the entire army.[28]

Philip trained his soldiers to be self-reliant and to do without luxury. He prohibited the use of carts and greatly reduced (and may

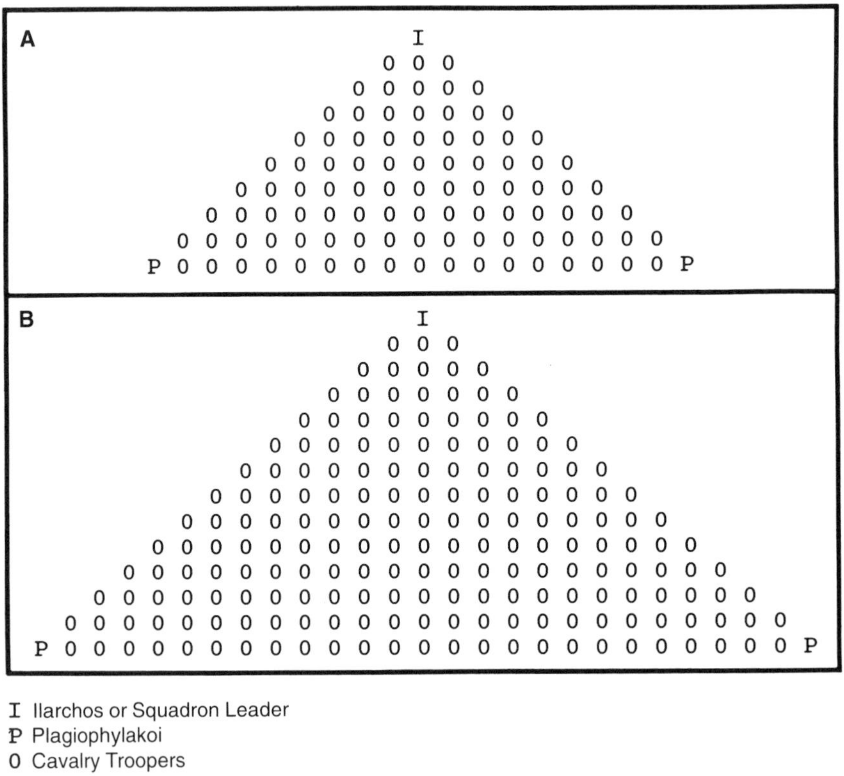

I   Ilarchos or Squadron Leader
P   Plagiophylakoi
0   Cavalry Troopers

Figure 7.1   *Macedonian wedge-shaped cavalry formation: (A) shows a prodromoi squadron wedge of 100 men, and (B) shows a territorial squadron of the Companion Cavalry of 200 men in a wedge.*

have eliminated) the extra, unnecessary equipment and items of comfort the soldiers took on campaign. After this reform, soldiers had to carry all their own personal gear. Obviously, the wealthy cavalrymen were far more affected by this order than the average infantryman. Philip also decreased the number of servants allowed within the army. Instead of every soldier having as many as he could afford, each cavalryman was allowed a single attendant or squire, and the 10 men of a file had to share the services of a single servant who was responsible for the communal equipment of the file, namely, the handmill used to grind grain into flour and the rope, possibly used for the file tent and other purposes.[29] With the exception of the number of servants permitted, officers and presumably the cavalrymen were expected to endure virtually the same conditions and rigors on campaign as the infantry soldiers. Philip required that each man in the army carry his own thirty-day supply of grain, along with his arms or armor.[30] He also sought to curtail elitism and special privileges by disciplinary action: In fact, officers were punished for using their rank to obtain luxuries not available to the average soldier. The Macedonian king, for example, demoted an officer for bathing with warm water and dismissed 2 commanders for bringing a song-girl into the camp for their personal enjoyment.[31]

The training of the Macedonian army was a year-round activity, in times of peace or war. Philip personally checked on the condition and proficiency of his soldiers at frequent intervals by conducting surprise training exercises. During these, units were decamped, mustered with full field equipment (including arms, armor, and rations), and marched 300 furlongs, or about 37 miles.[32] In short, Philip built a professional army and cavalry.

In 338 B.C. at Chaeronea, Philip's army demonstrated the results of the buildup and training with a coordinated infantry-cavalry attack. His opponent was a coalition of Greek city-states, including Thebes, Athens, and Corinth. This coalition fielded an army of about 35,000 infantry and 2,000 cavalry. The infantry formed a phalanx, consisting of roughly 30,000 hoplites, with its right wing anchored on the Cephissus River. This position was held by some 12,000 Theban hoplites, with the Sacred Band on the extreme right. This wing was no doubt fairly deep, deeper than the rest of the phalanx, as was customary with the Thebans. The center was composed of various allies and 5,000 mercenaries. Ten thousand Athenians formed the left wing, and the center and the left were probably 8 to 10 shields deep. The entire Greek phalanx stretched for about 2 miles. Greek light-armed soldiers were positioned in the foothills on the Athenian left, and the Greek cavalry was held in reserve, possibly some distance behind the phalanx, to guard the Kerata Pass, which was the Greeks' avenue of escape.[33]

Philip's forces at Chaeronea consisted of 30,000 infantry and at least 2,000 cavalry. The Macedonian king's light-armed soldiers took a position on the right of the Macedonian line in the foothills, confronting their Greek counterparts. The Macedonian phalanx con-

tained about 24,000 infantrymen with the hypaspists, or Shield Bear-
ers, on the right and the *pezhetairoi,* or foot-companions, in the
center and on the left. The Macedonian cavalry was positioned on
the left wing, opposite the Theban contingent. Philip commanded
the right, Antipater the left, and Alexander the cavalry.[34]

Philip advanced with his right (Figure 7.2A). The Macedonian
phalanx thus advanced obliquely in relation to the Greek line, with
the left refused. After the two lines met, the fighting was confined
for some time to the hypaspists and the right battalions of the foot-
companions versus the Athenian hoplites. The ancient sources tell
us that Philip deliberately did this because he knew the Athenians
were inexperienced and impetuous. At the appropriate command,
the Macedonian right began a slow, careful withdrawal. As Philip's
soldiers backed up farther and farther, the Athenians pressed forward, attempted to advance more quickly, and began to lose their order. The Athenians were moving not only forward but also more and
more to their left (Figure 7.2 B). This caused the units of the center
to move left as well, in order to maintain the cohesion and integrity
of the phalanx.[35]

As the center units of the Greek phalanx tried to conform to the
movement of the Athenians, a point of weakness or disorder appeared (Figure 7.2C). This may have been at the junction of the center and the Thebans on the right wing. The latter had to be very reluctant to move to the left because this would take them away from
the river and expose their right flank, thereby providing the Macedonian horsemen an avenue of attack. As it was, when the weakness in
the Greek line was perceived by Alexander, he immediately led the
Macedonian cavalry across the field and charged this point. The
sarissa-armed horsemen created a hole and widened this into a gap,
as their long spears impaled Greek infantrymen and caused panic.
The horsemen fought hard, drove their wedge into the enemy phalanx, and finally broke through. Alexander turned his mounted units
to the left and fell on the rear of the Thebans. At the same time,
Philip halted his calculated withdrawal and advanced the Macedonian phalanx. The Athenians were pushed back and broken. The
center also broke as the pezhetairoi pushed into the hole created by
their cavalry. For a time, the Thebans were surrounded with Mace-

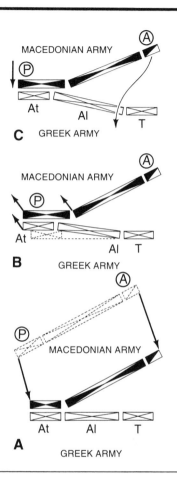

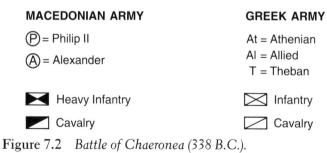

MACEDONIAN ARMY

(P) = Philip II

(A) = Alexander

▰ Heavy Infantry

◼ Cavalry

GREEK ARMY

At = Athenian

Al = Allied

T = Theban

⊠ Infantry

◩ Cavalry

Figure 7.2 *Battle of Chaeronea (338 B.C.).*

donian infantry in front and cavalry in the rear, but eventually, they broke and fled, with the exception of the Sacred Band, who apparently died almost to the last man. Contrary to the standard practice, Philip ordered his cavalry not to pursue the fleeing soldiers, in order to prevent any political repercussions from a needless slaughter. As it was, 1,000 Athenians lay dead upon the field, and 2,000 were prisoners. The Theban casualties were even heavier, although the exact numbers are unknown, and the Sacred Band was annihilated.[36]

At Chaeronea, Philip's coordinated infantry-cavalry attack worked perfectly and proved decisive. The Macedonian infantry of the right wing initiated the battle and fought for some time, while the Macedonian horsemen remained idle and waited for their opportunity. A controlled, slow withdrawal by the Macedonian right drew the Greek left wing and center forward and to the left. This shifting of position caused a point of weakness or disorder in the Greek line, and the Macedonian cavalry soon charged this point. Through the use of the sarissa, the wedge formation, and shock, the weakness was exploited and widened, and the Greek phalanx was broken. Philip's use of his cavalry to break an intact phalanx was innovative and unprecedented.[37]

It should be noted that some military historians do not believe that cavalry could break an infantry line. These individuals generally advance two arguments: first, that horses will not run into a mass of foot soldiers and, second, that even if they would, the riders would turn them rather than face certain death.[38] These points, though valid in some respects, seem to ignore or discount the exceptional conditions of war and the charge. Although no horse or any other domesticated animal would run into a wall or mass of men under normal conditions, stampeding horses or cattle will trample virtually anything in their path. Their only purpose is to move forward. And the final stage of a cavalry charge, with horses running as fast as they could, was nothing but a controlled stampede.

For men, discipline, training, leadership, and a cause cannot overcome fear, but they *have* resulted in heroic efforts. In response to these factors, men have sacrificed themselves in wars for centuries. Leonidas and 300 Spartans remained at Thermopylae in the face of certain death. A handful of men defended the Alamo to the last man against a large Mexican army. The Light Brigade rode into the valley of death. And U.S. Marines disembarked from landing craft into neck-deep water, endured merciless enemy fire, and waded 800 yards to the beaches of Tarawa. Thus, although the limitations of horses and men prevented cavalry charges from being pressed home and breaking an infantry line on many occasions, to deny that the charge was ever successful against formed infantry is an overstatement.

In fact, the *Drill Regulations for Cavalry, United States Army,* published in 1909, recognized the contradictions between the limitations of horses and men and use of the cavalry charge as a means of projecting force. However, it clearly showed that the direct cavalry assault or charge against an infantry line was possible, preferably when the foot soldiers of the attacking infantry had exhausted their ammunition, were retreating in disorder, or were shaken badly by artillery fire. The cavalry charge could also be successful against poor-quality infantry or as part of a coordinated infantry-cavalry attack. Finally, the charge could be employed to cut through a hostile surrounding infantry force. Most importantly, the mounted charge had to be executed with cohesion, rapidity, surprise, impetuosity, and vigor in the shock in order to be successful. Each trooper had to have complete control of his horse, be able to ride straight to the front, and maintain uniform speed and alignment.[39] Without a doubt, Philip's cavalry at Chaeronea met these criteria very well.

Five years after his father's victory at Chaeronea, Alexander used a coordinated infantry-cavalry attack at the Battle of Issus. This time, the Macedonian cavalry faced the challenge of massed Persian and Greek mercenary infantry. Alexander's army consisted of about 30,000 infantry and 5,000 cavalry.[40] As his army emerged from the Jonah Pass and the coastal plain east of the Pinarus River gradually opened, the Macedonian king deployed his army from line-of-column into a battleline (Figure 7.3—Position A). His initial deployment of the Macedonian phalanx had the hypaspists on the right, with the pezhetairoi forming the rest of the infantry line (Figure 7.3—Position B). On the right wing was the bulk of the cavalry, including the Companion Cavalry, the prodromoi, and the Thessalian squadrons. This wing was screened by some archers. The Greek al-

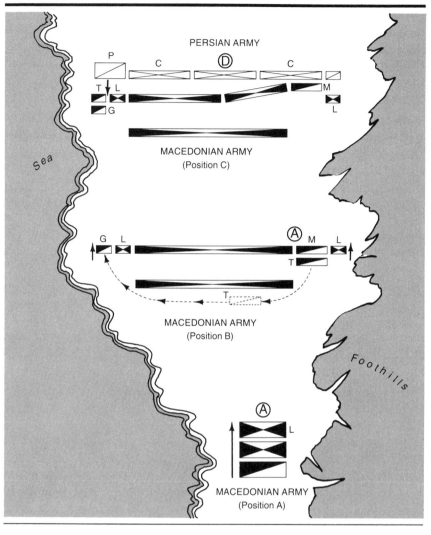

Figure 7.3   *Battle of Issus (333 B.C.).*

lied and mercenary horse was placed on the left wing. Alexander's Greek hoplites, allied and mercenary, formed a second infantry line behind the Macedonian phalanx, probably almost as long as the first and 100 yards or so back. To counter Persian skirmishers in the foot-hills on the Macedonian right flank, Alexander deployed a screening force of Agrianian peltasts, archers, and cavalry.[41]

At the approach of Alexander, Darius began to form his battleline. The ancient sources exaggerated the size of the Persian army, but Darius' force certainly outnumbered Alexander's army and probably had about 200,000 men, including at least 20,000 cav-alry.[42] Darius used light-armed soldiers and cavalrymen to screen his deployment and sent some light infantry into the foothills. The Per-sian king placed a large force of Greek mercenary hoplites, report-edly numbering 30,000 in the center of his line. These were flanked on both sides by 60,000 specially trained Persian peltasts, called Cardaces. Darius positioned the remainder of his foot soldiers, mostly tribal or ethnic levies from various parts of the empire, a little way behind his front line in tribal or ethnic formations. When he re-called his screening forces, a few of the mounted units took positions on the Persian left wing, but most of the Persian horsemen massed on the right wing at the shoreline.[43]

With the Persian screening forces removed, Alexander saw, for the first time, the Persian deployment of massed cavalry on the right wing. He therefore transferred the Thessalian cavalry from his right to his left (Figure 7.3—Position C). In the process of moving, the Thessalian horsemen rode behind the Macedonian infantry to hide this shift from Darius. Thracian javelin-men and Cretan archers were also positioned on the left front to support the horsemen. On the right wing, the prodromoi and the Paeonian cavalry were placed in front of the Companion Cavalry. To further extend the battleline to the right and fill the place vacated by the Thessalians, Alexander shifted two squadrons of the Companion Cavalry from the center of the mounted formation to the extreme right wing. Additional sup-port for the right wing was obtained by redeploying the Agrianians and the archers from the screening force.[44]

Alexander advanced his army slowly in order to maintain good order. When the Macedonian line was within missile range, Alexander led a charge of the right wing cavalry, followed by the remainder of the army. Alexander hoped in this way to lessen the casualties from the Persian arrows and cause panic among the Persian infantry. On Alexander's left wing, a desperate cavalry battle ensued between the Persian horsemen, on one side, and the Thessalian-Greek horsemen, on the other. Although the numbers and weight were on the side of the Persians, the Thessalians and Greeks held their own. This kept the Persian horsemen from penetrating the rear of the Macedonian phalanx and causing severe casualties. In the center, the Macedonian phalanx broke due to rough terrain, which gave Darius' Greek mercenaries an opportunity to rush in and exploit the gaps. In fact, the Greek mercenaries killed a number of Macedonian phalangites. However, before serious problems occurred either on the left or in the center, the cavalry with Alexander on the right wing gained victory.[45]

Alexander's cavalry charged forward and crossed the Pinarus River. The Macedonian horsemen drove the Persian archers back into the Cardaces, causing confusion and disorder. Then, the leading units of the cavalry, the prodromoi, hit the Persian peltasts. The Cardaces broke and fled almost immediately under the shock. With the Persian left routed, Darius fled the field. The Macedonian infantry and cavalry on the right curved around and enveloped the exposed flank of Darius' Greek mercenary formation. Many of the Greek mercenaries fell, and a general rout resulted. According to Arrian, some 100,000 Persian infantrymen and 10,000 Persian horsemen died in this battle.[46]

At Issus, Alexander gave his cavalry an even greater role than his infantry in the tactical and operational phases of the battle. The infantry was expected to advance, attack, and hold the enemy in a fighting stalemate, whereas the cavalry was expected to win the battle. To accomplish this, Alexander's horsemen had to perform two separate and distinct tasks. First, the Persian massed cavalry had to be neutralized or negated. This job was assigned to the Thessalians, who had a cavalry tradition stretching back some four hundred years, and to the Greek mercenary horsemen, whose profession was war. This force of about 2,500 horsemen outrode and outfought a far greater number of enemy horsemen. Although hard pressed at times, the Thessalian-Greek mounted squadrons on the left wing prevented the enemy cavalry from turning the flank of the Macedonian phalanx and reaching the rear of the Macedonian army.

Alexander assigned his Macedonian cavalry the second task, the task of charging an unbroken infantry line, breaking through, and destroying the integrity of the Persian army by either killing the king or forcing the Persians to flee. There was no room to maneuver, so this required a direct assault and shock. Arrian reported that Alexander hoped "to strike panic into the Persians by the swiftness of the attack."[47] Alexander used the prodromoi as the leading element of the assault because the long spears of the sarissophoroi were more effective than the cavalry sarissa against an unbroken line. The Macedonian horsemen performed as expected: They charged and hit the Persian Cardaces, who gave way immediately. After fighting through the confused, fleeing Persians, the Macedonians turned toward the Persian center, only to find that Darius had fled. As a result, the integrity of the Persian army dissolved. The speed and weight of Alexander's cavalry charge were the decisive elements at Issus.

Alexander continued to employ his cavalry as the critical force in his battles throughout his conquest of the Persian Empire, and the charge of the Macedonian horsemen gained him victories in major battles. The third stage of development for Greek cavalry was now fully in place. Philip had built a truly remarkable and proficient mounted force, composed of light and heavy cavalry units. The adoption of special weapons and the wedge formation made the Macedonian horsemen an implement of force and shock. In coordinated infantry-cavalry attacks, the charge of the Macedonian horsemen decided the outcome of the battle. Indeed, the speed, weight, and force of the Macedonian cavalry charge, the "hammer," broke even intact infantry lines. Philip broke a hoplite line at Chaeronea, and Alexander broke a Persian line at Issus. The cavalry charge and the projection of force made these Macedonian kings two of the greatest figures in military history.

8

Conclusion

Over the span of about one thousand years, Greek cavalry progressed through three recognizable stages. At first, the horse was used by the mounted warrior simply as a means of transportation to and from the battlefield. Next, the horse provided a platform from which cavalrymen fought and, at times, dominated the battlefield. And finally, the Greeks discovered that the cavalry charge, employing the weight and speed of the horse, was a means to project force in battle against either cavalry or infantry and gain victory.

The first tentative steps in this process began in the Mycenaean period. From about 1400 B.C. onward, the Greeks began to mount warriors on horseback. The evidence indicates mounted warriors were employed on Crete, Cyprus, and the Peloponnesus. The principal arms and armor for these horsemen included the sword, spear, and body armor—equipment indicative of mounted, close combat. Yet this was not an isolated phenomenon but part of a general trend throughout the eastern Mediterranean. Mounted warriors also appeared in the armies of Egypt, Syria, Hatti, and Mitanni. The search for greater mobility on the battlefield than the chariot provided likely spurred the experimentation with and employment of the horse and rider as instruments of war.

The fall of the Mycenaean world slowed the evolution of the mounted warrior but did not terminate it. Although the evidence is scanty, it suggests that the single spear was replaced by the javelin or, in most cases, two or more javelins as the principal offensive weapon of the armed horsemen. As the Dark Age ended and some light began to shine, the aristocratic cavalryman emerged in metal helmet and bell-shaped corslet, ready to dominate the battlefield of Greece for some time. In fact, the institutions of aristocracy and cavalry warfare were so ingrained in Greek society that they were among the first to be transplanted in the colonization movement that expanded the horizons of the Greek world.

The second stage of cavalry development coincided with the Archaic and Classical periods. The early Archaic period saw the hippeis preeminent on the battlefields of the Greek world. In the First Messenian War, both sides employed cavalry until the rigors of combat decimated the horsemen. The Lelantine War was fought primarily by cavalry and was concluded when the Chalcidians gained an overwhelming superiority in horsemen through an alliance with the Thessalians. With their large corps of horsemen and the deployment of the rhomboid or diamond formation, the Thessalians were the strongest and most proficient cavalry for several centuries. Yet other ethne and poleis deployed strong mounted forces also, including Eretria, Chalcis, Magnesia, Colophon, and Thebes.

Also during this period, the types of cavalry solidified, with their respective arms, armor, and tactics. Light cavalrymen wore no armor and used javelins with harassing tactics. Heavy cavalrymen used various pieces and combinations of armor and either javelins or thrusting spears. At times, these hippeis also employed shock tactics. And the dragoon, equipped in the complete panoply, fought on horseback or on foot as circumstances dictated. However, the cavalryman gradually lost his preeminence on the battlefield to the hoplite and the phalanx. By the Battle of Plataea, shock was too costly and ineffective against the disciplined, compact phalanx. Yet cavalry troops still had important roles to play as scouts, screens, harassers, and pursuers.

Although cavalry was now not the decisive element in warfare, at least two major political entities strengthened their mounted assets in the first half of the fifth century B.C. The Boeotian Confederacy formed a federal military force that included 1,100 horsemen. Cavalry was so important that each district was required to provide 100 hippeis. Athens also built up a strong cavalry. This was very difficult for the city because its cavalry had never been strong and Attica was unsuitable for raising large numbers of horses. But through a system of state subsidies paid to the hippeis, Athens created a force of 1,000 citizen cavalrymen, which was supplemented by 200 mercenary mounted archers. This force was organized and trained to be battle ready.

The Peloponnesian War provided the opportunities for the cavalrymen to put their training to use and for cavalry to demonstrate its worth. Cavalry was the first and principal means of countering invasions and incursions. Athens used its hippeis against the Spartan invaders from the first year of the war until the last. Even Sparta, which had disbanded its mounted units almost two centuries before, was forced to recognize this need and create a cavalry force for the defense of Laconia and Messenia. On the battlefield, cavalry was sometimes important and, on occasion, decisive. At the Battle of Delium (424 B.C.), the Theban cavalry provided valuable intelligence on the movement of the Athenian army and, during combat, attacked the Athenian rear, gaining victory. At the Battle of Mantinea (418 B.C.), the Athenian horsemen prevented the envelopment of the left flank of the Athenian phalanx and saved the hoplites from serious casualties and possible annihilation. And at the battles around Syracuse, the Athenian Sicilian Expedition was unsuccessful, in large part, because of the presence and performance of the Syracusan cavalry.

The cavalry charge as the decisive element in battle—the third and last stage in the development of Greek cavalry—appeared in the fourth century B.C. as part of the coordinated infantry-cavalry attack. The mounted force that was created and trained by Xenophon for Agesilaus' Asian campaign proved equal to the larger Persian cavalry of Tissaphernes at Sardis in 395 B.C. The Greek horsemen first contained and then led the combined assault against the Persian cavalry. Epaminondas used the charge of the Theban mounted troops at the Battle of Leuctra (371 B.C.) to push the inferior Spartan cavalry back into their own hoplites. This created a weak point that was exploited by the Sacred Band and the Theban hoplites for victory. At Mantinea (362 B.C.), the Theban horsemen again created the opportunity for victory by driving away the cavalry on the right wing of the Mantinean phalanx, thus exposing it to attack. Only the death of Epaminondas saved the Mantineans and their allies from destruction.

Finally, Philip II and Alexander III used the excellent Macedonian cavalry as the hammer in their hammer-and-anvil tactics. Although this was a coordinated infantry-cavalry attack, the cavalry was designed and employed to deliver the decisive blow that gained victory. Philip built the Macedonian cavalry from about 600 into a force of more than 3,000. He armed most of his horsemen with the cavalry sarissa, and a special unit of light horse was armed with the long infantry sarissa. Philip also adopted the wedge as the battle formation. These innovations gave the Macedonian cavalry the ability to penetrate and break infantry and cavalry formations alike. At Chaeronea (338 B.C.), the Macedonian infantry initiated the fighting, while the cavalry waited for the right opportunity to deliver the decisive blow. When a weakness appeared in the enemy line, the Macedonian cavalry assaulted this point and broke the Greek phalanx. Five years later, Alexander, while using part of his cavalry to counter the Persian horse, opened the battle of Issus by launching a direct mounted assault with the Companion Cavalry against the Persian infantry. The long spears, the speed, and the shock of the assault broke the Persians and won the day. Subsequently, this type of attack won Alexander the Persian Empire.

In contrast to what has often been written, the Greeks did not ignore cavalry or its role on the battlefield. They began to experiment with the mounted warrior as early as any civilization or society, proceeded to develop their horsemen and tactics, and finished by producing the finest cavalry in the world. Although their progress was slower than that of their Near Eastern counterparts, the end result—the cavalry of Philip and Alexander—was instrumental in conquering the Persian Empire, and nothing like it would be seen on the battlefields of Europe again until the Napoleonic Wars.

Abbreviations

AHB	*Ancient History Bulletin*
AJA	*American Journal of Archaeology*
AJAH	*American Journal of Ancient History*
AJP	*American Journal of Philology*
AncW	*Ancient World*
Andoc.	Andocides
Archil.	Archilochus
Ar. *Clouds*	Aristophanes *Clouds*
Ar. *Eq.*	Aristophanes *Knights*
Arr. *Anab.*	Arrian *Anabasis*
Arr. *Tact.*	Arrian *Tactica*
Arist. *Ath. Pol.*	Aristotle *Athenaion Politeia*
Arist. *Pol.*	Aristotle *Politica*
Asclep.	Asclepiodotus
Ath.	Athenaeus
BCH	*Bulletin de Correspondance Hellénique*
BSA	*Annual of the British School at Athens*
CA	*Classical Antiquity*
Caes. *BCiv.*	Caesar *Bellum Civile*
Caes. *BGall.*	Caesar *Bellum Gallicum*
CAH	*Cambridge Ancient History*
CJ	*Classical Journal*
CP	*Classical Philology*
CQ	*Classical Quarterly*
CR	*Classical Review*
CSCA	*California Studies in Classical Antiquity*
Curt.	Curtius
CVA	*Corpus Vasorum Antiquorum*

Dem.	Demosthenes
Diod.	Diodorus Siculus
Dion. Hal.	Dionysius of Halicarnassus
FGrH	F. Jacoby, *Die Fragemente der griechischen Historiker* (Leiden: E.J. Brill, 1940–1958)
Frontin. *Str.*	Frontinus *Strategemata*
G&R	*Greece and Rome*
Hdt.	Herodotus
Hell. Oxy.	*Hellenica Oxyrhynchia*
Hom. *Il*	Homer *Iliad*
HSPh	*Harvard Studies in Classical Philology*
IG	*Inscriptiones Graecae*
Isoc.	Isocrates
JEA	*Journal of Egyptian Archaeology*
JHS	*Journal of Hellenic Studies*
JNES	*Journal of Near Eastern Studies*
Lucr.	Lucretius
Nep. *Iph.*	Nepos *Iphicrates*
Nep. *Pelop.*	Nepos *Pelopidas*
OCD	*Oxford Classical Dictionary*
Paus.	Pausanias
Plut. *Ages.*	Plutarch *Agesilaus*
Plut. *Alex.*	Plutarch *Alexander*
Plut. *Arist.*	Plutarch *Aristides*
Plut. *Artax.*	Plutarch *Artaxerxes*
Plut. *Cim.*	Plutarch *Cimon*
Plut. *Lyc.*	Plutarch *Lycurgus*
Plut. *Nicias*	Plutarch *Nicias*
Plut. *Pel.*	Plutarch *Pelopidas*
Plut. *Per.*	Plutarch *Pericles*
Plut. *Sol.*	Plutarch *Solon*
Plut. *Thes.*	Plutarch *Theseus*
Poll. *Onom.*	Pollux *Onomasticon*
Polyaenus *Strat.*	Polyaenus *Strategemata*
Polyb.	Polybius

SO	*Symbolae Osloenses*
Strab.	Strabo
TAPA	*Transactions and Proceedings of the American Philological Association*
Theophr.	Theophrastus
Thuc.	Thucydides
Verg. G.	Virgil *Georgics*
Xen. *Ages.*	Xenophon *Agesilaus*
Xen. *An.*	Xenophon *Anabasis*
Xen. *Hell.*	Xenophon *Hellenica*
Xen. *Hipparch.*	Xenophon *Hipparchikos*
Xen. *Hippik.*	Xenophon *Peri Hippikes*
Xen. *Lace.*	Xenophon *Lakedaimonion Politeia*
Xen. *Oec.*	Xenophon *Oeconomicus*
YClS	*Yale Classical Studies*
ZPE	*Zeitschrift für Papyrologie und Epigraphik*

Notes

Chapter 1

1. L. E. Nolan, *Cavalry: Its History and Tactics* (London: Bosworth and Harrison, 1860), p. 2.

2. J. M. Brereton, *The Horse in War* (New York: Arco Publishing, 1976), p. 16. A concurring opinion was stated by Paul F. Gauaghan, *The Cutting Edge—Military History of Antiquity and Early Feudal Times* (New York: Peter Lang, 1990), p. 439: "Down through the centuries until the close of their independent existence, the Greek city-states were proverbially weak in cavalry."

3. G. L. Cawkwell, *Philip of Macedon* (Boston: Faber and Faber, 1978), p. 151.

4. W. Kendrick Pritchett, *The Greek State at War*, 5 vols. (Berkeley: University of California Press, 1971–1991), 1:132f. A more negative appraisal was given by John Lazenby, "Hoplite Warfare," in *Warfare in the Ancient World*, ed. by John Hackett (New York: Facts On File, 1989), p. 71: "Only once, perhaps, in three centuries of hoplite warfare, did cavalry play a decisive part in a pitched battle, and that in a negative way." Here, Lazenby referred to Tanagra in 458/457 B.C.

5. P.A.L. Greenhalgh, *Early Greek Warfare: Horsemen and Chariots in the Homeric and Archaic Ages* (London: Cambridge University Press, 1973), argued through most of the book that there were both mounted hoplites and cavalrymen as shown in the representations by Greek vase painters. W. Helbig, "Les hippeis Athéniens," *Mémoires de l'Institut National de France* 37(1904):157–264, maintained that Athenian cavalry did not exist until after the Persian Wars and thus that mounted warriors on Archaic vase paintings were foreign mercenaries, mounted hoplites, or mounted squires accompanying mounted hoplites. A. Alföldi, "Die Herrschaft der Reiterei in Griechenland und Rom nach dem Sturz der Könige," *Gestalt und Geschichte, Festschrift Karl Schefold*, beiheft 4 (Bern: Herausgegeben von der Vereinigung der Freunde Antike Kunst, 1897), argued that all representations were of cavalry.

6. Glenn Richard Bugh, *The Horsemen of Athens* (Princeton, N.J.: Princeton University Press, 1988), thoroughly examined the Athenian cavalry from the Archaic period to Hellenistic times but said nothing about its tactics or military functions.

7. George T. Denison, A *History of Cavalry from the Earliest Times* (1913; reprint ed., Westport, Conn.: Greenwood Press, 1977), p. 87, said, "We have seen that the first idea was simply the rapid conveyance of the warrior to the place of combat; then the use of the horse mounted for the same object—then the fighting from the horse itself, and lastly the development of the idea of the charge and the use of the weight and speed of the horse as an element of force."

8. J. H. Crouwell, *Chariots and Other Means of Land Transport in Bronze Age Greece* (Amsterdam: Allard Pierson Museum, 1981), p. 23.

9. D. H. Gordon, "Swords, Rapiers and Horse-Riders," *Antiquity* 27(1953):76.

Chapter 2

1. Greenhalgh, *Warfare*, chap. 1, argued that the Mycenaeans did not employ chariots as Homer described but rather used massed chariot attacks like the peoples of the Near East. However, I find it extremely difficult to believe in the massed chariot idea because the terrain in Greece is so broken and hilly, unlike much of the Near East.

2. Lucr. 5.1297–1299, proposed that the riding of horses in war preceded the driving of chariots. M.S.F. Hood, "A Mycenaean Cavalryman," *BSA* 48 (1953):91, stated that the chariot probably was decisively superior to early riding because it provided a more stable platform. J. Weisner, *Fahren und Reiten*, band 1, kapitel F, Archaeologica Homerica (Gottingen: Vandenhoeck & Ruprecht, 1968), p. 129, pointed out that if the Greeks had been able to use the ridden horse effectively in war when they first entered Greece, there would have been no need to invent and use the chariot. J. K. Anderson, *Ancient Greek Horsemanship* (Berkeley: University of California Press, 1961), p. 184, seemed to agree with Weisner's conclusion.

3. Arthur Evans, *Scripta Minoa*, 2 vols. (Oxford: Oxford University Press, 1909 and 1952), vol. 2, no. 222; idem, *The Palace of Minos*, 4 vols. (London: Oxford University Press, 1921–1936), 4:787.

4. Crouwell, *Chariots*, p. 128.

5. Greenhalgh, *Warfare*, pp. 45f.

6. Ibid., p. 45; Allard Pierson Museum, Amsterdam no. 1856; CVA Pays-Bas 1, pl. 127.

7. Hood, *BSA* 48, p. 84, figs. 47 and 48, reported on one figurine and suggested that carrying a dagger in this fashion apparently occurred in the Aegean, judging from other figurines found in the Middle Minoan sanctuary at Petsopha. A. M. Snodgrass, *Early Greek Armour and Weapons* (Edinburgh: Edinburgh University Press, 1964), p. 163, n. 18, reported on a second figurine. H. L. Lorimer, *Homer and the Monuments* (London: Macmillan, 1950), p. 225, showed the conical helmet was characteristically Mycenaean.

8. Hood, *BSA* 48, p. 88; W. Lamb, "Excavations at Mycenae—Palace Frescoes," *BSA* 25(1921):164–165; Greenhalgh, *Warfare*, p. 46, pl. 27.

9. Carl Blegen, *Prosymna*, vol. 2 (London: Cambridge University Press, 1937), fig. 615, no. 760; Hood, *BSA* 48, p. 86.

10. Hood, *BSA* 48, p. 86. J. L. Benson, *Horse, Bird and Man* (Amherst: University of Massachusetts Press, 1970), p. 23, suggested that such figurines are abbreviated chariot groups; however, Crouwell, *Chariots*, p. 45, believed this was unlikely considering the marked differences between rider figurines and chariot groups among Mycenaean terra-cottas.

11. A. M. Snodgrass, *Arms and Armour of the Greeks* (Ithaca, N.Y.: Cornell University Press, 1967), pp. 19–20, 26, 32, pl. 10–11.

12. Ibid., pp. 12, 20.

13. Ibid., pp. 84–85, 97, 109, 119.

14. Ibid., pp. 15–16, 18, 33; H. Peake and H. J. Fleure, *The Horse and the Sword* (New Haven, Conn.: Yale University Press, 1933), p. 86, said that the short dirk gave way to the slashing sword among the horse-riding men of the late Bronze Age. Lorimer, *Homer*, p. 228, fig. 23b, stressed the suitability of the Minoan rapier as a cutting weapon. Gordon, *Antiquity* 27, pp. 75f, though agreeing with Lorimer's assessment, did not believe that the existence of mounted warriors proved that the cut-and-thrust weapons were developed as cavalry weapons or that cavalry existed before the ninth century B.C. in Europe.

15. Arther Ferrill, *The Origins of War* (New York: Thames and Hudson, 1985), p. 73; John Hackett, ed., *Warfare in the Ancient World* (New York: Facts On File, 1989), p. 11.

16. Yigael Yadin, *The Art of Warfare in Biblical Lands*, 2 vols. (New York: McGraw-Hill, 1963), 1:218.

17. A. R. Schulman, "Egyptian Representations of Horsemen and Riding in the New Kingdom," *JNES* 16(1957):264.

18. James Henry Breasted, *The Battle of Kadesh*, 1st series, vol. 5, The Decennial Publication of the University of Chicago (Chicago: University of

Chicago Press, 1904), p. 32, called the mounted archer shown on pl. 5 a messenger.

19. Hood, *BSA* 48, p. 87, said that one of the reliefs from Luxor showed an officer carrying a bow and quiver and that the Abu Simbel reliefs showed 3 mounted warriors, 1 with a bow and quiver and another with just a quiver. Schulman, *JNES* 16, p. 263, believed that the representations show a small but important unit of scouts. Other scholars deny the existence of cavalry completely. H. E. Winlock, *The Rise and Fall of the Middle Kingdom in Thebes* (New York: Macmillan, 1947), pp. 153ff, believed that horses were too weak for heavy work and cavalrymen, and O. R. Faulkner, "Egyptian Military Organization," *JEA* 39(1953):43, stated that cavalry was unknown in the New Kingdom, possibly because the horses were too small and thus, that riders were no more than mounted orderlies.

20. Breasted, *Kadesh*, pl. 5, upper right of the plate shows several archers on foot, leading horses.

21. Richard F. Starr, *Nuzi* (Cambridge, Mass.: Harvard University Press, 1939), p. 542.

22. Hood, *BSA* 48, pp. 86f; O. R. Gurney, *The Hittites* (London: Penguin Books, 1952), p. 106, reported that the Hittites had no cavalry but that, on occasion, messengers were mounted on horseback.

23. Greenhalgh, *Warfare*, p. 44. Crouwell, *Chariots*, p. 51, disagreed with the idea that the depiction represents cavalry. A. F. Rainey, "The Military Personnel of Ugarit," *JNES* 24(1965):17–27, examined the military of Ugarit in the thirteenth century B.C. and found only infantry and chariots; thus cavalry was a later development.

24. Yadin, *Warfare*, 2:287.

25. Anderson, *Horsemanship*, p. 9.

26. A. M. Snodgrass, *The Dark Age of Greece* (Edinburgh: Edinburgh University Press, 1971), p. 415, dated this to the Sub-Minoan period. Lorimer, *Homer*, p. 153, fig. 10, dated the Mouliana crater to the Proto-Geometric period. V. R. d'A. Desborough, *Protogeometric Pottery* (Oxford: Oxford University Press, 1952), p. 269, argued that the Mouliana crater belongs to the Geometric period. Greenhalgh, *Warfare*, p. 46, fig. 31.

27. Snodgrass, *Arms and Armour*, p. 33.

28. Crouwell, *Chariots*, p. 50.

29. Polyb. 6.25.10; Martin W. Frederiksen, "The Campanian Cavalry," *Dialoghi di Archeologia* 2(1968):20.

30. Charles Oman, A *History of the Art of War in the Middle Ages*, 2 vols. (London: Methuen, 1924), 1:46; 1:56 also showed that the Franks used shields while mounted.

31. V. R. d'A. Desborough, *The Greek Dark Age* (London: Ernest Benn, 1972), p. 306.

32. Snodgrass, *Arms and Armour*, p. 38; idem, *Early Greek Armour*, pp. 136–139.

33. Snodgrass, *Dark Age of Greece*, p. 265.

34. Ibid., pp. 43, 415.

35. Snodgrass, *Arms and Armour*, p. 38.

36. J. K. Brock, *Fortetsa* (London: Cambridge University Press, 1957), p. 97, pl. 75, no. 1085.

37. Snodgrass, *Arms and Armour*, p. 58.

38. Desborough, *Greek Dark Age*, p. 306.

39. Buffalo Museum of Science C12847; A. M. Snodgrass, "The First European Body-Armour," in *The European Community in Later Prehistory, Studies in Honour of C.F.C. Hawkes*, ed. by J. Boardman, M. A. Brown, and T.G.E. Powell (Totowa, N.J.: Rowman & Littlefield, 1971), pp. 45f, pl. 5; Crouwell, *Chariots*, pp. 48f.

40. A. M. Snodgrass, "The Hoplite Reform and History," *JHS* 85(1965):112; idem, *Dark Age of Greece*, p. 271; idem, *Arms and Armour*, pl. 17.

41. Snodgrass, "Body-Armour," pp. 45f, pl. 4; idem, *Early Greek Armour*, p. 73, pl. 30.

42. Hom. *Il*. 2.220–232; here, I follow the translation of Richmond Lattimore, *The Iliad of Homer* (Chicago: Chicago University Press, 1951), p. 119.

43. Hom. *Il*. 11.266–274; Lattimore, *Homer*, p. 241.

44. Hom. *Il*. 20.495–502; Lattimore, *Homer*, p. 417.

45. Greenhalgh, *Warfare*, chap. 3. For a contrasting view, see Lorimer, *Homer*, p. 328: "Homer's treatment of the chariot is strictly Mycenaean." For other opinions on Homeric warfare, see Joachim Latacz, *Kampfparänese, Kampfdarstellung und Kampfwirklichkeit in der Ilias, bei Kallinos und Tyrtaios* (München: C. H. Beck, 1977); J. K. Anderson, "Greek Chariot-Bourne and Mounted Infantry," *AJA* 79(1975):175–187; G. S. Kirk, "War and Warrior in the Homer Poems," in *Problèmes de la guerre en Grèce ancienne*, ed. by Jean-Pierre Vernant (Paris: Mouton, 1968); B. Fenik, *Typical Battle Scenes in the Iliad, Studies in the Narrative Technique of Homeric*

Battle Description, in *Hermes* suppl. 21(1968); J. B. Hainesworth, "Joining Battle in Homer," *G&R* 13(1966):158–166; and P. C. Wilson, "Battle Scenes in the Iliad," *CJ* 47(1951):269–274, 299–300.

46. Greenhalgh, *Warfare,* p. 41.

47. Ibid., pp. 53–61.

48. Ibid., p. 61.

49. Arist. *Pol.* 1289b.36f.

50. Frederiksen, *Dialoghi* 2:20.

51. Frederiksen, *Dialoghi* 2:3–31, made a convincing argument for the origins of the Campanian Cavalry being found in the influence that Greek Cumae had on military affairs.

52. Polyb. 6.25.9–11; here, I follow the translation of W. R. Paton, *Polybius—The Histories,* vol. 3, Loeb Classical Library (Cambridge, Mass.: Harvard University Press, 1979), pp. 325 and 327.

53. Dion. Hal. 7.3.11.

Chapter 3

1. Arist. *Pol.* 1297b.16–19; Robert Sallares, *The Ecology of the Ancient Greek World* (London: Gerald Duckworth, 1991), p. 400, concluded that Aristotle's statement "is an anachronistic reconstruction if the 'cavalry' are thought of in terms of the knights in mediaeval Europe." Sallares's reasoning here was based upon the small size of the Greek horse, see pp. 398ff. However, this horse-size argument assumes that throughout the medieval period or the period of knights, the horses were all large, and this was not the case. See R.H.C. Davis, *The Medieval Warhorse* (London: Thames and Hudson, 1989), pp. 21ff.

2. Helbig, "Les hippeis," pp. 15ff. Crouwell, *Chariots,* p. 49, stated that Helbig was the first to introduce the concept of the mounted hoplite but that he went too far in his assertions concerning the exclusivity of the mounted hoplite and in denying the existence of any true mounted troops in mainland Greece prior to the fifth century B.C.

3. Greenhalgh, *Warfare,* p. 75.

4. J.A.O. Larsen, *Greek Federal States* (London: Oxford University Press, 1967), pp. 106f.

5. There is considerable controversy about the value of Pausanias' account of the Messenian Wars. Lionel Pearson, "The Pseudo-History of Messenia and Its Authors," *Historia* 11(1962):397–426, generally asserted that Pausanias and others fabricated a Messenian history and on p. 413 stated

that the battle descriptions had no real factual details, were too general and were set pieces. *CAH* III³, p. 328, here, N.G.L. Hammond proclaimed, "The detailed account in Pausanias IV is worthless" and maintained that only Tyrtaeus was of value. On the other side of the argument is W. Kendrick Pritchett, *Studies in Ancient Greek Topography*, vols. 1–6 (Berkeley: University of California Press, 1965–1989), vol. 7 (Amsterdam: J. C. Gieben, 1991), 5:4, who stated, "There is no reason to question his [Pausanias'] account in matters relating to the style of warfare and topography"; more recently, in 7:180, he concluded that Pausanias' topographical framework was sound for both wars. In this matter, I concur with Pritchett because I do not believe that all the battles were set pieces (one with a ravine or glen as an obstacle is hardly common or a set piece); Hammond's indictment was too all-inclusive, and all Tyrtaeus told us about the First Messenian War was that it was long and hard fought.

6. Pritchett, *Studies*, 5:5, recorded that William Martin Leake, *Travels in the Morea*, advanced this conclusion, but he did not confirm it.

7. Paus. 4.7.3ff.

8. Paus. 4.8.12.

9. Paus. 4.11; Denison, *Cavalry*, pp. 19f.

10. A. R. Burn, *The World of Hesiod—A Study of the Greek Middle Ages c. 900–700* (London: Routledge & Kegan Paul, 1936), p. 161, stated that Sparta provided its kings with a mounted life-guard regiment some 300 strong, but, as in some other Greek cavalry forces, these guards operated only as mounted infantry and fought in the phalanx; in the end, the horses were discarded completely, though the name *hippeis* was retained by the conservative society. J. F. Lazenby, *The Spartan Army* (Warminister, England: Aris & Phillips, 1985), p. 12, stated it is doubtful that the hippeis ever fought as cavalry. John Ellis, *Cavalry—The History of Mounted Warfare* (New York: G. P. Putnam's Sons, 1978), p. 11, proposed that the Spartan elite fought as heavy infantry but referred to themselves as hippeis to indicate that they had the ability to provide themselves and others with horses. Strab. 10.4.18, observed that some Spartan offices were not only administered in the same fashion as those of the Cretans but also carried the same names, *hippeis* being one of these. The term *hippeis*, as well as the soldier-type itself, was undoubtedly older in Crete because these warriors still retained their horses, whereas the Spartans preserved only the name.

11. Plut. *Lyc.* 23.1. Xen. *Lace.* 11.4, stated that Lycurgus organized the infantry and cavalry alike into 6 morai or regiments each.

12. Xen. *Lace.* 11.4, showed that there were 24 officers in each infantry mora. It thus seems reasonable that some system of command was used for the cavalry, possibly one as elaborate as that used for the infantry.

13. Great Britain, War Office, *Cavalry Training* (London: H. M. Stationery Office, 1921), p. 24, showed that a standard interval between ranks was 1 horse's length or approximately 3 yards; United States Army, *Drill Regulations for Cavalry, United States Army* (Washington: Government Printing Office, 1909), p. 100, stated that 1 horse is considered to occupy a space 3 yards long and 1 yard wide; on p. 15, it was stated that an open interval can have 3 yards between files.

14. Artemis Orthia, "The Sanctuary of Artemis Orthia at Sparta," *JHS*, suppl. 5(1920):206, pl. 92.3; Greenhalgh, *Warfare*, p. 94f, fig. 49.

15. Tyrtaeus 6; Ath. 14.630f; Diod. 8.36; *OCD* s.v. Tyrtaeus.

16. Thuc. 4.55.2.

17. Arist. *Pol.* 1286b.33ff.

18. Thuc. 2.13.8; P. Salmon, "L'armée fédérale des Béotiens," *L'Antiquité Classique* 22(1953):351; Larsen, *States*, p. 35.

19. Strab. 10.1.10, 12. P. Gardner, "A Numismatic Note on the Lelantian War," *CR* 34(1920):91, accepted the validity of the inscription described by Strabo, but this is rejected by W. G. Forrest, "Colonisation and the Rise of Delphi," *Historia* 6(1957):163, who believed this inscription belonged to a later war. Greenhalgh, *Warfare*, p. 92, acknowledged Strabo's account of the accord as a means of saving horses but still seemed to conclude that the *hippeis* dismounted to fight; however, this makes little sense because, once dismounted, the horses would have been kept out of harm's way for the most part. Everett L. Wheeler, "Ephorus and the Prohibition of Missiles," *TAPA* 117(1987):157–182, believed that Ephorus, Strabo's source for this treaty, created a fictional treaty to provide a precedent for a ban on catapults and catapult missile fire.

20. Thuc. 6.22.

21. Xen. *An.* 3.3.7, 4.17.

22. Arr. *Anab.* 2.9.2.

23. Frederick H. Russell, *The Just War in the Middle Ages* (Cambridge: Cambridge University Press, 1975), pp. 156ff; James Turner Johnson, *Just War Tradition and the Restraint of War* (Princeton, N.J.: Princeton University Press, 1981), pp. 128f; Philippe Contamine, *War in the Middle Ages*, trans. by Michael Jones (Oxford: Basil Blackwell, 1984), pp. 71f, 274f.

24. Snodgrass, *Early Greek Armour*, p. 192.

25. Archil. frag. 51.

26. Idem, frag. 3; Plut. *Thes.* 5.3.

27. Xen. *Hell.* 3.4.14, showed that it was common for cavalry (at least in Ionia) to use javelins; the Persians used ones made of cornel wood, which proved to be stronger than the Greek spears.

28. Greenhalgh, *Warfare*, p. 90, suggested that the sword was the least likely weapon for use on horseback; Arr. *Anab.* 1.15.8, showed that, in fact, the sword was very deadly when properly used against other horsemen, for Cleitus the Black cut Spithridates' arm off at the shoulder with his sword.

29. Snodgrass, *Arms and Armour*, p. 70.

30. Thuc. 1.15.3.

31. Plut. *Moralia* 760 E–F; A. R. Burn, "The So-Called 'Trade Leagues' in Early Greek History and the Lelantine War," *JHS* 49(1929):35f, believed the Thessalian cavalry was the decisive element in the war. For more discussion on this war, see also D. W. Bradeen, "The Lelantine War and Pheidon of Argos," *TAPA* 78(1947):223–241, and J. Boardman, "Early Euboean Pottery and History," *BSA* 52(1957):1–29.

32. Verg. G. 3.115.

33. Burn, *Hesiod*, p. 160, placed the coming of the Kimmerioi at the end of the eighth century B.C.; Gordon, *Antiquity* 27, p. 76, cited Burn.

34. Later reforms called for each kleros to provide 40 horsemen, with the total mounted force of the national army equaling 6,000. This seemed to indicate that there were 150 kleroi, and each was probably dominated by a single family.

35. H. D. Westlake, *Thessaly in the Fourth Century B.C.* (London: Methuen, 1935), chap. 2, for a discussion of the early people of Thessaly.

36. Larsen, *States*, p. 14; Burn, *Hesiod*, p. 217.

37. Westlake, *Thessaly*, p. 25, n. 1, stated "An important passage in Aristotle (frag. 497, Rose) does not mean, as it is commonly interpreted, that Aleuas divided an existing unity into four *moirai* but rather he found Thessaly consisting of four *moirai* and—the extant fragment does not record this further step—united them into a single state"; also see pp. 27f, 110.

38. Ibid., pp. 25, 104f; Larsen, *States*, p. 17; Xen. *Hell.* 6.1.9, 19.

39. Aelian 18.1–3.

40. Aelian 18.1ff; Asclep. 7.2 and 7.6–10, showed a theoretical rhomboid formation with about 40 men; by Alexander's day, the troop size may well have risen to 50 because the Thessalian cavalry squadrons in Alexander's army seem to number about 200 men or 4 troops of 50 men each.

41. Aelian 18.1ff; Asclep. 7.2.

42. Asclep. 7.3.

43. Richard A. Gabriel and Karen S. Metz, *From Sumer to Rome—The Military Capabilities of Ancient Armies* (New York: Greenwood Press, 1991), p. 32.

44. Ferrill, *Origins*, p. 70. Crouwell, *Chariots*, p. 48, stated that "an active role of riding in warfare is documented beyond any doubt only from the 9th century B.C. onwards, by texts and representations, especially the detailed, large-scale, Assyrian palace reliefs."

45. H.W.F. Saggs, *The Might That Was Assyria* (London: Sidgwick and Jackson, 1984), p. 72, gave credit to Tukulti-Ninurta for the first large-scale use of cavalry in the Assyrian army. Yadin, *Warfare*, 2:382ff, showed some of the reliefs from Ashurnasirpal's palace, where the reins of the archer's horse are held by a second rider; on 2:384, he showed an ivory plaque on which the relief clearly features a rider wearing a helmet but no body armor. Crouwell, *Chariots*, p. 48, believed that the mounted archer and squire were simply the charioteer and chariot warrior on horseback.

46. Yadin, *Warfare*, 2:425f, revealed a relief from Sargon's palace that depicts the head of a horse and the bridle, but also shown is the right hand of the rider, which is holding a spear; on 2:458f, he showed a relief depicting Sennacherib's cavalry, which included mounted archers, mounted archers using spears while their bows are in the quivers on their backs, and a column of cavalry armed with spears only moving through some woods, all the cavalrymen having the same type of armor.

47. Denison, *Cavalry*, pp. 13f; Yadin, *Warfare*, 2:442f.

48. J. N. Postgate, *Taxation and Conscription in the Assyrian Empire* (Rome: Biblical Institute Press, 1974), p. 17; Ferrill, *Origins*, pp. 71f.

49. Ferrill, *Origins*, p. 70, estimated the size of the Assyrian army between 100,000 and 200,000. Saggs, *Assyria*, p. 253, gave the figures for Shalmaneser III's army. Terence Wise, *Ancient Armies of the Middle East*, Men-At-Arms Series, no. 109 (London: Osprey Publishing, 1981), p. 34, provided the size of the armies of both Shalmaneser and Sennacherib.

50. Wise, *Ancient Armies*, p. 34, proposed these proportions.

51. Ferrill, *Origins*, p. 78.

52. Saggs, *Assyria*, p. 94.

53. Yadin, *Warfare*, 2:303, 2:442ff.

54. Arist. *Pol.* 1286b.33ff, 1289b.

55. Aelian 14.46; cf. Poll. *Onom.* 5.46 and Polyaenus *Strat.* 7.1 for the use of dogs in war.

56. Burn, *Hesiod,* p. 168.

57. Hdt. 1.79; P. Vigneron, *Le cheval dans l'antiquité gréco-romaine* (Nancy: La Faculté des Lettres et des Sciences humaines de l'Université de Nancy, 1968), p. 240; Burn, *Hesiod,* p. 168, n. 7.

58. Strab. 14.1.28.

59. G.M.A. Richter, *Archaic Greek Art* (New York: Oxford University Press, 1949), p. 95, fig. 161, called these horsemen hunters after hares, but this seems to be clearly wrong because all the horsemen carry shields, a useless item during a hare hunt.

60. British Museum 1969.12–15.1. Greenhalgh, *Warfare,* p. 58, fig. 37, saw this depiction as an early example of the *hippobatas* and *hippostrophos,* or knight and squire, motif. However, no second horse is indicated and, contrary to Greenhalgh's appraisal, the rider seems to be armed with a spear.

61. Greenhalgh, *Warfare,* p. 112, fig. 56; J. D. Beazley, *Attic Black-Figure Vase Painters* (Oxford: Clarendon Press, 1956), p. 101, no. 119; Anderson, *Horsemanship,* pl. 29.

62. Staatliche Museum Berlin 1797; Greenhalgh, *Warfare,* pp. 122f., fig. 65; Beazley, *Black-Figure,* p. 227; Helbig, "Les hippeis," pl. 2.2.

63. Greenhalgh, *Warfare,* p. 115, fig. 65; Beazley, *Black-Figure,* p. 81; Anderson, *Horsemanship,* pl. 30a.

64. British Museum 1814.7–4.91; Greenhalgh, *Warfare,* p. 99, fig. 52. On p. 100, Greenhalgh placed the armored riders into four categories, and the riders of fig. 52 are in category one—those who would fight only on horseback because they lack greaves, breastplates, and shields.

65. British Museum B375; Greenhalgh, *Warfare,* p. 125, fig. 66. On p. 101, Greenhalgh questioned whether greaves might not denote mounted infantry for they might cut into the horse or interfere with the grip of the rider's legs. Snodgrass, *Early Greek Armour,* p. 88, said that greaves were rounded and fitted and thus would not interfere with a rider in any way.

66. Martin von Wagner-Museum der Universitat Würzburg 206; Greenhalgh, *Warfare,* p. 129, fig. 70; Beazley, *Black-Figure,* p. 282.

67. Herzog Anton Ulrich-Museum, Braunschweig (AT)235; *CVA Deutschland* 4 (Braunschweig), pls. 149, 150. Greenhalgh, *Warfare,* p. 100, fig. 53, said that the cavalryman on fig. 53a, the one with only the helmet and spear, was placed in category one, as one who will only fight mounted, but that the riders in fig. 52b, with shields, are in category two because of their shields. On p. 102, Greenhalgh was uncertain exactly how category two cavalry would fight because the use or interference of the shield while

mounted is hard to determine. Yet these could well be dragoons for the absence of breastplates does not preclude them from serving in a phalanx, nor would the shield keep them from fighting mounted.

68. Musée Royaux d'Art et d'Histoire, Brussel R300; CVA Belgium 3 (Brussels 3) pl. 117.2b; Beazley, *Black-Figure*, p. 288; Greenhalgh, *Warfare*, p. 132, fig. 71. On p. 131, Greenhalgh commented that if the realism of this scene could be accepted, it would explain why most cavalrymen chose to fight without shields.

69. Musée du Louvre F72; CVA France 14 (Louvre 9), pl. 621; Greenhalgh, *Warfare*, pp. 121f, fig. 64, said this painting had been restored and so there was some question about its validity.

70. Great Britain, War Office, *Cavalry Training*, p. 280, advised that the spike on the butt end of the cavalry lance could be used when the point could not be brought to bear, such as when one's opponent was close.

71. Greenhalgh, *Warfare*, p. 122, said that the portrayal of a shield being used by a cavalryman is rare, and on p. 131, he speculated that if the portrayal of a horseman using a hoplite shield was accurate, considering shape, size, and weight, "it is not surprising that the evidence of the vase-paintings reveals that it was generally considered more trouble than it was worth."

72. Hdt. 1.79, reported that Lydian cavalry used shock tactics against Cyrus' army; cf. Plut. *Artax.* 10–11, Xen. *An.* 1.8.25–29, Nep. *Pelop.* 5.4, and Curt. 4.9.24–25 for examples of shock tactics used in single combat.

73. Hdt. 5.64.

74. Oman, *Art of War*, 2:261, 2:262f.

75. Arist. *Ath. Pol.* 7.3–4; here, I follow the translation of J. M. Moore, *Aristotle and Xenophon on Democracy* (Berkeley: University of California Press, 1975), pp. 151f.

76. C. Cichorius, "Zu den Namen der attischen Steuerklassen," in *Griechische Studien H. Lipsius dargebracht zum sechzigsten Geburtstag* (Leipzig: Teubner, 1894), pp. 135–140; J. E. Sandys, *Aristotle's Constitution of Athens* (London: Macmillan, 1912), p. 28; A. Andrewes, *Greek Tyrants* (London: Hutchinson's University Library, 1960), p. 87; L. H. Jeffrey, *Archaic Greece* (New York: St. Martin's Press, 1976), pp. 93, 107, n. 6; V. Ehrenberg, *From Solon to Socrates*, 2d ed. (London: Methuen, 1973), pp. 65–67; R. Sealey, *A History of the Greek City-States 700–338 B.C.* (Berkeley: University of California Press, 1976), pp. 128, 212, n. 2; D. Whitehead, "The Archaic Zeugitai," *CQ* 31(1981):282–286.

77. Greenhalgh, *Warfare*, p. 99, believed this scene may, indeed, show how the introduction of the phalanx caused the creation of organized cav-

alry—namely true mounted troops developed in response to the phalanx because of the inability to attack the phalanx head-on and the need to use mobility; thus, Greenhalgh did not seem to believe that cavalry existed before the hoplite revolution.

78. Greenhalgh, *Warfare*, p. 87, fig. 48, reported that this was the only example of a figure fighting on horseback from the seventh century B.C., and proposed that the rider might be attempting to dismount. T. J. Dunbabin, ed., *Perachora: The Sanctuaries of Hera Akraia and Limenia*, vol. 2 (London: Oxford University Press, 1962), n. 1590, pl. 61, concluded that curious mistakes, caused by lack of experience, occur in drawing human figures and pointed out that the shield is drawn so that the inside is turned outward and the warrior sits sidesaddle; thus, for Dunbabin, this painting was a misrepresentation, rather than an accurate portrayal of cavalry dismounting.

79. Frontin. *Str.* 4.1.6, reported that Philip II of Macedon limited each cavalryman to a single servant, as a means of streamlining the Macedonian army. In contrast, each Greek hoplite had at least 1 servant according to Hdt. 7.229, Thuc. 3.17.4. Cf. Thuc. 4.16.1, 7.75.5, Theophr. 25.4. Also, the Spartiates at times had 7 servants each, Hdt. 9.10, 29.

80. Greenhalgh, *Warfare*, p. 111f, believed this depiction provides valuable evidence for mounted hoplite and light cavalry. Anderson, *Horsemanship*, pl. 29, called the dismounting warrior a heavy dragoon in his commentary on that plate.

81. Hdt. 5.63.

82. Thuc. 4.96.5, recorded that 2 squadrons of Boeotian cavalry raised enough dust and made enough noise approaching the rear of the Athenian army at Delium (424 B.C.) that the Athenians were warned of the presence of the horsemen.

83. Arr. *Anab.* 3.9.4–5, showed Alexander inspecting the plain of Arbela and finding indications it had been leveled and cleared. Further, it seems totally improbable that the Spartans were not informed as to Hippias' preparations considering the number of executions and exiles that the tyrant ordered and his subsequent lack of support among the citizens of the city. After all, the Athenians later allowed Hippias to be besieged on the Acropolis by the Spartans.

84. Thuc. 4.11–12, revealed just how difficult an amphibious landing was against opposition in ancient times when he recorded Demosthenes' successful repulsion of the Spartans.

85. W. W. How and J. Wells, *A Commentary on Herodotus*, 2 vols. (Ox-

ford: Oxford University Press, 1928), 2:31, stated the sense of Herodotus' passage was that the Spartans were ridden down.

86. Hdt. 5.64.

87. Hdt. 8.113 for the barbarian components of Mardonius' army. For the cavalry equipment: see Hdt. 7.61, 84, for the Persians; see Hdt. 7.62, 86, for the Medes, the Bactrians, and the Indians. G. B. Grundy, *The Great Persian War and Its Preliminaries, A Study of the Evidence, Literary and Topographical* (New York: Charles Scribners' Sons, 1901), p. 418, proposed that one must either accept Herodotus' figures for the Persian army or make corresponding reductions in the figures for both armies. Henry Burt Wright, *The Campaign of Plataea* (New Haven, Conn.: Tuttle, Morehouse & Taylor, 1904), pp. 58f, recorded the variations in the estimates for the sizes of the Greek and Persian forces from his contemporaries, who all thought Herodotus exaggerated the size of both armies. C. Hignett, *Xerxes' Invasion of Greece* (London: Oxford University Press, 1963), p. 267, believed it unlikely that Mardonius' Asiatic troops exceeded 60,000 men. However, even assuming that Herodotus exaggerated, it seems likely that Mardonius had between 10,000 and 30,000 cavalrymen.

88. Hdt. 9.28f. Grundy, *Persian War*, p. 459, accepted Herodotus' numbers for the Greek army.

89. Hdt. 9.21.

90. Hdt. 9. 20–23; How and Wells, *Commentary*, 2:295, accepted 800 as the most likely number of Athenian archers but acknowledged that Athens had twice that number.

91. Hdt. 9.23; here I follow the translation of A. D. Godley, *Herodotus IV*, Loeb Classical Library (Cambridge, Mass.: Harvard University Press, 1981), pp. 183 and 185.

92. Grundy, *Persian War*, p. 461, thought that the Persian aim with this attack was to break through the Greek army at an appropriate place and thus cut it in two. Yet this sort of divide-and-conquer approach would seem to call for an assault at an appropriate moment, which never occurred.

93. Grundy, *Persian War*, p. 462, believed that the Persian cavalry was taught a lesson by this encounter and subsequent defeat—the folly of close combat with hoplites—and that the Persians did not make the same mistake again. Hignett, *Xerxes' Invasion*, p. 300, stated it was clear that cavalry could not operate against an unbroken phalanx.

94. Hdt. 9.39. Herodotus had a Theban named Timagenides advise Mardonius to set a watch on the passes through the mountains because the Greeks were getting reinforcements and supplies by these routes. It seems

logical for the Theban cavalry to have been part of any such action, possibly with Timagenides as its commander. Denison, *Cavalry*, p. 223, believed that this may have been the first time that cavalry operated independently behind enemy lines.

95. Hdt. 9.49.

96. Hdt. 9.57, 60.

97. Hdt. 9.68.

98. Hdt. 9.69.

Chapter 4

1. See Hdt. 7.87 for the size of the Persian cavalry.

2. J.F.C. Fuller, *A Military History of the Western World*, 3 vols. (New York: Funk and Wagnalls, 1954–1956), 1:103, 372.

3. See Hdt. 9.28f for the size of the Greek army at Plataea.

4. Hdt. 1.192. This number of animals at one farm is far too many for normal, everyday needs because horses were not customarily used as farm animals in the ancient world; thus, this stud farm and others like it must have been set up to supply the needs of the military.

5. Hdt. 7.196.

6. Hdt. 5.111, reported that the horse of Artybius, a Persian general, was trained to rear and kick at infantrymen.

7. Hdt. 9.20–23.

8. Hdt. 9.49. Ferrill, *Origins*, p. 8, thought that two distinct lines of military development existed simultaneously in the eastern Mediterranean, one involving cavalry in the Near East and the other involving heavy infantry in Greece, and that the two tentatively came together for the first time in the Persian Wars, with the Greeks acquiring some knowledge of cavalry as a result.

9. Hdt. 9.20, clearly stated that all Mardonius' cavalry was involved in the attack on the Athenians to recover the dead man's body.

10. Hdt. 9.31, gave Mardonius' initial battle order with the Boeotians facing the Athenians; on 9.47, he showed Mardonius shifting his forces in response to Pausanias' deployments, but the Boeotians always faced the Athenians.

11. Hdt. 9.67, recorded the Boeotians fighting the Athenians, and on 9.68f, he showed the Boeotian cavalry screening the withdrawal and attacking the pursuing infantry when it became disordered.

12. Thuc. 4.95.2; Xen. *Hell.* 6.4.10; Salmon, *L'Antiquité* 22:351. There are also many representations of cavalry on Boeotian funeral monuments.

Cf. A. Körte, "Die antike Sculpturen aus Boeotian," *Mittlungen des deutschen archäologischen Institutes in Athens* 3(1878):360f, 376f.

13. See Hdt. 9.31, 47, 67, 68, for usage of Boeotian or Boeotian cavalry; 9.38, 40, 67, 69, for usage of Theban or Theban cavalry; and 9.69 for hipparchos. Some scholars believe the Boeotian League was established in the mid-sixth century B.C. See R. J. Buck, "The Formation of the Boeotian League," *CP* 67(1972):94–101; idem, *A History of Boeotia* (Edmonton: University of Alberta Press, 1979), chap. 7; and Hammond, *History*, pp. 196ff. For an opposing view, see Nancy H. Demand, *Thebes in the Fifth Century* (Boston: Routledge & Kegan Paul, 1982), pp. 19ff.

14. *Hell. Oxy.* 12.24f; Paul Roesch, *Thespies et la confédération Béotienne* (Paris: E. de Boccard, 1965), p. 109; Larsen, *States*, p. 35; Roland Etienne and Paul Roesch, "Convention militaire entre les cavaliers d'Orchomène et ceux de Chéronée," *BCH* 102(1978):367.

15. Diod. 15.26.4; Michel Feyel, *Polybe et l'histoire de Béotie au IIIe siècle avant notre ère* (Paris: E. de Boccard, 1942), p. 217.

16. Salmon, *L'Antiquité* 22:350; Roesch, *Thespies*, pp. 109f; Etienne and Roesch, *BCH* 102:367; Feyel, *Polybe*, p. 197.

17. Roesch, *Thespies*, p. 110.

18. Ibid., p. 37; on p. 47, he showed the changes in the districting that took place in the fourth century B.C., wherein Thebes had 4 districts and Plataea was not listed at all.

19. Salmon, *L'Antiquité* 22:350; Etienne and Roesch, *BCH* 102:369.

20. Asclep. 7.4; Aelian 18.9; Xen. *Hell.* 3.4.13f. All showed that the Greeks liked to have their cavalry in a rectangular formation similar to that of the phalanx.

21. Herodotus showed that all the barbarian cavalry at Plataea were mounted archers (cf. chapter 3, n. 86), and yet on 9.49, he stated that both arrows and javelins were used by Mardonius' horsemen against the Greek hoplites. Thus, Boeotian, Thessalian, and Macedonian cavalry units must have used the javelin. Xen. *Hell.* 5.4.39f, reported that the Theban cavalry was armed with javelins in the fourth century B.C.

22. Thuc. 5.57.2; Xen. *Hell.* 7.5.24; Denison, *Cavalry*, p. 24; Salmon, *L'Antiquité* 22:352.

23. Caes. *BCiv.* 3.84; Denison, *Cavalry*, p. 24.

24. Caes. *BGall.* 1.48; here, I follow the translation of H. J. Edwards, *Caesar—The Gallic War*, Loeb Classical Library (Cambridge, Mass.: Harvard University Press, 1979), pp. 79 and 81.

25. M. A. Martin, *Les cavaliers Athéniens*, Bibliothèque des Ecoles françaises d'Athènes et de Rome, fasc. 47 (Paris: Ernest Thorin, 1886), pp. 71–78, 295–307.

26. Helbig, "Les hippeis," pp. 158ff.

27. Snodgrass, *Arms and Armour*, p. 85. Others who support Helbig's conclusion include G. Busolt and H. Swoboda, *Griechische Staatskunde*, 2 vols., Handbuch der Altertumswissenschaft, vierte abteilung, erster teil, erster band (Munich: C. H. Beck'sche Verlags Buchhandlung, 1920–1926), 2:978, n. 3; 2:1128; Larsen, *States*, p. 106f.

28. Greenhalgh, *Warfare*, pp. 111–136.

29. Bugh, *Horsemen*, pp. 3–38, presented an examination of the evidence for an Archaic Athenian cavalry.

30. Arist. *Ath. Pol.* 7.3–4; Plut. *Sol.* 18.1–2. Bugh, *Horsemen*, p. 22, believed that Solon was the author of this system.

31. Arist. *Ath. Pol.* 7.4, and Plut. *Sol.* 18.1, both said that the hippeis were those individuals who could afford to keep horses. Martin, *Les cavaliers*. pp. 72f, thought the title *hippeis* was highly significant.

32. Greenhalgh, *Warfare*, p. 111, reported that Attic black-figure vase painters maintained an almost total silence on contemporary warfare until the second decade of the sixth century B.C., at which time the war-horse and mounted warrior were immediately represented; on pp. 191–194, he listed all the Attic black-figure vases known to Greenhalgh that contained mounted warriors.

33. Greenhalgh, *Warfare*, p. 1, said, "In the seventh and especially the sixth centuries it is true that vase-painting of at least two states provides us with a good many mounted warriors whose accurate portrayal from contemporary life need not be doubted." John Boardman, *Athenian Red Figure Vases—the Archaic Period a Handbook* (London: Thames and Hudson, 1975), p. 218, asserted that both black-figure and red-figure artists were explicit and accurate in their depictions.

34. Hdt. 1.63; How and Wells, *Commentary*, 1:85.

35. Plut. *Cim.* 5.2–3. Cimon's family was well known for its horses, and several members of his family had won the 4-horse chariot event at the Olympic Games. Cf. Hdt. 6.63, 103; Paus. 6.10.8.

36. Plato *Meno* 94B, 93D.

37. Poll. *Onom.* 8.108; Busolt and Swoboda, *Griechische*, 2:824, n. 1, doubted the value of Pollux's evidence. However, Bugh, *Horsemen*, p. 5, accepted Pollux.

38. Bugh, *Horsemen*, p. 38. Of course, in classical Athens, liturgies included the trierarchy, the financing of a trireme for one year (which cost as much as six thousand drachmas), and sponsoring a playwright for the City Dionysia.

39. F. J. Frost, "The Athenian Military Before Cleisthenes," *Historia* 33(1984):284, believed that the most effective means of mobilizing the army would have been the phratry roasters; on p. 285, he stated that men in a phratry lived in the same district, were friends, and trained together and recalled that Nestor believed that men fought better when fighting alongside friends and acquaintances (*Iliad* 2.362). Though there is some controversy about the true nature of the phratry, I accept the traditional view at present.

40. Arist. *Ath. Pol.* 61.5; C. Fornara, *The Athenian Board of Generals from 501 to 404 B.C.* (Wiesbaden: Franz Steiner, 1971), p. 1.

41. Arist. *Ath. Pol.* 15.4; Polyaenus *Strat.* 1.21.2.

42. Hammond, *History,* pp. 105ff, 179ff.

43. Hdt. 1.64, 5.62, 6.103; Arist. *Ath. Pol.* 19.1.

44. Arist. *Ath. Pol.* 18.4, 19.1; cf. Hdt. 5.62; Bugh, *Horsemen*, p. 35.

45. Hdt. 5.63. Bugh, *Horsemen*, p. 35, maintained that at least some aristocrats made peace with Pisistratus because the names of Alcmeonids and Philaids appeared on the list of eponymous archons. However, this does not mean that cavalry service was continued or restored.

46. Arist. *Ath. Pol.* 21, 22.1ff; Hdt. 5.66ff; Hammond, *History,* pp. 185ff.

47. Anderson, *Horsemanship*, p. 130, made a convincing point that cavalry was felt to be an unnecessary luxury after the expulsion of Hippias. Bugh, *Horsemen*, p. 6, said there was no evidence for post-Cleisthenic naucraries being connected with cavalry.

48. Hdt. 9.54; Alföldi, "Die Herrschaft," p. 30, said the messenger at Plataea was an aristocratic hippeus because the message was too important to trust to anyone else.

49. Martin, *Les cavaliers*, pp. 121ff.

50. Plut. *Arist.* 21.1.

51. Busolt and Swoboda, *Griechische*, 2:978, n. 3 and 2:1128, n. 5.

52. Paus. 1.29.6, recorded the presence in the Kerameikos of a grave stele on which horsemen were depicted fighting, and Melanopus and Marcartatus were recorded as being killed while fighting the Lacedaemonians and Boeotians on the borders of Eleon and Tanagra. This most likely dates to 458/457 B.C. Cf. Martin, *Les cavaliers*, p. 126, and Bugh, *Horsemen*, pp. 43f. A.W. Gomme, *A Historical Commentary on*

Thucydides, 5 vols. (Oxford: Oxford University Press, 1945–1981), 1:316, thought it likely that Athenian cavalry participated at Tanagra. B. D. Meritt, "Greek Inscriptions," *Hesperia* 16(1947):147f, no. 36, pl. 23, challenged the dating of this inscription due to the discovery of a similar inscription that he believed was the one Pausanias recorded, but it has Ionic lettering, which dates it after 458/457 B.C.

53. Thuc. 1.107.4–108.1.

54. Diod. 11.80.1–6.

55. Andoc. 3.5; Bugh, *Horsemen,* pp. 39f; Anderson, *Horsemanship,* pp. 130ff; Gomme, *Commentary,* 1:328, n. 1.

56. IG I² 400. A. Raubitschek, *Dedications from the Athenian Acropolis* (Cambridge, Mass.: Archaeological Institute of America, 1949), p. 151, concluded that the three hipparchs held office simultaneously. Bugh, *Horsemen,* p. 49, placed the date of the inscription at 457–445 B.C.

57. Anderson, *Horsemanship,* p. 131.

58. During the Classical period, the Athenians often made all commanders equal and rotated commands on a daily basis. Cf. Hdt. 6.110, Thuc. 6.8.2. This practice very well could have been applied to the cavalry at this time.

59. Diod. 12.6.1f; Thuc. 1.113; Hammond, *History,* p. 308.

60. Thuc. 1.114; Hammond, *History,* p. 308.

61. Scholiast to Ar. *Eq.* 627. B. Keil, *Anonymous Argentinensis: Fragmente zur Geschichte des perikleischen Athens aus einem Strasburger Papyrus* (Strasburg: K. J. Trübner, 1902), p. 144, n. 1, proposed that the cavalry figures on the Parthenon frieze are symbolic of a squadron and, thus, that in 440 B.C., the Athenian cavalry numbered 600. Bugh, *Horsemen,* p. 40, contended that the Athenian cavalry jumped from 300 to 1,000 without an intermediate step; on p. 40, n. 9, he called the counting of figures on the Parthenon "risky." Though I acknowledge the risk, a 600-man cavalry force seems to me to be a logical step that would allow for a reorganization for better control of the larger force.

62. The basic unit of the Thessalian cavalry was a 40-man troop, and that of the Theban horse was a 50-man squadron. In modern times, the British cavalry troop consisted of 3 sections, or 25 men. See Great Britain, War Office, *Cavalry Training,* p. 32.

63. See Arist. *Ath. Pol.* 49.2, 61.4f for the hipparchoi and phylarchoi; Xen. *Hell.* 2.4.31 for phyle as the name of a military unit, *Hipparch.* 1.8 for phylarchoi, 2.2 for 10 phylai, and 8.17 for 2 troops per phyle. Though this organization was surely in place by the start of the Peloponnesian War, I

think it took some time to effect and probably was begun when the cavalry numbered 600.

64. Ar. *Eq.* 225, Andoc. 3.7, and Philochorus (*FGrH* 328 F 39), all stated the cavalry had 1,000 men. Scholiast to Ar. *Eq.* 627, Arist. *Ath. Pol.* 24.3, and Thuc. 2.13.8, all recorded the cavalry strength as 1,200. Anderson, *Horsemanship*, p. 131, placed the Athenian cavalry at 10 squadrons of 100 men each, plus 200 horse-archers who were paid troops. L. G. Spence, "Athenian Cavalry Numbers in the Peloponnesian War; IG I³ 375 Revisited," *ZPE* 67(1987):167, agreed with Anderson.

65. Thuc. 5.84.1f, spoke of 20 hippotoxotai being sent as a unit on an expedition to Melos (416 B.C.); this may not have been a composite but rather an organized troop.

66. Hdt. 9.13, had Mardonius withdraw from Attica because the country was ill suited to cavalry and horses. Thuc. 1.2.5, spoke of the poor quality of the Attic soil. A. M. Andreades, *A History of Greek Public Finance*, vol. 1 (Cambridge, Mass.: Harvard University Press, 1933), p. 218, n. 6, noted that there may have been no more than 3,000 horses in all Attica.

67. Bugh, *Horsemen*, p. 56, and idem, "The Three Hundred Athenian Cavalrymen," *Phoenix* 36(1982):309–311, believed this loan started when Athens increased its cavalry to 300. J. H. Kroll, "An Archive of the Athenian Cavalry," *Hesperia* 46(1977):99, connected the katastasis with the later 1,000-man cavalry.

68. Ar. *Clouds* 21ff, had a 300-drachma price for a good horse. Xen. *An.* 7.8.6, recorded that Xenophon's prized stallion cost 50 daric or 1,200 drachmas. Bugh, *Horsemen*, p. 57, showed that cavalry horses were normally valued at much less than 1,200 drachmas. Also see John M. Camp, *The Athenian Agora—Excavations in the Heart of Classical Athens* (London: Thames and Hudson, 1986), p. 119. For a discussion of the value of horses, see Anderson, *Horsemanship*, p. 136.

69. *IG* I³ 375, lines 4, 8, 9, 11, 12, and 24, attested to the sitoi in 410/409 B.C. However, this allowance probably started earlier, perhaps as early as 450 B.C. Cf. Bugh, *Horsemen*, pp. 60f.

70. Xen. *Hipparch.* 1.19; Bugh, *Horsemen*, pp. 60 and 155. Dem. *Fourth Philippic* 28, recommended that each cavalryman sent on an expedition receive a grain allowance of 1 drachma per day. Andreades, *Finance*, p. 218, accepted Demosthenes' figures of 1 drachma per day as the sitos and, on p. 219, he placed the total expenditure for the cavalry at 40 to 80 talents. Because this was an overseas expedition in the fourth century B.C., the allow-

ance of 1 drachma per day was probably higher than that in the fifth century.

71. Polyb. 6.39.13f. Donald Engles, *Alexander the Great and the Logistics of the Macedonian Army* (Berkeley: University of California Press, 1978), p. 18, estimated that the horses in Alexander's army needed 10 pounds of straw and 10 pounds of grain per day. Brereton, *Horses*, p. 70, said Frederick the Great provided his cavalry mounts with 8 pounds of oats and 11 pounds of hay each day. United States Army, *Drill Regulations*, p. 369, par. 886, set the rations for a cavalry horse at 12 pounds of grain and 14 pounds of hay per day. Great Britain, War Office, *Cavalry Training*, p. 91, recommended 10 pounds of grain and 10 pounds of hay daily.

72. Bugh, *Horsemen*, p. 58f.

73. Camp, *Agora*, p. 119.

74. Bugh, *Horsemen*, pp. 57f.

75. Poll. *Onom.* 8.130.

76. John K. Davies, *Wealth and the Power of Wealth in Classical Athens* (Salem, N.H.: Ayer, 1984), p. 36, thought this statement by Pollux "represents capitalization of some kind for the Solonian property qualification."

77. John K. Davies, *Athenian Propertied Families 600–300 B.C.* (Oxford: Oxford University Press, 1971), p. xxvi, was uncertain that all the pentacosiomedimnoi belonged to the liturgical class because of questions about the nature of the archonship and the difficulty of translating the return or income into monetary wealth.

78. Davies, *Families*, pp. xxi–xxii.

79. Davies, *Wealth*, p. 27.

80. Twelve hundred was the number of men who, for at least part of the fourth century B.C., were responsible for the syntrierarchies or cooperative trierarchies where more than 1 man was liable for the 1-talent maintenance cost, or the 1,200 wealthiest citizens (cf. Isoc. 15.145, and Dem. 14.16). This number was probably not selected at random but may well represent the traditional size of the upper classes. Though estimates of the Athenian population vary, A. W. Gomme, *The Population of Athens in the Fifth and Fourth Centuries B.C.* (Oxford: Basil Blackwell, 1933), p. 26, table 1, estimated that Athens had approximately 43,000 male citizens in 431 B.C.

81. Davies, *Wealth*, p. 16, believed that a man did not have to perform two liturgies simultaneously and thus did not have to be trierarch and serve in the cavalry. Bugh, *Horsemen*, p. 71, thought it likely the trierarchy exempted men from cavalry service. P. J. Rhodes, "Problems in Athenian

eisphora and Liturgies," *AJAH* 7(1982):4–5, took a different view, believing that the cavalrymen were exempt from the trierarchy.

82. Plut. *Per.* 11.4.

83. Thuc. 2.24.2.

84. Thuc. 2.13.8.

85. Ar. *Eq.* 731.

86. Xen. *Hipparch.* 1.9ff.

87. *IG* II² 6217.

88. Bugh, *Horsemen*, p. 63, and appendix A (pp. 207–208), believed that the average age was even younger in the fifth century B.C.

89. Gomme, *Population*, p. 29, table 2, proposed that between 49 and 68 percent of the male population reached forty and that 3 to 45 percent reached fifty-nine. It seems likely that a higher percentage of the upper classes reached these ages because they could afford better food and care.

90. Xen. *Hipparch.* 7.3, spoke of the pride of the Athenian cavalry.

91. When addressing topics of drill, weapons, training, formations, and so forth, Xenophon consistently used the term *phyle* when referring to the unit with the responsibility for these functions. See Xen. *Hipparch.* 1.21, 25, 26, 2.2, 3.2, 6, 11, among others.

92. Xen. *Hipparch.* 2.2, 5, 4.9.

93. Xen. *Hipparch.* 2.2f, discussed the route of a parade through the streets of Athens. The Dipylon Gate and the connecting street were about 23 yards wide, enough to permit the cavalry to parade in this formation.

94. *IG* II² 6217, recorded a dedication to Dexileos, a cavalryman killed in a battle near Corinth in 396 B.C., who was called "one of five." This did not refer to cavalry casualties at this battle because *IG* II² 5222 showed that 11 hippeis were killed. I believe this "one of five" refers to a file of 5 cavalrymen and that Dexileos was either the only one of the file killed or that he was the "first" of the 5 or the leader. Other opinions on this are: Martin, *Les cavaliers*, p. 416, who proposed that Dexileos was one of 5 cavalrymen who distinguished themselves; M. N. Tod, *A Selection of Greek Historical Inscriptions*, 2 vols. (Oxford: Oxford University Press, 1933–1948), vol. 2, no. 105, who suggested Dexileos was one of the 5 best horsemen who formed a special unit to fall upon an advancing enemy (cf. Xen. *Hipparch.* 8.25); K. Friis Johansen, *The Attic Grave-Reliefs of the Classical Period* (Copenhagen: E. Munksgaard, 1951), p. 48, who commented that the meaning is unknown; and Bugh, *Horsemen*, pp. 137f, who concluded this referred to 5 men from the tribe of Akamantis who died.

95. Xen. *Hipparch.* 1.21, showed that the weapon of the Athenian cavalry was the javelin. This is confirmed by the depictions on the stele of Dexileos, which show the horseman in the act of throwing his spear down at a prone hoplite (cf. G.M.A. Richter, *The Sculptures and Sculptors of the Greeks* [New Haven, Conn.: Yale University Press, 1950], fig. 215), and on the Attic red-figure crater in the Louvre, which depicts the cavalrymen practicing throwing javelins from horseback (cf. CVA France 8 [Louvre 5], pl. 382/4.

96. The Athenian cavalry deployed on the left at Solygea (425 B.C.), Amphipolis (422 B.C.), and Mantinea (418 B.C.). See Thuc. 4.43–44.2, 5.10, 5.67, and J. MacInnes, "The Athenian Cavalry in the Peloponnesian War," CR 25(1911):194.

97. Xen. *Hipparch.* 1.18.

98. Xen. *Hipparch.* 1.13.

99. Xen. *Hipparch.* 1.17.

100. Camp, *Agora*, pp. 118f.

101. Ath. 9.402ff.

102. Paus. 6.24.2, reported that the agora of Elis was called the *Hippodrome* and that horses were trained there.

103. Xen. *Hipparch.* 1.21, placed the responsibility on the phylarchos for having good javelin-throwers, which clearly implied that this officer had the ultimate responsibility for the necessary drill.

104. Xen. *Hippik.* 12.13.

105. Musée du Louvre G528; CVA France 8 (Louvre 5), pl. 382/4. This fourth-century B.C. crater clearly shows the cavalrymen practicing throwing their javelins at a suspended shield. Note that the horses in some cases pass to the left of the pole, causing the rider to throw across the neck of the horse.

106. Even though the horseman's spear is missing, the stele of Dexileos clearly shows a light cavalryman getting ready to throw his javelin down at a fallen hoplite. Richter, *Sculptures*, fig. 215; Bugh, *Horsemen*, fig. 12.

107. E. N. Gardiner, "Throwing the Javelin," JHS 27(1907):258, showed that a throw of 20 meters was not uncommon for a javelin without a throwing thong. A. W. Lawrence, *Greek Aims in Fortifications* (London: Oxford University Press, 1979), p. 40, estimated a distance of 30 to 40 meters for the effective range of a javelin thrown without a throwing thong. Because both of these estimates are for peltasts or infantry javelin-men, the distance for a mounted throw was probably shorter since the horseman had less balance and leverage.

108. Xen. *Hipparch.* 3.10, had the entire cavalry deploy in a formation to sweep across the hippodrome.

109. Xen. *Hipparch.* 3.6; R. E. Wycherley, "Xenophon Hipparchicus 3.6–7: Cavalry at the Lyceum," *CR* 13(1963):14–15; Donald G. Kyle, *Athletics in Ancient Athens* (Leiden: E. J. Brill, 1987), p. 80.

110. Xen. *Hipparch.* 3.14.

111. Xen. *Hipparch.* 3.10–13; *IG* II^2 3130 (mid–fourth century B.C.), *IG* II^2 379 (late fourth century B.C.), and *IG* II^2 3079 (early third century B.C.), all showed the popularity of the anthippasis and placed it during the Greater Panathenaia and the Olympieia. Camp, *Agora*, pp. 120f, fig. 96 and 97, discussed the fragment of a victory trophy for the tribe of Leontis. See Bugh, *Horsemen*, pp. 59f, fig. 6 and 7; H. W. Parke, *Festivals of the Athenians* (Ithaca, N.Y.: Cornell University Press, 1977), pp. 143f; Kyle, *Athletics*, p. 46; E. Vanderpool, "Victories in the Anthippasis," *Hesperia* 43(1974):311–313, for the anthippasia in the third century B.C.

Chapter 5

1. Thuc. 2.19.1f.

2. Denison, *Cavalry*, p. 23, basing a verdict on the Athenian cavalry performance during the initial Spartan invasion, did not believe the quality of the Athenian horse was very good.

3. Thuc. 2.22.2. I. G. Spence, "Perikles and the Defence of Attika during the Peloponnesian War," *JHS* 110(1990):97, concluded that "the use of cavalry to bear the brunt of a hoplite invasion runs counter to the general assumption that Greek cavalry was really only of peripheral value prior to Philip and Alexander because of its inability to charge into formed bodies of heavy infantry." For a full discussion of Periclean strategy and tactics, cf. H. D. Westlake, "Sea-borne Raids in Periclean Strategy," *CQ* 39(1945):75–84; M. H. Chambers, "Thucydides and Pericles," *HSPh* 62(1957):79–92; P. A. Brunt, "Spartan Policy and Strategy in the Archidamian War," *Phoenix* 19(1965):255–280; B. X. de Wet, "The So-called Defensive Policy of Pericles," *Acta Classica* 12(1969):103–119; D. W. Knight, "Thucydides and the War Strategy of Pericles," *Mnemosyne*, 4th series, 23(1970):150–161; G. L. Cawkwell, "Thucydides' Judgment of Periclean Strategy," *YClS* 24(1975):53–70; A. J. Holladay, "Athenian Strategy in the Archidamian War," *Historia* 27(1978):399–427; T. E. Wick, "Megara, Athens, and the West in the Archidamian War: A Study in Thucydides," *Historia* 28(1979):1–14; Victor Hanson, *Warfare and Agriculture in Classical Greece* (Pisa: Giardini

Editori Stampatori, 1983); Josiah Ober, "Thucydides, Pericles and the Strategy of Defense," in *The Craft of the Ancient Historian—Essays in Honor of Chester G. Starr,* ed. by John W. Eadie and Josiah Ober (New York: University Press of America, 1985).

4. Xen. *Hell.* 7.1.20f; here, I follow the translation of Carleton L. Brownson, *Xenophon II: Hellenica V–VII,* Loeb Classical Library (Cambridge, Mass.: Harvard University Press, 1968), p. 241.

5. For examples of cavalry destroying small or disorganized infantry units, cf. Thuc. 2.79.6, 5.10.9, and Xen. *Hell.* 4.8.18f, 7.2.4, 21f.

6. Hanson, *Warfare,* p. 126, concluded that none of the first five invasions did lasting damage to Attica. Ober, "Thucydides," p. 179, stated that the Athenian tactics were successful because Archidamus withdrew without having entered the main Attic plain.

7. Thuc. 2.56.1, showed Pericles as strategos, leading a naval expedition the next year.

8. Thuc. 2.9.3.

9. Thuc. 2.10.2f. The Boeotian Confederacy had 11 regiments or 1,100 cavalrymen; two-thirds of the latter figure is 732 men, but it seems unlikely that a regiment would have been split to obtain exactly two-thirds.

10. Thuc. 2.22.3.

11. Thuc. 2.22.2; here, I follow the translation of Charles Forster Smith, *Thucydides I,* Loeb Classical Library (Cambridge, Mass.: Harvard University Press, 1980), p. 303.

12. Gomme, *Commentary,* 2:77, said the size of the Athenian force is unknown, but Thucydides did use the term *telos,* which may mean a single phyle.

13. Thuc. 3.90.1, specified that the author would only mention noteworthy events with regard to fighting in Sicily, and this seems to be his practice for the entire war. Simon Hornblower, *Thucydides* (Baltimore, Md.: Johns Hopkins University Press, 1987), pp. 37f, acknowledged this trait in Thucydides' writing.

14. Thuc. 2.23.1–3.

15. Thuc. 3.1.1.

16. Thuc. 2.23.2f, 25.1–5.

17. Thuc. 2.56.1–6.

18. Thuc. 2.56.1f; Gomme, *Commentary,* 2:163, gave three possible translations of the Greek in this passage: (1) for the first time in this war, (2) for the first time in Athens or Greece, and (3) for the first time ever.

19. Cecil Tor, *Ancient Ships* (1895; reprint ed., Chicago: Argonaut Press, 1964), pp. 14f; J. S. Morrison and J. F. Coates, *The Athenian Trireme* (Cambridge: Cambridge University Press, 1986), pp. 157, 226f.

20. Thuc. 2.25.2, showed that in 431 B.C., Brasidas had a guard party of 100 men near Methone and was able to save it; on 2.25.3, he revealed that at Elis, a locally raised rescue party of 300 men opposed the Athenians and was defeated; on 2.30.1–3, he showed the Athenians capturing several towns without any opposition; on 3.1.2f, 16.2 he recorded that a 30-ship Athenian fleet ravaged the Laconian coast unopposed and that the Spartan army returned from Attica; and on 4.6.1, he stated that the Spartan army left Attica and returned in haste when the Athenians landed and fortified Pylos.

21. At times, infantry could march rapidly, and the Spartans, being professional soldiers, were as proficient as any, but the maximum rate of march was and is about 50 miles per day. Hdt. 6.120, showed the Spartans marching from Sparta to Athens, a distance of about 150 miles, in three days. By comparison, cavalry could travel much faster, at least for short intervals. Arr. 3.21.9, showed that Alexander and a detachment of mounted Macedonians covered 400 stades, or about 40 miles, in one night in pursuit of Darius.

22. Thuc. 4.3.1–4.2, 41.1–3.

23. Thuc. 4.53.1–54.4.

24. Thuc. 4.55.1.

25. Thuc. 4.55.2. Gomme, *Commentary*, 3:510, noted that for the Spartans to need the support of bows and arrows was a sign of weakness. Interestingly, Gomme made no comment about the need to reestablish a cavalry.

26. Xen. *Hell.* 6.4.11, related that the richest men owned and maintained the cavalry horses and that the cavalrymen were supplied with the horses and equipment only when the army was called out. See Lazenby, *Army*, p. 47.

27. Xen. *Hell.* 4.4.10, 5.12 for *hipparmostes*; at 5.2.41, Xenophon used the term *hipparchos* for the Laconian commander of cavalry, but he may have been referring to the Spartiate who commanded all the mounted forces in this army, which included Boeotian and Macedonian units. See Lazenby, *Army*, p. 12.

28. Xen. *Hell.* 4.2.16; Lazenby, *Army*, p. 12, thought the 600 Spartan cavalry at Nemea were 5 morai because there were only 5 morai of infantry present. Probably, however, the Spartans sent all their horsemen because of the threat and numbers of the opposing Boeotian and Athenian mounted forces.

29. See Anderson, *Military*, pp. 225–251 and Ferrill, *Origins*, p. 105, for the Spartan infantry organization.

30. Ferrill, *Origins*, p. 105, showed the infantry mora formation, with each enomotia formed in 3 files of 8 men each.

31. Thuc. 2.79.1–2.

32. Xen. *Hell.* 5.3.1, showed 600 Olynthian cavalry raiding Apollonia in 381 B.C. Dem. 19.267, stated 500 Olynthian horsemen surrendered to Philip in 340 B.C.

33. Dem. 19.230, 266, gave the strength of the Olynthian military as 10,000 hoplites and 1,000 cavalry. N.G.L. Hammond and G. T. Griffith, *A History of Macedonia*, 3 vols. (London: Oxford University Press, 1972–1988), 2:316, stated that Demosthenes' numbers represented the strength of the Chalcidian League forces. Hammond, *History*, p. 468, placed the establishment of the Chalcidian League early in the Peloponnesian War.

34. Dem. 8.40, reported Euthyrates and Lasthenes betrayed Olynthus; on 9.56, he said Philip's partisan betrayed the Olynthian cavalry, and on 9.66, named Lasthenes as a hipparchos. Diod. 16.53.2, named Euthyrates and Lasthenes as chief officials of Olynthus. J. R. Ellis, *Philip II and Macedonian Imperialism* (London: Thames and Hudson, 1976), p. 99, called Euthyrates and Lasthenes hipparchs.

35. Thuc. 2.79.3–4.

36. Thuc. 2.79.6.

37. Thuc. 2.79.5–7.

38. Gomme, *Commentary*, 2:213, called this battle the first intelligent use of peltasts combined with cavalry against a hoplite force.

39. Thuc. 4.90.1–4.

40. Thuc. 4.91.1–5, 93.1.

41. Pritchett, *Greek States*, 1:127ff, did not believe that Greek armies employed scouts before the time of Xenophon.

42. Pritchett, *Studies*, 2:30, placed Delium near modern Dilesi and noted the distance on the ancient road from Tanagra to Dilesi was about 9,000 meters or 6 miles.

43. Hdt. 6.106, recorded that Phidippides, who ran from Athens to Sparta to seek help for the Athenians at Marathon, arrived in Sparta the day after he left Athens; thus, he covered 150 miles in no more than 36 hours, averaging a little more than 4 miles per hour.

44. The Boeotian Confederacy had 1,100 cavalrymen, but Thuc. 4.93.3, reported that Pagondas had only 1,000 with his army, so it seems likely that 1 regiment had been detached to act as scouts.

45. Thuc. 4.93.1–3. Gomme, *Commentary*, 3:563, believed that the Athenian cavalry left at fortified Delium could have played a decisive role but that Pagondas acted too quickly to counter this threat.

46. Thuc. 4.93.3–5. Diod. 12.69.3, reported that Pagondas had at least 20,000 infantry and 1,000 cavalry, and on 12.70.1, he showed the Thebans on the right of the phalanx, with the Orchomenians on the left and an elite group forming the front rank. Feyel, *Polybe,* pp. 187–218, and Roesch, *Thespies,* pp. 109–121, discussed the organization of Boeotian forces at Delium.

47. Thuc. 4.94.1. Diod. 12.69.4, said the Athenians were more numerous than the Boeotians but less well equipped. Probably, Diodorus here referred to the Athenian invasion force, which included a general levy of all eligible citizens and metics, but the light-armed troops had already returned to Attica. Gomme, *Commentary*, 3:564, suggested that Athens was not able to maintain 1,000 cavalry and 200 mounted archers after the plague. In fact, Thuc. 3.87.3, recorded that 300 cavalrymen were lost in the plague, and on 4.68.5, he showed only 600 cavalry in the campaign against Megara in early 424 B.C., when all available horsemen could have been used because of Megara's close proximity to Athens.

48. Thuc. 4.95.2.

49. Thuc. 4.96.1–4. Diod. 12.70.2, had a cavalry battle, which the Athenian horsemen won, occur before the armies advanced, but this does not seem likely considering that Thucydides made no mention of it, and it would have been important for Athenian morale with the overall outcome of the battle and campaign. Gomme, *Commentary*, 3:562ff, ignored Diodorus' account. And Pritchett, *Studies,* 2:34, n. 38, said Diodorus' cavalry battle did not deserve credence.

50. Thuc. 4.96.5.

51. Thuc. 4.96.6–8. Diod. 12.70.2f, had the right wing of both hoplite phalanxes defeating its opponent and then the Theban right stopping its pursuit to turn and fall on the pursuing Athenian right and gain victory.

52. Thuc. 4.101.2. Gomme, *Commentary*, 3:571, suggested that the Boeotian cavalry caught the Athenian light-armed forces and workers before the pursuit was stopped by night.

53. Donald Kagan, *The Archidamian War* (Ithaca, N.Y.: Cornell University Press, 1974), p. 285, stated that Pagondas showed a touch of tactical genius in his use of cavalry. V. Hanson, "Epameinondas, the Battle of Leuctra (371 B.C.) and the 'Revolution' in Greek Battle Tactics," CA 7(1988):196, listed Delium as one of the first occurrences of a truly novel coordination between cavalry and infantry.

54. See Thuc. 5.61.1 for the size of the Athenian contingent and 67.2 for the Mantinean battle order. See Pritchett, *Studies,* 2:62, for the location of the battle. Gomme, *Commentary,* 4:101, basically agreed with Pritchett's location; on 4:116, he placed the strength of the Mantinean army at 10,000 hoplites. Hammond, *History,* p. 385, also thought the Mantineans and allies numbered 10,000.

55. See Thuc. 5.66.2 for Agis and the Spartans caught by surprise, 67.1 for Agis' battle order, and 68.1 for Thucydides' comment about the size of the Spartan army. Gomme, *Commentary,* 4:116, estimated the size of Agis' army at 11,000 or more hoplites.

56. Thuc. 5.70.1–72.4. Gomme, *Commentary,* 4:119, believed that the 2 Spartan *lochoi* were to come from the right of the Spartan center, not from the far right wing of the phalanx.

57. Thuc. 5.72.4–73.1; Gomme, *Commentary,* 4:123, suggested that Thucydides' statement about panic may have been exaggerated or that the author was misled for his Spartan informers were no doubt contemptuous of the defeated enemy.

58. Thuc. 5.73.1–2.

59. Gomme, *Commentary,* 4:124, called this a typical harassing cavalry action but nowhere attempted to explain how it was done.

60. Thuc. 5.73.2–4.

61. Thuc. 5.74.2.

62. See Hdt. 6.117 for the Persian casualties, and Ferrill, *Origins,* p. 108, for the strength of the Persian army at Marathon.

63. Polyb. 3.107.9–15, showed the Roman army had 80,000 infantrymen and 9,600 cavalry troops, and on 117.1–3 he stated there were 70,000 dead out of 79,000 who took part in the battle.

64. I recognize that the armies at both Marathon and Cannae were enveloped on both wings and that the casualty rates were therefore unusually high. But these provide some working figures to illustrate the point.

65. Thuc. 6.21.1.

66. Thuc. 6.67.2.

67. Thuc. 6.72.4, stated that the Syracusans had 15 generals. This implies that the Syracusan military had 15 major components or units of infantry and cavalry, in the same way the Athenians had 10 generals and 10 phylai in infantry and cavalry. Thus, 1,200 divided by 15 equals 80-man squadrons.

68. Because Syracuse was a Dorian city, it had the characteristic three Dorian tribes, and the military mirrored the social organization. Thuc. 6.73.1, showed that 3 generals were elected, obviously 1 from each tribe,

and on 7.4.6 he showed a triton of cavalry sent out as a unit to garrison the Olympieium. Gomme, *Commentary*, 4:348f, noted 1 general per tribe.

69. Polyaenus *Strat.* 1.39.2, recorded that Ecphantus was the sole commander of the Syracusan cavalry.

70. Thuc. 6.22.1.

71. Thuc. 6.43.1. Diod. 13.2.5, listed the expedition's forces as 140 triremes and many transport ships loaded with troops, horses, food, and equipment, and there were hoplites, slingers, and cavalry, as well as more than 7,000 allies, not including the crews of the ships.

72. MacInnes, *CR* 25:195f.

73. Bugh, *Horsemen*, pp. 99f.

74. Gomme, *Commentary*, 4:257f, concluded that it was not practical to ship enough cavalry to make any difference.

75. Thuc. 2.56.2, 58.1; Bugh, *Horsemen*, p. 90.

76. Thuc. 6.20.1–23.4.

77. Thuc. 6.26.1.

78. Thuc. 3.87.3.

79. Thuc. 4.68.5, showed only 600 cavalry took part in a campaign against Megara. Megara is so close to Athens that there would have been no reason for all the cavalry not to take part in this campaign.

80. Thuc. 6.52.2.

81. Plut. *Nicias* 16.1; Thuc. 6.63.3, reported much the same taunt.

82. Plut. *Nicias* 16.1.

83. Thuc. 6.64.1–66.3.

84. Thuc. 6.67.1–3.

85. Thuc. 6.69.1–70.2.

86. Polyaenus *Strat.* 1.39.2, named Ecphantus as commander of the Syracusan cavalry; on 1.39.2, he also said that the Athenians successfully employed caltrops to impede the Syracusan horsemen, but this seems unlikely because Thucydides did not mention it and he surely would not have overlooked this success.

87. Plut. *Nicias* 16.4; Thuc. 6.70.1ff; Diod. 13.6.6.

88. Thuc. 6.74.2; Gomme, *Commentary*, 4:346, stated this cavalry action was one of the decisive moments in the entire campaign.

89. Thuc. 6.94.4; Diod. 13.6.6. *IG* I^2 302, recorded this expenditure.

90. Thuc. 6.88.6.

91. The discrepancy in the numbers is due to a disagreement between our two sources. Thuc. 6.98.1, listed 300 Egestans, 100 Naxians, Sicels, and others, along with horses for the Athenian riders, for a total of 650

cavalrymen. Diod. 13.7.4, recorded 300 Egestans but 250 Sicels, for a total of 800.

92. Thuc. 6.97.1–98.3.

93. Thuc. 6.98.3f. Gomme, *Commentary*, 4:372, noted that 1 phyle of hoplites may have encompassed only about 150 men because there were just 1,500 Athenian hoplites total in all 10 tribes, and tribal organization was probably maintained.

94. Thuc. 6.101.4; E. A. Freeman, *History of Sicily*, 3 vols. (1891–1894; reprint ed., New York: Burt Franklin, 1965), 3:220–222.

95. Thuc. 6.101.4–6; Plut. *Nicias* 18.1ff; Freeman, *Sicily*, 3:223f.

96. Thuc. 6.102.2, 7.15.1; Freeman, *Sicily*, 3:221. Gomme, *Commentary*, 4:375, noted that Thuc. 6.102.2 was the first mention of Nicias' illness and that he must have been fit during the early part of the campaign.

97. Thuc. 6.8.4, 9.1–14.1.

98. Freeman, *Sicily*, 3:224.

99. Thuc. 7.1.5. Diod. 13.7.7, gave the reinforcements as 3,000 infantry and 200 cavalry.

100. Thuc. 7.2.1.

101. Thuc. 7.3.1–3.

102. Thuc. 7.3.4, 4.1.

103. Thuc. 7.5.1f.

104. Thuc. 7.5.1–3. Gomme, *Commentary*, 4:384, compared Gylippus with Brasidas and Lysander in his diplomatic ability to work with and command allies.

105. Thuc. 7.6.1–3.

106. Thuc. 7.6.3.

107. Thuc. 7.6.4.

108. Thuc. 7.4.1–6.

109. Thuc. 7.4.6.

110. Thuc. 7.11.4.

111. Thuc. 7.13.2.

112. Thuc. 7.11.1–15.2.

113. Thuc. 7.22.1–24.3.

114. Thuc. 7.37.1–41.5.

115. Thuc. 7.43.1–4. Diod. 13.2.3, said that Demosthenes used 10,000 hoplites and the same number of light-armed troops. Gomme, *Commentary*, 4:422, suspected the light-armed forces were left at the foot of the ascent to the Epipolae, to be brought up to counter cavalry in the morning.

116. Thuc. 7.43.5–44.7.

117. Thuc. 7.44.8.

118. Thuc. 7.47.1–50.4

119. Thuc. 7.51.1f. Gomme, *Commentary*, 4:429, noted the horses were left so the riders could escape on foot into the fortifications.

120. Thuc. 7.52.1–72.5.

121. Thuc. 7.73.1–74.2.

122. Thuc. 7.75.1–78.4.

123. Thuc. 7.78.5.

124. Thuc. 7.78.6f; here, I follow the translation of Charles Forster Smith, *Thucydides IV*, Loeb Classical Library (Cambridge, Mass.: Harvard University Press, 1986), p. 161.

125. Thuc. 7.79.1–5.

126. Thuc. 7.79.5; Smith, *Thucydides IV*, p. 163.

127. Thuc. 7.79.6.

128. Thuc. 7.80.1–82.3.

129. Thuc. 7.83.1–85.4. Gomme, *Commentary*, 4:460, concluded that the cavalry killed all the Athenians who managed to escape the slaughter at the river.

130. Thuc. 7.19.1–2.

131. Thuc. 7.27.4.

132. Thuc. 7.27.4–5. Gomme, *Commentary*, 4:406, did not seem to consider this an excessive number.

133. Thuc. 7.27.5, 28.2.

134. Spence, ZPE 67:174.

135. Thuc. 8.71.1–2. Xen. *Hell.* 4.5.11–18, showed a similar engagement by the Athenians outside Corinth in 395 B.C.

136. Diod. 13.72.3–6.

137. The highest number of Athenian cavalry that Spence, ZPE 67:174, reported for the year 410/409 B.C. is 666; it seems highly unlikely that conditions after two years of besiegement had improved for anyone.

138. Diod. 13.72.7–9.

Chapter 6

1. See Xen. *An.* 1.2.9, 7.10 for the number of Greek hoplites and peltasts with Cyrus.

2. Xen. *An.* 1.7.10f, said Cyrus' army totaled 100,000 men and 20 scythed chariots, and on 1.8.5f, listed 1,000 Paphlagonian horsemen on the right of the Greeks and 600 horsemen in the center. There must have been

an equal number of cavalry on both the left and right. Ferrill, *Origins,* p. 152, gave slightly lower numbers.

3. Xen. *An.* 2.4.6.

4. Xen. *An.* 3.2.18; here, I follow the translation of Carleton L. Brownson, *Xenophon III,* Loeb Classical Library (Cambridge, Mass.: Harvard University Press, 1980), p. 205.

5. Xen. *An.* 3.3.6–8.

6. Xen. *An.* 3.3.9–11; by comparison, see 1.2.5, where Cyrus' army was said to cover 22 parasangs or 72.5 miles in three days (or 24.2 miles per day) and 1.2.7, where he recorded 20 parasangs in three stages for approximately the same daily march rate.

7. Xen. *An.* 3.3.15–20.

8. Xen. *An.* 3.4.1–3.

9. The Persian light-armed infantry no doubt crossed the ravine first and formed a screen for the horsemen, who may have been slowed by this obstacle. Also, Xen. *An.* 3.4.5, reported only the capture of 18 horsemen but no casualties among the riders, which also seems to indicate they were behind the light-armed troops.

10. Xen. *An.* 3.4.4f.

11. Xen. *An.* 3.4.13–16, reported such a skirmish and said Mithradates did not have the courage to close the Greek formation.

12. Xen. *Ages.* 1.7, *Hell.* 3.4.2; Plut. *Ages.* 6.2. Diod. 14.79.1, listed Agesilaus' army as being composed of 6,000 soldiers and a council of 30 Spartan citizens.

13. Diod. 14.37.4, 79.2. Xen. *Hell.* 3.2.7, showed an anonymous commander for the Cyreans, and *An.* 7.3.7, showed Xenophon as commander of the Cyreans. J. K. Anderson, "The Battle of Sardis," *CSCA* 7(1974):30, believed that Xenophon probably retained command of the Cyreans under Agesilaus until 396 B.C.

14. Diod. 14.79.1, said Agesilaus had 400 horsemen. Xen. *Ages.* 1.15, stated that Tissaphernes believed that Agesilaus had no cavalry, *Hell.* 3.4.12, said Agesilaus had no cavalry. Plut. *Ages.* 9.3, recorded that Agesilaus' force was inferior to the Persians in cavalry.

15. Xen. *Hell.* 3.4.13f; Vivienne J. Gray, "Two Different Approaches to the Battle of Sardis in 395 B.C.," *CSCA* 12(1979):188.

16. Thuc. 2.13.8; Aeschines 2.174. See also Chapter 5 of this work.

17. H. W. Parke, *Greek Mercenary Soldiers* (Oxford: Oxford University Press, 1933), p. 4, noted that it is certain that Greek mercenaries served the

Egyptian pharaoh Psammetichus (early seventh century B.C.) and that some probably were employed earlier.

18. Xen. *Oec.*, writing a half century after the Peloponnesian War, clearly showed that Athens had not fully recovered its economic prosperity, with the mines still closed, the metics and foreign merchants staying away, and land in the city available.

19. Xen. *An.* 6.4.8.

20. Isoc. 4.167f.

21. For a brief biography of Xenophon, see George Cawkwell's introduction to Xenophon, *A History of My Times* (New York: Penguin Books, 1988). For a full biography, see J. K. Anderson, *Xenophon* (London: Gerald Duckworth, 1974).

22. Xen. *Ages.* 1.24, *Hell.* 3.4.15; Plut. *Ages.* 9.3.

23. Xen. *Lace.* 12.5.

24. Paul Cartledge, *Agesilaos and the Crisis of Sparta* (London: Gerald Duckworth, 1987), p. 20; Charles D. Hamilton, *Agesilaus and the Failure of Spartan Hegemony* (Ithaca, N.Y.: Cornell University Press, 1991), pp. 13ff.

25. Xen. *Hell.* 6.1.5; Pritchett, *Greek States*, 2:213.

26. Xen. *Ages.* 1.27, *Hell.* 3.4.18.

27. Frontin. *Str.* 4.1.9.

28. Frontin. *Str.* 4.1.16, reported that a soldier had his hand cut off for theft.

29. Frontin. *Str.* 4.1.17; here, I follow the translation of Charles E. Bennett, *Frontinus*, Loeb Classical Library (Cambridge, Mass.: Harvard University Press, 1980), p. 275.

30. Frontin. *Str.* 3.12.2.

31. Nep. *Iph.* 2.1f, reported on the strictness of the mercenary commander Iphicrates, which resulted in his having the best-drilled troops in Greece. Polyaenus, *Strat.* 3.9.35, showed that Iphicrates constantly drilled and worked his mercenaries.

32. Nep., *Iph.* 2.1ff.

33. Xen. *Ages.* 1.25, *Hell.* 3.4.16.

34. Thuc. 4.55.

35. Thuc. 5.66.1–73.2.

36. Xen. *Ages.* 2.9ff, *Hell.* 4.3.15ff.

37. Xen. *Hell.* 6.4.11ff.

38. Plut. *Ages.* 26.3. Diod. 15.33.1ff, and Plut. *Ages.* 26.2, both said that the Thebans became proficient infantrymen because of the number of expeditions made against them by the Spartans.

39. Xen. *An.* 3.3.16ff.

40. Xen. *An.* 4.8.9ff.

41. Xen. *An.* 7.3.3f.

42. Xen. *Hell.* 3.4.20. Because Xenophon led the Cyreans until the reshuffling of commands in 395 B.C., he obviously commanded them in the 396 B.C. campaign.

43. P. A. Rahe, "The Military Situation in Western Asia on the Eve of Cunaxa," *AJP* 101(1980):95, stated "One must wonder whether Xenophon was Agesilaus' tutor in the coordinated use of infantry and cavalry." Hamilton, *Agesilaus*, p. 97, said "It is tempting to think that Agesilaus had the advice in this matter [the improvement of the cavalry] of Xenophon."

44. Both *Xenophontos peri Hippikes* and *Xenophontos Hipparchikos* were written between 371 B.C. and 365 B.C.

45. Xen. *Hipparch.* 2.2–6.

46. Xen. *Hipparch.* 2.6, 4.3, 5.5ff.

47. Xen. *Hipparch.* 2.7f, 4.3.

48. Great Britain, War Office, *Cavalry Training*, p. 451; Brereton, *Horses*, p. 69, reported that Frederick the Great expected his cavalry to charge from 1 mile and in the last 800 yards to be at full speed.

49. Xen. *Hipparch.* 1.5, 18, 20, *Hippik.* 3.7.

50. Xen. *Hippik.* 12.1–13.

51. Xen. *Hell.* 3.4.20. Anderson, *Xenophon*, p. 155, believed that the Greek text implied that "another" referred to another Spartiate, like Xenocles. However, this can be read as simply another person, and Xenophon on at least one other occasion referred to himself in this fashion; cf. n. 13 earlier.

52. Xen. *Ages.* 1.24, said Agesilaus took selected citizens from a few cities into his army, so the cavalry was composed of two distinct elements.

53. Plut. *Ages.* 9.5; Frontin. *Str.* 1.11.17.

54. There are no exact numbers available on the size of Agesilaus' army, but these reflect the figures for the 396 B.C. campaign, with a substantial increase in cavalry.

55. Xen. *Ages.* 1.29f, *Hell.* 3.4.22f.

56. Xen. *Hell.* 3.4.24; here, I follow the translation of Carleton L. Brownson, *Xenophon I*, Loeb Classical Library (Cambridge, Mass.: Harvard University Press, 1985), pp. 241 and 243.

57. Xen. *Ages.* 1.31f, *Hell.* 3.4.23f; Plut. *Ages.* 10.3, showed light infantry with the cavalry. Diod. 14.80.1–6, and the *Hellenica Oxyrhynchia* gave a totally different account of this battle. In fact, the two accounts are so differ-

ent they cannot be reconciled. For a discussion of this problem, cf. I.A.F. Bruce, *An Historical Commentary on the Hellenica Oxyrhynchia* (Cambridge: Cambridge University Press, 1967), pp. 77–92, J. K. Anderson, "The Battle of Sardis in 395 B.C.," *CSCA* 7(1974):27–53, and Vivienne J. Gray, "Two Different Approaches to the Battle of Sardis in 395 B.C.," *CSCA* 12(1979):183–200. I chose Xenophon's account because of his known relationship to Agesilaus and his close proximity to and probable participation in the events, whereas the author of the *Hellenica Oxyrhynchia*, which formed the basis of Diodorus, is unknown. However, he was obviously not in Asia at the time of the battle; cf. Hamilton, *Agesilaus*, pp. 97ff.

58. Plut. *Pel.* 20.1, provided the very reasonable figures of 10,000 hoplites and 1,000 cavalry. Xen. *Hell.* 6.4.9, listed Heiron's mercenaries, Phocian peltasts, and the horsemen of Heraclea; and Phlius, 6.4.10, listed the Lacedaemonian horse. Pritchett, *Studies*, 1:58, n. 47, concluded there were 2,300 Lacedaemonians, as did Anderson, *Military*, p. 196. Hammond, *History*, p. 493, said the Spartans numbered over 2,000; Ferrill, *Origins*, p. 166, agreed with the numbers of Plutarch. Other ancient sources provided higher numbers for the Spartan army. Polyaenus, *Strat.* 2.3.8, recorded 40,000 Spartans and allies took the field. Frontin. *Str.* 4.2.6, credited Cleombrotus with 24,000 infantry and 1,600 cavalry.

59. Paus. 9.13.6f, showed only 7 Boeotarchs at Leuctra and thus 7,000 infantry and 700 cavalry. Polyaenus *Strat.* 2.3.12, said the Theban army numbered 6,000; Plut. *Pel.* 31.4, 35.2, showed 7,000 hoplites taking the field against Jason of Pherae shortly after Leuctra, so the Thebans could field an army this size. Diod. 15.52.2, recorded that the Theban army totaled no more than 6,000 men. G. Busolt, "Spartas Herr und Leuktra," *Hermes* 40(1905):444f, concluded 3,000 Theban hoplites out of a total of 6,000 to 6,500 and 600 to 800 cavalry. Anderson, *Military*, p. 198, reasoned that Cleombrotus' army outnumbered Epaminondas' army by 3 to 1. Ferrill, *Origins*, p. 166, proposed 6,000 hoplites and 800 cavalry for the Theban army.

60. Paus. 9.13.8; Xen. *Hell.* 6.4.9.

61. Xen. *Hell.* 6.4.10f; Anderson, *Military*, p. 402; Ferrill, *Origins*, pp. 166f.

62. Xen. *Hell.* 6.4.10, 12; Anderson, *Military*, p. 402; Ferrill, *Origins*, pp. 166f.

63. Xen. *Hell.* 6.4.13f; Plut. *Pel.* 23.1f.

64. A. M. Devine, "EMBOLON: A Study in Tactical Terminology," *Phoenix* 37(1983):207–231, believed the Thebans used a wedge-shaped formation at Leuctra. P. Krentz, "The Nature of Hoplite Warfare," *CA*

4(1985):59, also believed the wedge formation was used. James Devoto, "Pelopidas and Kleombrotos at Leuktra," *AHB* 3(1989):116, placed the Sacred Band on the left front corner of the Theban formation.

65. Plut. *Pel.* 23.3f.

66. Xen. *Hell.* 6.4.13.

67. Polyaenus *Strat.* 2.3.3; Xen. *Hell.* 6.4.14; Ferrill, *Origins*, p. 168.

68. Xen. *Hell.* 6.4.15.

69. Xen. *Hell.* 6.4.10, said the Spartan cavalry deployed in front of the Lacedaemonians because the plain between the two armies was level; however, most plains between phalanxes were level at the time of battle, so Xenophon's meaning is unclear. Anderson, *Military*, p. 216, concluded that the Spartan cavalry was being used to conceal the movement of the morai. See also Ferrill, *Origins*, p. 167.

70. G. Cawkwell, "Epameinondas and Thebes," *CQ* 66(1972):262f, stated this was an unusual role for cavalry and the first time a major Greek battle showed the coordination of army units that Philip and Alexander perfected. See also Cawkwell, *Philip*, p. 155. Agreeing with this view was J. Buckler, "Plutarch on Leuktra," *SO* 55(1980):89, and idem, "Epameinondas and the EMBOLON," *Phoenix* 39(1985):143. For an opposing opinion, cf. V. Hanson, "Epameinondas, the Battle of Leuktra (371 B.C.) and the 'Revolution' in Greek Battle Tactics," *CA* 7(1988):195, who saw no deliberate move by the Theban commanders but only reaction to poor Spartan performance.

71. Xen. *Hell.* 7.5.14; Polyb. 9.8.9; Diod. 15.84.2. Hans Delbrück, *History of the Art of War Within the Framework of Political History*, vol. 1, trans. by Walter J. Renfroe, Jr. (Westport, Conn.: Greenwood Press, 1975), pp. 169f, discounted the validity of Diodorus' account and claimed the battle may be recounted only as described by Xenophon.

72. Xen. *Hell.* 7.5.15ff. Diod. 15.84.2, had 6,000 Athenians under Hegesileus arrive and save the city.

73. Diod. 15.84.4, 85.1f; Xen. *Hell.* 7.5.23; Johannes Kromayer, *Antike Schlachtfelder in Griechenland*, vols. 1 and 2 (Berlin: Weidmannsche Buchhandlung, 1903–1907), 1:52; Pritchett, *Studies*, 2:64f; Hammond, *History*, p. 507.

74. Xen. *Hell.* 7.5.21f; Diod. 15.84.4, 85.2; Polyaenus *Strat.* 2.3.14.

75. Xen. *Hell.* 7.5.22f; Arr. *Tact.* 11.2; Kromayer, *Schlachtfelder*, 1:64, estimated that the Boeotian and Theban hoplites numbered 7,000. See also Hammond, *History*, pp. 508f.

76. Xen. *Hell.* 7.5.23f; here, I follow the translation of Carleton L.

Brownson, *Xenophon II*, Loeb Classical Library (Cambridge, Mass.: Harvard University Press, 1968), p. 335.

77. Xen. *Hell.* 7.5.24; Diod. 15.85.3–7; Hammond, *History*, p. 509.

78. Xen. *Hell.* 7.5.25; Diod. 15.85.8–87.2; Paus. 8.11.5; Pritchett, *Studies*, 2:66; Hammond, *History*, p. 509.

Chapter 7

1. Ellis, *Cavalry*, p. 13, stated, "Two thousand years before European generals were even beginning to realize that cavalry might act as skirmishers or shock troops, scouts or reserves, Alexander of Macedon had built an army that made full allowance for all these functions."

2. Diod. 16.4.3–7; Frontin. *Str.* 2.3.2; Hammond, *History*, p. 538; Hammond and Griffith, *Macedonia*, 2:213. Griffith thought Bardylis employed the square formation because this was perhaps the first appearance of the phalanx armed with the sarissa. However, a square was a defensive formation for all-around, flank and rear, protection, which seems to indicate the threat was a mobile one, cavalry. M. M. Markle, "Use of the Sarissa by Philip and Alexander of Macedon," *AJA* 82(1978):486, thought it unlikely the sarissa was used this early. Eugene N. Borza, *In the Shadow of Mt. Olympus—The Emergence of Macedon* (Princeton, N.J.: Princeton University Press, 1990), p. 202, believed there were two new elements in Philip's army—its size and the coordinated attack.

3. Hdt. 9.31.

4. Thuc. 2.98.4.

5. Diod. 15.19.3.

6. Arr. *Anab.* 1.2.5, referred to Macedonian cavalry squadrons from Amphipolis and Bottiaia. See also G. T. Griffith, "The Macedonian Background," *G&R* 12(1965):134ff; Ellis, *Philip*, pp. 54f; A. B. Bosworth, *Conquest and Empire—The Reign of Alexander the Great* (New York: Cambridge University Press, 1988), p. 261.

7. Theopompus (*FGrH* 115 F224–225), observed that Greeks and Thessalians were *hetairoi*, or Companions, and these served as cavalry in battle. Plut. *Alex.* 10.3, recorded the names of Harpalus, Erigyios, and Nearchus as Companions of Alexander, and Arr. *Anab.* 3.6.5, included Laomedon. These young men were Alexander's age, and so their fathers were made Companions by Philip. Ellis, *Philip*, pp. 54, 218, identified Harpalus as probably Elimiote, Erigyios and Laomedon as Mytilenean, and Nearchus as Cretan. See also Bosworth, *Conquest*, p. 7.

8. Diod. 16.4.3.

9. Diod. 16.35.4; Hammond and Griffith, *Macedonia,* 2:410.

10. Diod. 16.85.5. Because Philip was unlikely to take all his mounted assets out of Macedonia and Alexander two years later mustered more than 3,000 horsemen, a two-thirds estimate seems correct.

11. Diod. 17.17.3–5, listed Alexander's invasion army, which included 1,800 Macedonian cavalry and 900 Thracians, Paeonians, and prodromoi, and showed Alexander left 1,500 Macedonian cavalry with Antipater. N.G.L. Hammond, *Alexander the Great King, Commander, and Statesman* (Park Ridge, N.J.: Noyes Press, 1980), p. 28, identified the prodromoi as Macedonians, as did Hammond and Griffith, *Macedonia,* 2:411. These countered an earlier view held by W. W. Tarn that the prodromoi were Thracians (W. W. Tarn, *Alexander the Great,* 2 vols. [London: Cambridge University Press, 1948], 2:157).

12. Arr. *Anab.* 1.2.5, showed squadrons from Bottiaia and Amphipolis, on 1.12.7, a squadron from Apollonia, and on 2.9.3, squadrons from Anthemas and Leugaia. See also Cawkwell, *Philip,* p. 32; N.G.L. Hammond, "A Cavalry Unit in the Army of Antigonus Monophthalmus," *CQ* 28(1978):128f; Bosworth, *Conquest,* pp. 261ff.

13. Arr. *Anab.* 1.2.5; Hammond, *CQ* 28:132; Bosworth, *Conquest,* pp. 261f.

14. Tarn, *Alexander,* 2:162f; Bosworth, *Conquest,* p. 262.

15. Arr. *Anab.* 2.5.9, 3.1.4, 11.8; Diod. 16.93.6; Ellis, *Philip,* p. 54; Bosworth, *Conquest,* p. 261.

16. Arr. *Anab.* 4.13.25, 7.5.16, 8.3; Plut. *Alex.* 32.5; Hammond, *Alexander,* p. 30; Bosworth, *Conquest,* p. 262.

17. Arr. *Anab.* 1.15.5, used the term *xyston* for the cavalry spear, and on 1.15.7–8, he had the terminology changed to *doru* for this weapon. Diod. 17.60.2, had Alexander throwing a javelin at Darius. W. W. Tarn, *Hellenistic Military and Naval Development* (Cambridge: Cambridge University Press, 1930), p. 71, stated Alexander's cavalry used the xyston or short cavalry spear. Hammond, *Alexander,* pp. 30f, listed the cornel-wood lance with metal tip and butt-spike as the cavalry weapon. More recently, P. A. Manti, "The Cavalry Sarissa," *AncW* 8(1983):73–80, argued convincingly for the existence of the cavalry sarissa.

18. Arr. *Anab.* 1.15.7f; Hammond, *Alexander,* pp. 30f.

19. Arr. *Anab.* 1.12.7, 14.6, 3.7.7; Hammond, *Alexander,* p. 28; Bosworth, *Conquest,* p. 262.

20. Markle, *AJA* 82:492; Hammond, *Alexander,* p. 31; Cawkwell, *Philip,* p. 35; Bosworth, *Conquest,* p. 262.

21. Theophr. 3.12.2; Polyb. 18.29.2; Asclep. 5.1; M. M. Markle, "The Macedonian Sarissa, Spear, and Related Armor," *AJA* 81(1977):324f; Hammond, *Alexander*, p. 32.

22. Arr. *Anab*. 1.14.6, reported that the prodromoi and Paeonians crossed the Granicus first and assaulted the Persians; on 2.9.2, he showed the prodromoi placed in front of the Companion Cavalry at Issus, thus leading the assault, and on 3.14.1, he had Alexander order Aretas, commander of the prodromoi, to charge the Persian cavalry; and when a gap appeared, the Companion Cavalry followed.

23. Diod. 17.17.4, reported that Alexander had a total of 900 Thracians, Paeonians, and prodromoi; Arr. *Anab*. 1.12.7, recorded there were 4 squadrons of prodromoi. Thus, it seems likely that the prodromoi numbered 100 per squadron and 400 total.

24. Arr. *Anab*. 3.12.3, showed a single commander for the prodromoi.

25. Asclep. 7.3; Aelian 18.4.

26. Hammond and Griffith, *Macedonia*, 2:414.

27. Asclep. 7.3; Aelian 18.4.

28. Frontin. *Str*. 4.2.4, stated, "Alexander of Macedon conquered the world, in the face of innumerable enemy forces, by means of forty thousand men long accustomed to discipline under his father Philip."

29. Frontin. *Str*. 4.1.6; Engels, *Logistics*, p. 12.

30. Frontin. *Str*. 4.1.6; Engels, *Logistics*, p. 12.

31. Polyaenus *Strat*. 4.2.1, 3.

32. Polyaenus *Strat*. 4.2.10.

33. Diod. 16.86.2; N.G.L. Hammond, "The Two Battles of Chaeronea (338 B.C. and 86 B.C.)," *Klio* 31(1938):206; idem, *History*, p. 569; W. Kendrick Pritchett, "Observations on Chaironeia," *AJA* 62(1958):309f; John Warry, *Warfare in the Classical World* (New York: St. Martin's Press, 1980), p. 68; Bosworth, *Conquest*, p. 10.

34. Diod. 16.85.5, 86.1; Hammond, *Klio* 31:210f; idem, *History*, pp. 568f; Warry, *Warfare*, pp. 68f.

35. Frontin. *Str*. 2.1.9; Polyaenus *Strat*. 4.2.4, 7; Hammond, *History*, p. 569; Warry, *Warfare*, pp. 68f.

36. Diod. 16.86.3–6; Frontin. *Str*. 2.1.9; Polyaenus *Strat*. 4.2.2, 7; Plut. *Alex*. 9.2; Plut. *Pel*. 18.5; Hammond, *Klio* 31:208ff; idem, *History*, pp. 569f; Markle, *AJA* 82:490f; Warry, *Warfare*, pp. 68f.

37. Markle, *AJA* 82:491. F. E. Adcock, *The Greek and Macedonian Art of War* (Berkeley: University of California Press, 1957), p. 50, stated, "For cavalry to be at all effective in shock tactics, the most skillful horsemanship was

needed together with most resolute and unflinching will to advance. This combination was achieved by the Companion Cavalry of Alexander. ... But, even so, if the attack was to succeed, it must be helped by a gap or weak place in the enemy line, or it must be directed against troops less well armed and prepared to resist a charge." Borza, *Olympus*, p. 203, believed that Philip's coordinated infantry-cavalry tactics reflect a Theban influence.

38. John Keegan, *The Face of Battle* (New York: Viking, 1976), passim, gave an excellent account of cavalry warfare but generally argued that the cavalry charge into a line was a romantic notion. Rahe, *AJP* 101:84f, believed that cavalry could not break an infantry line unless a horse or horses went mad and ran into the men. Ferrill, *Origins*, p. 84, stated that cavalry would not force its way through an unbroken line but acknowledged a cavalry charge could lead to a line breaking. In contrast, Spence, *JHS* 110:99, n. 50, did not believe there was anything in the nature of the horse to preclude its running into a body of men.

39. United States Army, *Drill Regulations*, p. 154, par. 339; and p. 341, par. 847. Nolan, *Cavalry*, p. 302, stated, "[If] the cavalry put their horses to their utmost speed, ride home, ... then the [infantry] square must go down." This experienced cavalry officer, writing in the nineteenth century, clearly implied that the cavalrymen, not the horses, were the deciding factor in the successful cavalry charge and shock tactics against an infantry line. If the riders did not falter, then the horses would not.

40. Tarn, *Alexander*, 1:26, calculated that Alexander had only 20,000 to 24,000 infantry and 5,000 cavalry, fewer men than he had at Granicus. Ulrich Wilcken, *Alexander the Great*, trans. by C. G. Richards (New York: W. W. Norton, 1967), p. 103, believed Alexander had the same number of men as at Granicus. Hammond, *History*, p. 610, placed Alexander's army at 30,000 foot soldiers and 5,000 horsemen. For the battle, I will principally follow the account of Arrian for it is more coherent and precise than those of Diodorus and Curtius.

41. Arr. *Anab.* 2.8.2–4; Curt. 3.9.7–11; Hammond, *History*, p. 610; A. M. Devine, "Grand Tactics at the Battle of Issus," *AncW* 12(1985):47ff; idem, "Alexander the Great," in *Warfare in the Ancient World*, p. 113.

42. Arr. *Anab.* 2.8.8, placed Darius' strength at 600,000. Diod. 17.31.2, said Darius had 400,000 infantry and at least 100,000 cavalry. Justin 11.9.1, gave 400,000 as the size of the Persian force.

43. Arr. *Anab.* 2.8.5–8; Curt. 3.9.1–6; Polyb. 12.17.6; Strab. 15.3.18f; J.F.C. Fuller, *The Generalship of Alexander the Great* (1960; reprint ed., New

York: Da Capo Press, 1989), p. 159; Hammond, *History*, p. 160. Some historians prefer to follow Diodorus and Curtius for this battle, and both of these ancient authors placed all the Cardaces on the left of the Greek mercenaries. Cf. Devine, *AncW* 12:47f; idem, "Alexander," p. 114.

44. Arr. *Anab*. 2.9.1–4; Hammond, *History*, p. 610; Fuller, *Generalship*, pp. 159f; Bosworth, *Conquest*, p. 60; Curt. 3.11.1–3, had the shift of the Thessalians occur after the battle began. Cf. Devine, *AncW* 12:49ff; idem, "Alexander," pp. 114f.

45. Arr. *Anab*. 2.10.1–11.3; Curt. 3.11.14f; Diod. 17.33.2; Fuller, *Generalship*, p. 161; Hammond, *History*, p. 611; Bosworth, *Conquest*, p. 61. For a slightly different reconstruction, cf. Devine, *AncW* 12:49ff; idem, "Alexander," pp. 115f.

46. Arr. *Anab*. 2.10.4f, 11.1–4; Diod. 17.33.5, 34.7f; Fuller, *Generalship*, pp. 161f; Hammond, *History*, p. 611. Bosworth, *Conquest*, p. 61, said the momentum of Alexander's cavalry could not have been great, because it was attacking across a stream, but the Persian infantry was unable to withstand the shock. Devine, *AncW* 12:52, believed that no cavalry charge took place but rather that Alexander's light infantry and light cavalry crossed the Pinarus at a ford first and forced the Persian guards away, then the Companion Cavalry crossed slowly, squadron by squadron, and reformed on the Persian side and charged the Persian formation. See idem, "Alexander," pp. 115ff.

47. Arr. *Anab*. 2.10.3.

Selected Bibliography

Adcock, F. E. *The Greek and Macedonian Art of War.* Berkeley: University of California Press, 1957.

Alföldi, A. "Die Herrschaft der Reiterei in Griechenland und Rom nach dem Sturz der Könige." In *Gestalt und Geschichte: Festschrift Karl Schefold.* Edited by Martha Rohde-Liegle, Herbert A. Cahn, and H. Chr. Ackermann. Berne: Francke Verlag, 1967.

Anderson, J. K. *Ancient Greek Horsemanship.* Berkeley: University of California Press, 1961.

––––––. *Military Theory and Practice in the Age of Xenophon.* Berkeley: University of California Press, 1970.

––––––. "The Battle of Sardis in 395 B.C." *CSCA* 4(1974):27–53.

––––––. *Xenophon.* London: Gerald Duckworth, 1974.

––––––. "Greek Chariot-Bourne and Mounted Infantry." *AJA* 79(1975):175–187.

Andreades, A. M. *A History of Greek Public Finance.* Cambridge, Mass.: Harvard University Press, 1933.

Andrewes, A. *The Greek Tyrants.* London: Hutchinson's University Library, 1960.

Artemis Orthia. "The Sanctuary of Artemis Orthia at Sparta." *JHS* suppl. 5(1920).

Beazley, J. D. *Attic Black-Figure Vase Painters.* Oxford: Clarendon Press, 1956.

Benson, J. L. *Horse, Bird and Man.* Amherst: University of Massachusetts Press, 1970.

Blegen, Carl. *Prosymna.* 2 vols. London: Cambridge University Press, 1937.

Boardman, John. "Early Euboean Pottery and History." *BSA* 52(1957):1–29.

––––––. *Athenian Red-Figure Vases—The Archaic Period a Handbook.* London: Thames and Hudson, 1975.

Borza, Eugene. *In the Shadow of Olympus—The Emergence of Macedon.* Princeton, N.J.: Princeton University Press, 1990.

Bosworth, A. B. *Conquest and Empire—The Reign of Alexander the Great.* New York: Cambridge University Press, 1988.
Bradeen, D. W. "The Lelantine War and Pheidon of Argos." *TAPA* 78(1947):223-241.
Breasted, James Henry. *The Battle of Kadesh.* The Decennial Publications of the University of Chicago. First series, vol. 5. Chicago: University of Chicago Press, 1904.
Brereton, J. M. *The Horse in War.* New York: Arco Publishing, 1976.
Brock, J. K. *Fortetsa.* London: Cambridge University Press, 1957.
Bruce, I.A.F. *A Historical Commentary on the Hellenica Oxyrhynchia.* London: Cambridge University Press, 1967.
Brunt, P. A. "Spartan Policy and Strategy in the Archidamian War." *Phoenix* 19(1965):255-280.
Buck, R. J. "The Formation of the Boeotian League." *CP* 67(1972):94-101.
_____ . *A History of Boeotia.* Edmonton: University of Alberta Press, 1979.
Buckler, J. "Plutarch on Leuktra." *SO* 55(1980):175-193.
_____ ."Epameinondas and the EMBOLON." *Phoenix* 39(1985):134-143.
Bugh, Glenn R. "Andocides, Aeschines, and the Three Hundred Cavalrymen." *Phoenix* 36(1982):306-312.
_____ . *The Horsemen of Athens.* Princeton, N.J.: Princeton University Press, 1988.
Burn, A. R. "The So-called 'Trade League' in Early Greek History and the Lelantine War." *JHS* 49(1929):14-37.
_____ . *The World of Hesiod—A Study of the Greek Middle Ages c. 900-700 B.C.* London: Routledge & Kegan Paul, 1936; reprint ed., New York: Benjamin Blom, 1966.
Busolt, G. "Spartas Herr und Leuktra." *Hermes* 40(1905):387-449.
Busolt, G., and Swoboda, H. *Griechische Staatskunde.* 2 vols. Handbuch der Altertumswissenschaft, vierte abteilung, erster teil, erster Band. Munich: C. H. Beck'sche Verlags Buchhandlung, 1920-1926.
Camp, John M. *The Athenian Agora—Excavations in the Heart of Classical Athens.* London: Thames and Hudson, 1986.
Cartledge, Paul. *Agesilaos and the Crisis of Sparta.* London: Gerald Duckworth, 1987.
Cawkwell, George L. "Epameinondas and Thebes." *CQ* 66(1972):254-278.
_____ ."Thucydides' Judgment of Periclean Strategy." *YClS* 24(1975):53-70.
_____ . *Philip of Macedon.* Boston: Faber and Faber, 1978.
Chambers, M. H. "Thucydides and Pericles." *HSPh* 62(1957):79-92.

Cichorius, Conrad. "Zu den namen der attischen Steuerklassen." In *Griechische Studien H. Lipsius dargebracht zum sechsigsten Geburtstag.* Leipzig: Teubner, 1894.

Contamine, Philippe. *War in the Middle Ages.* Translated by Michael Jones. Oxford: Basil Blackwell, 1984.

Crouwell, J. H. *Chariots and Other Means of Land Transport in Bronze Age Greece.* Amsterdam: Allard Pierson Museum, 1981.

Davies, John K. *Athenian Propertied Families, 600–300 B.C.* Oxford: Oxford University Press, 1971.

_____ . *Wealth and the Power of Wealth in Classical Athens.* Salem, N.H.: Ayer, 1984.

Davis, R.H.C. *The Medieval Warhorse.* London: Thames and Hudson, 1989.

Delbrück, Hans. *History of the Art of War Within the Framework of Political History.* Vol. 1. Translated by J. Renfroe, Jr. Westport, Conn.: Greenwood Press, 1975.

Demand, Nancy H. *Thebes in the Fifth Century.* Boston: Routledge & Kegan Paul, 1982.

Denison, George T. *A History of Cavalry from the Earliest Times.* London: MacMillan, 1913; reprint ed., Westport, Conn.: Greenwood Press, 1977.

Desborough, V. R. d'A. *Protogeometric Pottery.* London: Oxford University Press, 1952.

_____ . *The Greek Dark Age.* London: Ernest Benn, 1972.

Devine, A. M. "EMBOLON: A Study in Tactical Terminology." *Phoenix* 37(1983):201–237.

_____ ."Grand Tactics at the Battle of Issus." *AncW* 12(1985):39–59.

Devoto, James. "Pelopidas and Kleombrotos at Leuktra." *AHB* 3(1989):115–118.

de Wet, B. X. "The So-called Defensive Policy of Pericles." *Acta Classica* 12(1969):103–119.

Dunbabin, T. J., ed. *Perchora: The Sanctuaries of Hera Akraia and Limenia.* 2 vols. London: Oxford University Press, 1940–1962.

_____ . *The Western Greeks.* London: Oxford University Press, 1948.

Ehrenberg, Victor. *From Solon to Socrates.* 2d ed. London: Metheun, 1973.

Ellis, John. *Cavalry—The History of Mounted Warfare.* New York: G. P. Putnam's Sons, 1978.

Ellis, J. R. *Philip II and Macedonian Imperialism.* London: Thames and Hudson, 1976.

Engels, Donald. *Alexander the Great and the Logistics of the Macedonian Army.* Berkeley: University of California Press, 1978.

Etienne, Roland, and Roesch, Paul. "Convention militaire entre les cavaliers d'Orchomène et ceux de Chéronée." *BCH* 102(1978):359–374.

Evans, Arthur. *The Palace of Minos.* 4 vols. London: Oxford University Press, 1921–1936.

_____. *Scripta Minoa.* 2 vols. London: Oxford University Press, 1909–1952.

Faulkner, R. O. "Egyptian Military Organization." *JEA* 39(1953):32–46.

Fenik, B. "Typical Battle Scenes in the Iliad, Studies in the Narrative Techniques of Homeric Battle Description." *Hermes* suppl. 21(1968).

Ferrill, Arther. *The Origins of War.* New York: Thames and Hudson, 1985.

Feyel, Michel. *Polybe et l'histoire de Béotie au IIIe siècle avant notre ère.* Paris: E. de Boccard, 1942.

Fornara, C. *The Athenian Board of Generals from 501 to 404 B.C.* Wiesbaden: Franz Steiner, 1971.

Forrest, W. G. "Colonisation and the Rise of Delphi." *Historia* 6(1957):160–175.

Frederiksen, M. W. "The Campanian Cavalry." *Dialoghi di Archeologia* 2(1968):3–31.

Freeman, E. A. *The History of Sicily.* 3 vols. Oxford: Oxford University Press, 1891–1894; reprint ed., New York: Burt Franklin, 1965.

Frost, F. J. "The Athenian Military Before Cleisthenes." *Historia* 33(1984):283–294.

Fuller, J.F.C. A *Military History of the Western World.* 3 vols. New York: Funk and Wagnalls, 1954–1956; reprint ed., New York: Da Capo Press, 1987.

_____. *The Generalship of Alexander the Great.* New Brunswick, NJ: Rutgers University Press, 1960; reprint ed., New York: Da Capo Press, 1989.

Gabriel, Richard A., and Metz, Karen S. *From Sumer to Rome—The Military Capabilities of Ancient Armies.* New York: Greenwood Press, 1991.

Gardiner, E. N. "Throwing the Javelin." *JHS* 27(1907):249–273.

Gardner, P. "A Numismatic Note on the Lelantian War." *CR* 34(1920):90–91.

Gauaghan, Paul F. *The Cutting Edge: Military History of Antiquity and Early Feudal Times.* New York: Peter Lang, 1990.

Gomme, A. W. *The Population of Athens in the Fifth and Fourth Centuries B.C.* Oxford: Basil Blackwell, 1933.

_____. A *Historical Commentary on Thucydides.* Vols. 1–3. Oxford: Oxford University Press, 1945–1956.

Gomme, A. W., Andrewes, A., and Dover, K. J. A *Historical Commentary on Thucydides.* Vols. 4–5. Oxford: Oxford University Press, 1970–1981.

Gordon, D. H. "Swords, Rapiers and Horse-Riders." *Antiquity* 27(1953):67–78.

Gray, Vivienne. "Two Different Approaches to the Battle of Sardis in 395 B.C." *CSCA* 12(1980):183–200.

Great Britain, War Office. *Cavalry Training.* London: H. M. Stationery Office, 1921.

Greenhalgh, P.A.L. *Early Greek Warfare: Horsemen and Chariots in the Homeric and Archaic Ages.* London: Cambridge University Press, 1973.

Griffith, G. T. "The Macedonian Background." *G&R* 12(1965):125–138.

Grundy, G. B. *The Great Persian War and Its Preliminaries, A Study of the Evidence, Literary and Topographical.* New York: Charles Scribner's Sons, 1901.

Gurney, O. R. *The Hittites.* London: Penguin Books, 1952.

Hackett, John, ed. *Warfare in the Ancient World.* New York: Facts On File, 1989.

Hainesworth, J. B. "Joining Battle in Homer." *G&R* 13(1966):158–166.

Hamilton, Charles D. *Agesilaus and the Failure of Spartan Hegemony.* Ithaca, N.Y.: Cornell University Press, 1991.

Hammond, N.G.L. "The Two Battles of Chaeronea (338 B.C. and 86 B.C.)." *Klio* 31(1938):186–218.

———. "A Cavalry Unit in the Army of Antigonus Monophthalmus." *CQ* 28(1978):128–134.

———. *Alexander the Great King, Commander and Statesman.* Park Ridge, N.J.: Noyes Press, 1980.

———. *A History of Greece to 322 B.C.* 3d ed. Oxford: Oxford University Press, 1986.

Hammond, N.G.L. and Griffith, G. T. *A History of Macedonia.* 3 vols. London: Oxford University Press, 1972–1988.

Hanson, V. *Warfare and Agriculture in Classical Greece.* Pisa: Giardini Editori e Stampatori, 1983.

———. "Epameinondas, the Battle of Leuktra (371 B.C.) and the 'Revolution' in Greek Battle Tactics." *CA* 7(1988):190–207.

Helbig, W. "Les Hippeis Athéniens." *Mémoires de l'Institut National de France.* Vol. 37. Paris: C. Klincksieck, 1904.

Hignett, C. *Xerxes' Invasion of Greece.* London: Oxford University Press, 1963.

Holladay, A. J. "Athenian Strategy in the Archidamian War." *Historia* 27(1978):399–427.

Hood, M.S.F. "A Mycenaean Cavalryman." *BSA* 48(1953):84–93.

Hornblower, Simon. *Thucydides*. Baltimore, Md.: Johns Hopkins University Press, 1987.

How, W. W., and Wells, J. *A Commentary on Herodotus*. 2 vols. Oxford: Oxford University Press, 1928.

Jeffrey, L. H. *Archaic Greece: The City-States c. 700–500 B.C.* New York: St. Martin's Press, 1976.

Johansen, K. Friis. *The Attic Grave-Reliefs of the Classical Period*. Copenhagen: E. Munksgaard, 1951.

Johnson, James Turner. *Just War Tradition and the Restraint of War*. Princeton, N.J.: Princeton University Press, 1981.

Kagan, Donald. *The Archidamian War*. Ithaca, N.Y.: Cornell University Press, 1974.

Keegan, John. *The Face of Battle*. New York: Viking, 1976.

Keil, Bruno. *Anonymus Argentinensis: Fragmente zur Geschichte des perikleischen Athens aus einem Strasburger Papyrus*. Strasburg: K. J. Trubner, 1902.

Kirk, G. S. "War and Warrior in the Homer Poems." In *Problèmes de la guerre en Grèce ancienne*. Edited by Jean-Pierre Vernant. Paris: Mouten, 1968.

Knight, D. W. "Thucydides and the War Strategy of Pericles." *Mnemosyne*. 4th series. 23(1970):150–161.

Krentz, P. "The Nature of Hoplite Warfare." *CA* 4(1985):50–61.

Kroll, J. H. "An Archive of the Athenian Cavalry." *Hesperia* 46(1977):83–140.

Kromayer, Johannes. *Antike Schlachtfelder in Griechenland*. 4 vols. Berlin: Weidmannsche Buchhandlung, 1903.

Kyle, Donald G. *Athletics in Ancient Athens*. Leiden: E. J. Brill, 1987.

Lamb, W. "Excavations at Myceanae—Palace Frescoes." *BSA* 25(1921):162–172.

Larsen, J.A.O. *Greek Federal States*. London: Oxford University Press, 1967.

Latacz, J. *Kampfparanese, Kampfdarstellung und Kampfwirklichkeit in der Ilias, bei Kallinos und Tyrtaios*. Munchen: C. H. Beck, 1977.

Lattimore, Richmond, trans. *The Iliad of Homer*. Chicago: University of Chicago Press, 1951.

Lawrence, Arnold W. *Greek Aims in Fortification*. Oxford: Oxford University Press, 1979.

Lazenby, J. F. *The Spartan Army*. Warminster, England: Aris & Phillips, 1985.

Lorimer, H. L. *Homer and the Monuments*. London: Macmillan, 1950.

MacInnes, J. "The Athenian Cavalry in the Peloponnesian War." *CR* 25(1911):193–195.

Manti, P. A. "The Cavalry Sarissa." *AncW* 8(1983):73–80.

Markle, Minor M. "The Macedonian Sarissa, Spear, and Related Armor." *AJA* 81(1977):323–339.

––––––. "Use of the Sarissa by Philip and Alexander of Macedon." *AJA* 82(1978):483–497.

Martin, M. A. *Les cavaliers Athéniens.* Bibliothèque des Ecoles françaises d'Athènes et de Rome. Vol. 47. Paris: Ernest Throin, 1886.

Meritt, B. D. "Greek Inscriptions." *Hesperia* 16(1947):147–183.

Metzger, Henri. *Les représentations dans la céramique Attique du IVᵉ siècle.* Bibliothèque des Ecoles françaises d'Athènes et de Rome. Vol. 112. Paris: E. de Boccard, 1951.

Moore, J. M. *Aristotle and Xenophon on Democracy.* Berkeley: University of California Press, 1975.

Morrison, J. S., and Coates, J. F. *The Athenian Trireme.* London: Cambridge University Press, 1986.

Nolan, L. E. *Cavalry: Its History and Tactics.* 3d ed. London: Bosworth & Harrison, 1860.

Ober, Josiah. "Thucydides, Pericles, and the Strategy of Defense." In *The Craft of the Ancient Historian—Essays in Honor of Chester G. Starr.* Edited by John W. Eadie and Josiah Ober. New York: University Press of America, 1985.

Oman, Charles. *A History of the Art of War in the Middle Ages.* 2 vols. London: Metheun, 1924.

Parke, H. W. *Festivals of the Athenians.* Ithaca, N.Y.: Cornell University Press, 1977.

Peake, Harold, and Fleure, Herbert J. *The Horse and the Sword.* New Haven, Conn.: Yale University Press, 1933.

Pearson, Lionel. "The Pseudo-History of Messenia and Its Authors." *Historia* 11(1962):397–426.

Postgate, J. N. *Taxation and Conscription in the Assyrian Empire.* Rome: Biblical Institute Press, 1974.

Pritchett, W. Kendrick. "Tribal Decree for Anthippasia Victor." *Hesperia* 9(1940):111–112, no. 21.

––––––. "Observations on Chaironeia." *AJA* 62(1958):307–311.

––––––. *Studies in Ancient Greek Topography.* Vols. 1–6. Berkeley: University of California Press, 1965–1990. Vol. 7. Amsterdam: J. C. Gieben, 1991.

––––––. *The Greek State at War.* 5 vols. Berkeley: University of California Press, 1971–1991.

Rahe, P. A. "The Military Situation in Western Asia on the Eve of Cunaxa." *AJP* 101(1980):79–96.

_____. "The Annihilation of the Sacred Band at Chaeronea." *AJA* 85(1981):84–87.

Rainey, A. F. "The Military Personnel of Ugarit." *JNES* 24(1965):17–27.

Raubitschek, A. *Dedications from the Athenian Akropolis.* Cambridge, Mass.: Archaeological Institute of America, 1949.

Rhodes, P. J. "Problems in Athenian *Eisphora* and Liturgies." *AJAH* 7(1982):1–19.

Richter, Gisela M.A. *Archaic Greek Art.* New York: Oxford University Press, 1949.

_____. *The Sculptures and Sculptors of the Greeks.* New Haven, Conn.: Yale University Press, 1950.

_____. *Archaic Gravestones of Attica.* London: Phardon Press, 1961.

Roesch, Paul. *Thespies et la confédération Béotienne.* Paris: E. de Boccard, 1965.

Russell, Frederick H. *The Just War in the Middle Ages.* Cambridge: Cambridge University Press, 1975.

Saggs, H.W.F. *The Might That Was Assyria.* London: Sidgwick & Jackson, 1984.

Sallares, Robert. *The Ecology of the Ancient Greek World.* London: Gerald Duckworth, 1991.

Salmon, P. "L'armée fédérale des Béotiens." *L'Antiquité Classique* 22(1953):347–360.

Sandys, J. E. *Aristotle's Constitution of Athens.* London: MacMillan, 1912.

Schulman, A. R. "Egyptian Representations of Horsemen and Riding in the New Kingdom." *JNES* 16(1957):263–271.

Sealey, R. *A History of the Greek City-States 700–338 B.C.* Berkeley: University of California Press, 1976.

Snodgrass, A. M. *Early Greek Armour and Weapons.* Edinburgh: Edinburgh University Press, 1964.

_____. "The Hoplite Reform and History." *JHS* 85(1965):110–122.

_____. *Arms and Armour of the Greeks.* Ithaca, N.Y.: Cornell University Press, 1967.

_____. *The Dark Age of Greece.* Edinburgh: Edinburgh University Press, 1971.

_____. "The First European Body-Armour." In *The European Community in Later Prehistory: Studies in Honour of C.F.C. Hawkes.* Edited by John Boardman, M. A. Brown, and T.G.E. Powell. Totowa, N.J.: Rowman & Littlefield, 1971.

Spence, I. G. "Athenian Cavalry Numbers in the Peloponnesian War; IG I^3 375 Revisited." *ZPE* 67(1987):167–175.

_____ . "Perikles and the Defence of Attika During the Peloponnesian War." *JHS* 110(1990):91–109.

Starr, Richard Francis. *Nuzi: Report on the Excavations at Yorgan Tepa Near Kirkuk, Iraq.* 2 vols. Cambridge, Mass.: Harvard University Press, 1939.

Tarn, W. W. *Alexander the Great.* 2 vols. London: Cambridge University Press, 1948.

_____ . *Hellenistic Military and Naval Development.* London: Cambridge University Press, 1930; reprint ed., New York: Biblio and Tannen, 1966.

Tausend, Klaus. "Der Lelantinische Krieg, ein Mythos." *Klio* 69(1987):499–514.

Tod, M. N. *A Selection of Greek Historical Inscriptions.* 2 vols. Oxford: Oxford University Press, 1933–1948.

Torr, Cecil. *Ancient Ships.* Cambridge: Cambridge University Press, 1895; reprint ed., Chicago: Argonaut, 1964.

Tupin, C. J. "The Leuctra Campaign." Klio 69(1987):84–93.

United States Army. *Drill Regulations for Cavalry, United States Army.* Washington, D.C.: Government Printing Office, 1909.

Vanderpool, E. "Victories in the Anthippasis." *Hesperia* 43(1974):311–313.

Vigneron, P. *Le cheval dans l'antiquité gréco-romaine.* 2 vols. Nancy: La faculté des Lettres et des Sciences Humaines de l'université de Nancy, 1968.

Warry, John. *Warfare in the Classical World.* New York: St. Martin's Press, 1980.

Westlake, H. D. *Thessaly in the Fourth Century B.C.* London: Methuen, 1935.

_____ . "The Sources of Plutarch's 'Pelopidas.'" *CQ* 33(1939):11–22.

_____ . "Sea-bourne Raids in Periclean Strategy." *CQ* 39(1945):75–84.

Wheeler, Everett L. "Ephorus and the Prohibition of Missiles." *TAPA* 117(1987):157–182.

Whitehead, D. "The Archaic Athenian Zeugitai." *CQ* 31(1981):282–286.

Wick, T. E. "Megara, Athens, and the West in the Archidamian War: A Study in Thucydides." *Historia* 28(1979):1–14.

Wiesner, Joseph. *Fahren und Reiten.* Archaeologia Homerica. Band 1, kapitel F. Gottingen: Vandenhoeck & Ruprecht, 1968.

Wilcken, Ulrich. *Alexander the Great.* Translated by G. C. Richards. New York: W. W. Norton, 1967.

Wilson, P. C. "Battle Scenes in the Iliad." *CJ* 47(1951/1952):269–274, 299–300.

Winlock, H. E. *The Rise and Fall of the Middle Kingdom in Thebes.* New York: Macmillan, 1947.

Wise, Terrance. *Ancient Armies of the Middle East.* Men-At-Arms Series. London: Osprey Publishing, 1981.

Wright, Henry Burt. *The Campaign of Plataea (September, 479 B.C.).* New Haven, Conn.: Tuttle, Morehouse & Taylor, 1904.

Wycherley, R. E. "Xenophon Hipparchicus 3.6–7: Cavalry at the Lyceum." *CR* 13(1963):14–15.

Yadin, Yigael. *The Art of Warfare in the Biblical Lands—In the Light of Archaeological Study.* 2 vols. New York: McGraw-Hill, 1963.

About the Book and Author

The achievements of Greek cavalry—hippeis—on the field of battle should be legendary. However, in most military histories of ancient Greece, the hoplite has received by far the most attention and praise. The modern preoccupation with the heavy infantry of Greece has led to a disregard of the important role played by cavalry. This book is the first to trace the history of Greek cavalry and offers a startling reassessment of the place of mounted troops in ancient Greek warfare.

The first tentative steps toward creating cavalry began as early as the Mycenaean period. Around 1400 B.C., the Greeks began to mount warriors on horseback. The original intent was to gain mobility rather than power on the battlefield. But even at this early stage, some hippeis were equipped to fight mounted and were employed for their "shock" effect in battle.

The early Archaic period saw the hippeis emerge preeminent on the battlefields of the Greek world. Cavalry played an important role in the first Messenian War and was decisive in the Lelantine War. Success led to specialization—heavy cavalry, light cavalry, and dragoons. Although the dominance of the hippeis was gradually eroded by the advent of the hoplite and the phalanx, the employment of cavalry actually increased in the Classical period.

Boeotia, Athens, and Syracuse all fielded formidable mounted forces that played a vital role in the Peloponnesian War. Xenophon's mounted units enabled the "Ten Thousand" to escape the Persians and permitted Agesilaus to conduct a successful campaign in Asia Minor. Epaminondas used the charge of the Theban horse to open the fighting and gain victories at the battles of Leuctra and Mantinea. Philip and Alexander used their cavalry as the "hammer" of the Macedonian army in campaigns that won them dominance of Greece and crushed the Persian Empire. Leslie Worley's *Hippeis* restores the skilled horsemen of Greece to their rightful position in the history of the ancient world.

Leslie J. Worley was born in San Diego, California. He served with the U.S. Marines in the Viet Nam War. Since receiving his Ph.D., he has taught ancient and military history at the University of Washington.

Index

Achaeans, 148
Aegospotami, 121
Aelian, 30
Age, 73–74, 198(nn 88, 89)
Agesilaus, 127–129, 131–136, 139–141,
    152, 209(nn 12, 14), 211(nn 43, 52,
    54)
Agis, King, 97–98, 99, 119, 120, 146
Agora, 78
Agrianians, 165
Akraiphai, 61
Alcibiades, 102, 103, 104, 120
Alcman, 26
Alcmeonids, 66, 67, 194(n45)
Aleuas the Red, 30, 185(n37)
Alexander I, 154
Alexander III, 27, 59, 160, 163–167,
    172, 202(n21), 214(n1)
Amphipolis, 102, 214(n6)
Amyntas, 154–155
Anchimolius, 51
Anderson, J. K., 13
Antander, 23
Anthippasis, 81, 200(n111)
Antipater, 160
Aramaic cavalry, 13, 15
Arbedo, Battle of, 49
Arcadians, 26, 96, 98, 99
Archaeological evidence
    Dark Age, 15–16, 17, 18, 19–20
    Mycenaean period, 11–12
    See also Representations

Archaic period
    art from, 25(fig.), 37(figs.), 39(fig.),
        40(fig.), 42(figs.), 43(fig.), 44(fig.),
        45(fig.), 46(fig.), 47(fig.), 187(nn 59,
        60, 64, 65, 67), 188(n68), 189(n78),
        193(nn 32, 33)
    Athenian cavalry during, 27, 36–49,
        63–66, 177(n5), 194(nn 39, 47)
    role of cavalry during, 1–3, 21–58,
        170, 182(n2)
    Spartan cavalry during, 24–26,
        183(nn 10, 11), 184(n12)
Archers
    Athenian use of mercenary
        mounted, 70, 81
    early use of mounted, 32, 180(n20)
    effectiveness against cavalry, 27, 127
    Spartan, 89, 202(n25)
Archidamian War, 103
Archidamus, 83–86, 87, 201(n6)
Archilochus, 27–28
Argives, 26
    and Battle of Mantinea, 148, 149
    and Peloponnesian War, 96, 97, 98,
        99, 104, 106
Argos, 17
Aristides, 68
Aristocles, 98
Aristocrats
    in Athens, 66–67, 194(n45)
    as cavalrymen, 3, 22, 24, 170
    Ionian, 134

Spartan, 89
use of horses during Archaic period,
29
See also Sociopolitical organization
Aristophanes, 73
Aristotle, 19, 21, 23, 27, 35, 49–50, 66,
182(n1)
Arrian, 167
Ashurbanipal, 35
Asia, 4, 123–141, 152. *See also* Near
East; Persians
Asopodorus, 57
Assyrians, 32–35, 186(nn 44, 45, 46, 49)
Athenian Empire, 59, 129
Athens
Archaic cavalry, 27, 36–49, 39(fig.),
40(fig.), 42(Fig. 3.8), 43(fig.),
45(fig.), 46–47(fig.), 63–66, 177(n5),
194(nn 39, 47)
and Battle of Chaeronea, 159–162
and Battle of Mantinea, 146–151,
213(n72)
and Battle of Phalerum, 189(n83)
and Battle of Plataea, 55–56, 60–61,
190(n90)
buildup/organization of cavalry
during Classical period, 68–81,
170–171, 194(n52), 195(nn 58, 59,
61, 63), 196(nn 64, 65, 67, 69, 70)
Classical period cavalry formations,
75–77, 76(fig.), 199(n96)
demographics, 73–74, 197(n80),
198(n89)
effect of Peloponnesian War on, 130,
210(n18)
equipment/weapons, 15, 199(n95)
Peloponnesian War, 83–122, 171,
201(n12), 202(n20), 204(nn 45, 47,
49, 51, 52), 205(n59), 206(nn 79,
86), 207(nn 93, 115), 208(n137)
quality of cavalry, 200(n2)
raising horses in, 196(n66)

role of cavalry for, 3, 103–104, 120,
208(n135)
sociopolitical organization, 49–50,
67, 72, 74, 193(n31), 194(nn 38, 45),
197(nn 77, 81)
Spartan invasions of, 83–87, 119–
121, 201(n6), 208(n137)

Bactrians, 54
Bardylis, 153–154, 214(n2)
Battles
Archaic period, 23–24, 34–35, 51–58
Athens-Sparta invasions, 83–88,
119–121
cavalry use, 3–4. *See also* Cavalry
Chaeronea, 159–162
Delium, 93–96
infantry use, 1. *See also* Infantry
Issus, 163–167
Leuctra, 141–145
Mantinea, 362 B.C., 146–151
Mantinea, 418 B.C., 96–100
of Middle Ages, 49
pentakontaetia period, 68–69
Philip II and Illyrians, 154
Sardis, 140–141
Siege of Syracuse, 100–119
Spartulos, 90–93
See also specific battles
Boeotia, 3
Athenian invasion of, 93–96
Athenian loss of, 69–70
and Battle of Leuctra, 141–145
and Battle of Mantinea, 146–150,
213(n75)
and Battle of Plataea, 54, 60–61,
191(nn 10, 11)
cavalry of, 144, 191(n12), 192(n21)
and Peloponnesian War, 86, 93–96,
114, 121, 204(nn 46, 52)
See also Thebans
Boeotian Confederacy, 59, 83, 170,
192(nn 13, 18)

cavalry, 27, 61–63, 201(n9), 203(n44)
threat to Athens of, 70, 81
Bottiaia, 214(n6)
Brasidas, 52, 87, 102
Brasideans, 97, 98
Brereton, J. M., 2
Bronze Age. *See* Mycenaean period
Bugh, Glenn, 2, 64, 73, 102–103,
    178(n6)
Bullthrowing, 29

Caesar, 62–63
Camarinaeans, 106
Campanian Cavalry, origins of,
    182(n51)
Cannae, Battle of, 99, 205(nn 63, 64)
Capua, 20
Cardaces, 166, 217(n43)
Carmagnola, 49
Casualty rates, 205(nn 63, 64)
    and Archaic period, 24, 49–50
    Battle of Leuctra, 145
    and Peloponnesian War, 99, 103–104,
    119–120
Cavalry
    Athenian Archaic, 27, 36–49, 63–66,
    177(n5), 194(nn 39, 47)
    Athenian buildup during Classical
    period, 68–81, 170–171. *See also*
    Athens
    Boeotian, 61–63. *See also* Boeotia
    definition of, 4–5
    evolution/roles of Greek, 1–4, 169–
    172, 177(nn 2, 4), 178(n7)
    and fourth-century Asian
    campaigns, 123–141, 209(n14),
    211(nn 52, 54)
    Greek battles in fourth century,
    141–152
    Macedonian use of, 153–167,
    214(n1). *See also* Macedonians
    and Persian Wars, 54–58, 59–61, 67–
    68

role in Peloponnesian War, 83–122,
    200(n3)
types of, 3. *See also* Dragoons;
    Heavy cavalry; Light cavalry
use during Archaic period, 21–53,
    170, 182(n2)
use during Dark Age, 13–20
use during Mycenaean period, 7–13
See also Equipment/weapons;
    specific city-states; Tactics; Troop
    organization
Cavalry charge
    as Archaic period shock tactics, 36,
    48–56, 58
    effectiveness of, 162–163, 216(n37),
    217(nn 38, 39)
    evolution of, 4, 123, 170
    fourth-century Greek use of, 126–
    127, 144–145, 149–150, 151, 152,
    171–172, 188(n72)
    Macedonians and refinement of,
    153, 162, 167, 172, 216(n37),
    218(n46)
    See also Tactics
Cawkwell, George, 2
Chaeronea, 61
Chaeronea, Battle of, 4, 155, 159–162,
    161(fig.), 167, 172
Chalcidian League, 90–91, 203(n33)
Chalcidians
    and Lelantine War, 170
    and Peloponnesian War, 90–93, 121
Chalcis, 2, 19, 26–28, 170
Chariots, 7, 11, 13, 22, 178(n2)
    massed attacks by, 178(n1)
Cheonaeans, 98
Chians, 87
Cimon, 65, 193(n35)
Cineas of Conium, 51
Classical period
    art from, 79(fig.), 80(fig.), 194(n52),
    195(n61), 199(nn 95, 105, 106)

role of cavalry during, 1–2, 3–4. *See also* Cavalry; Peloponnesian War; *specific battles*

Clearchus, 124, 133

Cleisthenes, 67

Cleitus the Black, 28, 185(n28)

Cleomachus, 28

Cleombrotus, 141, 142, 144–145

Cleomenes, 53

Cleon, 102

Cleonaeans, 96

Cleonnis, 23, 24

Cleonymus, 145

Cleophantus, 65

Colophon, 2, 36, 170

Companion Cavalry, 155–156, 157, 165, 214(n7), 216(n37), 218(n46)

Copaeans, 94

Corcyrans, 87

Corinth, 28, 59, 130, 159
    Archaic period cavalry, 36, 41, 42(Fig. 3.7), 44(fig.)

Corinthian War, 133

Coronea, 61, 94

Coronea, Battle of, 134

Crete, 2, 11, 165, 183(n10)
    cavalry during Mycenaean period, 169
    Dark Age archaeological evidence, 13–15

Crousis, 90, 92

Crouwell, J. H., 4, 14

Cumae, 15, 19–20, 182(n51)

Cunaxa, Battle of, 123–124, 135, 208(n2)

Cyprus, 2, 169

Cyreans, 136

Cyrus, 123–124, 208(n2)

Darius, 165–167

Dark Age
    art from, 14(fig.), 16(fig.), 180(n26)

role of cavalry during, 2, 13–20, 169–170

Davies, J. K., 72

Decelaea, 119

Defense, cavalry for, 89, 90, 93, 121, 171

Delian League, 59, 129

Delium, Battle of, 83, 93–96, 121, 171, 189(n82), 203(n42), 204(nn 45, 46, 47, 49, 51, 52, 53)

Demonstrations, 80–81

Demosthenes, 113–118, 189(n84), 207(n115)

Derkylidas, 136

Dexileos, 73

Diodorus, 61, 69, 120–121

Dionysius of Halicarnassus, 20

Discipline, 132–133, 138, 210(n28)
    Macedonian, 157–159, 216(n28)

Documentation, written
    Archaic period, 65, 182(n5)
    Classical period, 74
    Dark Age literary sources, 17–19, 20
    Mycenaean period tablets, 7–8
    Xenophon's works on cavalry, 74, 136–139, 198(n91), 211(n44)
    See also specific authors

Dragoons, 3, 26, 35, 170, 187(n67)

Drill Regulations for Cavalry, United States Army, 163

Ecphantus, 106, 206(nn 69, 86)

Egestans, 107, 206(n91)

Egypt, 7, 11–12, 169, 180(n19)

Elamites, 35

Eleans, 148, 149

Epaminondas, 123, 141, 142–152, 171, 172

Ephorus, 184(n19)

Equipment/weapons, 139, 185(nn 27, 28), 188(nn 70, 71)
    during Archaic period, 25–26, 27–28, 33, 41, 187(n65)

Athenian, 15, 199(n95)
   during Dark Age, 14–17, 18, 169–170
   fourth-century, 128, 192(n21)
   Macedonian, 156–157, 167, 215(n17)
   during Mycenaean period, 9–11,
      169, 179(n14)
Eretria, 2, 26–28, 170
Erigyios, 214(n7)
Eteobutads, 66, 67
Euboea, 19, 26–28
Euphaes, 23, 24
Eurymedon, 113
Euthyrates, 203(n34)
Evans, Arthur, 7–8

Ferrill, Arther, 32
Fighting styles
   Archaic period, 28, 32, 36, 38, 40
   Archaic period heavy cavalry, 41–48
   See also Equipment/weapons;
      Formation, troop; Tactics
Figurines, 9, 10, 10(Fig. 2.1), 179(nn 7,
   10)
First Messenian War, 21, 23–24, 170
Formation, troop, 184(n13)
   Athenian, 66, 75–77, 76(fig.)
   Classical Spartan, 90, 91(fig.)
   infantry, 203(n30), 214(n2). *See also*
      Phalanx
   Macedonian wedge-shaped, 157,
      158(fig.), 167, 172
   night-march, 135–136
   rectangular/square, 25, 62, 63, 66,
      75–77, 76(fig.), 90, 91, 91(fig.), 100–
      102, 101(fig.), 192(n20), 198(n94)
   Syracusan, 100–102, 101(fig.)
   Theban wedge-shaped, 212(n64)
   Thessalian rhomboid, 30–32, 31(fig.),
      170, 185(n40)
   Xenophon's works on, 137–138
   See also Fighting styles; Tactics
Fortetsa, Crete, 15
Frederick the Great, 211(n48)

Frontinus, 133

Gabriel, Richard A., 32
Geloans, 106, 110
Gordon, D. H., 4
Granicus, Battle of, 28
Great Panathenaia, 81
Greeks
   evolution of cavalry use, 1–4, 169–
      172, 177(nn 2, 4)
   See also specific city-states
Greenhalgh, P. A. L., 2, 18–19, 22, 23,
   64
Gylippus, 110–118, 207(n104)

Haliartians, 94
Haliartos, 61
Hamippe, 62–63
Hannibal, 59
Harassment
   by Athenian cavalry, 84–87, 119,
      205(n59)
   of retreating units, 115–117, 125. *See
      also* Screening
   Siege of Syracuse, 108
   See also Tactics
Harpalus, 214(n7)
Hatti, 169
Heavy cavalry
   Archaic period, 40–49, 42(figs.),
      43(fig.), 44(fig.), 45(fig.), 54, 170
   evolution of, 3, 35
   Philip II and Macedonian, 155–156
   See also Cavalry
Hegesileus, 213(n72)
Heiron, 142
Helbig, W., 21–22, 22–23, 64, 182(n2)
Heraclean, 141, 142
Heraeans, 97
Herippides, 139
Herodotus, 51–57, 61, 65, 67–68,
   190(n87)
Himeraeans, 110

Hipparchus, 65
Hippeis
    in Athens, 64, 67, 72, 74, 193(n31)
    Spartan use of term, 183(n10)
    See also Cavalry
Hippias, 51, 65, 67, 189(n83)
Hippocrates, 93, 94–95, 96
Hippodrome, 78, 199(n102)
Hippomedon, 20
Hipponoides, 98
Hittites, 7, 12, 180(n22)
Homer, 17–19
Hoplite
    as principal fighting force, 21, 23, 51,
        58, 59
    role of, 1, 3
    See also Infantry
Horse racing, 29
Horses
    Assyrian procurement, 33–34
    Athenian subsidies for purchase and
        care, 71–72, 196(nn 67, 69, 70)
    in Attica, 196(n66)
    care and training, 60, 138–139,
        191(n6), 197(n71), 211(n48)
    danger to/protective armor for, 27,
        33, 184(n19)
    Persian breeding, 60, 191(nn 4, 6)
    Siege of Syracuse and, 107
    size of, 182(n1)
    Thessaly and, 28–29
    value of, 196(n68)
Horse-transports, Athenian, 88, 103
Hounds, 36

Iliad, 17–19
Illyrians, 153–154
Indians, 54
Infantry
    development of Greek heavy,
        191(n8)
    formations, 203(n30), 214(n2). *See
        also* Phalanx

fourth-century changes in tactics
        for, 123
    mobility, 202(n21)
    See also Hoplite; Peltast
Ionians, 128–129, 131, 134
Iphicrates, 123, 210(n31)
Isocrates, 130
Issus, Battle of, 4, 27, 163–167,
        164(fig.), 172, 216(n22), 217(nn 40,
        42, 43), 218(nn 44, 46)

Jason of Pherae, 30, 132
Javelin, 199(n106)
    Athenian use of, 199(n95)
    general use of, 15, 27–28, 169–170,
        185(n27), 192(n21)
    range of, 199(n107)
    training with, 78–79, 79(fig.), 199(nn
        103, 105)
    use and tactical formations, 62, 77
    Xenophon on, 139
    See also Spears

Kadesh, Battle of, 12
Katastasis, 71, 74, 81, 196(n67)
Kimmerioi, 29, 185(n33)
Kopai, 61

Lacedaemonians. *See* Sparta
Laconia, 87, 88, 89, 171
Lamachus, 102, 103, 104, 106–110, 119
Laomedon, 214(n7)
Lapithae, 28
Larsen, J. A. O., 22, 23
Lasthenes, 203(n34)
Lebadeia, 61
Lelantine War, 3, 21, 26–28, 170,
        185(n31)
Lesbians, 87
Leuctra, Battle of, 4, 134, 141–145,
        143(fig.), 152, 171, 212(nn 58, 59,
        64), 213(nn 69, 70)

Light cavalry
  Archaic period, 36–40, 37(figs.),
    39(fig.), 40(fig.), 54, 170
  evolution of, 3, 35
  Philip II and Macedonian, 155, 156–
    157, 165, 166, 167, 215(n11), 216(nn
    22, 23, 24)
  See also Cavalry
Liturgies, 72, 73, 194(n38), 197(n81)
Locrians, 85, 96
Louis, Dauphin, 49
Lyceum, 80–81
Lycurgan Law, 132
Lycurgus, 24, 66, 135, 183(n11)
Lydians, 36, 188(n72)
Lysander, 132–133

Macedonians, 4, 153–167, 172
  and Battle of Issus, 216(n22),
    217(n40)
  and Battle of Plataea, 54, 55
  cavalry/army size, 215(nn 10, 11),
    216(n23)
  cavalry equipment, 15, 156–157,
    192(n21), 215(n17)
  troop organization, 155–156, 157,
    215(n12)
  wedge formation, 31–32, 157,
    158(fig.)
MacInnes, J., 102
Maenalians, 97
Magnesia, 2, 35–36, 170
Mantinea, Battle of (362 B.C.), 4, 146–
  151, 147(fig.), 152, 171–172, 213(nn
  72, 75)
Mantinea, Battle of (418 B.C.), 83, 96–
  100, 121, 134, 171, 205(nn 54, 55,
  56, 57)
Mantineans
  and Battle of Mantinea, 362 B.C.,
    146–151

and Battle of Mantinea, 418 B.C.,
  205(n54)
and Peloponnesian War, 96–99, 104
Marathon, 99, 205(n63)
Mardonius, 54, 55, 57, 60, 190(n87),
  191(n10)
Martin, M. A., 63
Masistius, 55
Medes, 54
Megacles, 66
Megara campaign, 206(n79)
Megarians
  and Battle of Plataea, 54–55, 57
  and Lelantine War, 28
Mercenaries, 209(n17)
  Athenian use of mounted archers,
    70, 81
  and Battle of Issus, 163, 166
  and Battle of Leuctra, 142
  pool created by Peloponnesian War,
    129–131
  the Ten Thousand, 123–128, 136
  training of, 210(n31)
Messengers/couriers
  cavalry as, 68, 194(n48)
  runners, 94, 203(n43)
Messenians
  and Messenian Wars, 23–24, 26
  and Peloponnesian War, 88, 171
Messenian War(s)
  documentation on, 182(n5)
  First, 21, 23–24, 170
  Second, 26
Middle Ages, 27, 49, 180(n30), 182(n1)
Mitanni, 12, 169
Mithradates, 125, 126, 127, 209(n11)
Mnesimachos, 78
Mobility
  chariots versus mounted horses for,
    7, 11, 19, 20, 169
  infantry versus cavalry, 202(n21)
  tactics and cavalry, 35, 56
Mouliana, Crete, 13–15, 180(n26)

Mycenaean period
  art from, 10(figs.), 179(nn 7, 10),
    180(nn 19, 23)
  chariots during, 178(n1)
  role of cavalry during, 2, 7–13, 169,
    179(n14)
Mygdon, 139

Naval forces, Peloponnesian War, 83,
    87–88, 104, 112–113, 121
Naxians, 107, 206(n91)
Nearchus, 214(n7)
Near East, 12–13, 191(n8). *See also*
    Asia
Nepos, 133
Nicias, 27, 100, 102–118, 207(n96)
Nolan, L. E., 1
Nuzi, 12

Olympic Games, 29, 81
Olympiodorus, 55
Olynthians, 90–93, 203(nn 32, 33)
Onomarchus, 155
Orchomenians, 94, 204(n46)
Orchomenus, 61
Orneates, 96, 98

Paeonians, 165, 215(n11)
Pagondas, 93–96, 204(nn 46, 53)
Pallene, Battle of, 65
Parades, 80–81, 198(n93)
Paralos, 65
Pausanias, 23–24, 54, 182(n5)
Pelopidas, 123, 144
Peloponnesian League, 59, 83
Peloponnesian War, 52, 83–122,
    201(n12), 202(n20)
  cavalry use during, 3, 121–122, 171,
    200(n3)
  mercenary pool resulting from, 129–
    131
Peloponnesus
  Athenian invasions of, 87–88

cavalry during Mycenaean period, 2,
    169
  See also Spartans
Peltast, 1, 62–63, 203(n38). *See also*
    Infantry
Pentacosiomedimnoi, 49, 50, 67, 72,
    73, 74, 197(n77)
Pentakontaetia, 68–81
Perdiccas II, 154
Perdiccas III, 153
Pergola, Angelo de la, 49
Periclean Age, 59–81
Pericles, 73, 85–86, 87, 201(n7)
Persians
  and Battle of Issus, 163, 165–167,
    171, 217(n42)
  and Battle of Plataea, 54–58, 59–60,
    190(nn 87, 92, 93)
  fourth-century Greek campaigns
    against, 123–141, 152, 209(nn 6, 9,
    11)
  at Marathon, 99
  weapons, 185(n27)
Persian Wars, 54–58, 60–61, 67–68,
    190(nn 87, 90, 92, 93, 94), 191(n8)
Pezhetairoi, 160, 163
Phalanx
  effect on cavalry of, 21, 51, 58,
    188(n77), 190(n93)
  See also Formation, troop; Tactics
Phalerum, Battle of, 51–53, 189(n83)
Pharsalus, 62
Phidippides, 203(n43)
Philaids, 67, 194(n45)
Philip II, 123, 153–163, 167, 172,
    189(n79)
Phliasians, 57, 141, 142
Phocians, 85, 141, 142
Phyle, 75–77, 76(fig.), 198(n91)
Pisistratus, 66–67, 194(n45)
Plataea, 192(n18)
Plataea, Battle of, 3, 54–58, 60–61, 67–
    68, 154, 170, 190(nn 87, 90, 92, 93,

94), 191(nn 9, 10, 11), 192(n21),
     194(n48)
Plato, 65
Pleistoanax, 70
Plutarch, 25, 65, 73, 104, 109, 144
Pollux, 65, 72
Polybius, 20
Pritchett, W. Kendrick, 2
Prodromoi, 155, 156–157, 165, 166,
     167, 215(n11), 216(nn 22, 23, 24)
Prosymna, 9
Pylos, Messenia, 88, 89
Pythaides, 73
Pytharatus, 23

Rapiers, 11
Representations
  Archaic period, 21–22, 22–23,
     25(fig.), 32, 35, 36–38, 37(figs.),
     39(fig.), 40–45, 40(fig.), 42(figs.),
     43(fig.), 44(fig.), 45(fig.), 46(fig.),
     47(fig.), 50, 51, 64–65, 177(n5),
     187(nn 59, 60, 64, 65, 67), 188(n68),
     189(n78), 193(nn 32, 33)
  Assyrian, 186(nn 44, 45, 46)
  Classical period, 78, 79(fig.), 80(fig.),
     194(n52), 195(n61), 199(nn 95, 105,
     106)
  Dark Age, 13–15, 14(fig.), 16–17,
     16(fig.), 180(n26)
  Mycenaean period, 8–9, 10(figs.), 12–
     13, 179(nn 7, 10), 180(nn 19, 23)
Retreat(s)
  cavalry screens for, 57–58, 61, 106–
     107, 109, 191(n11)
  from Siege of Syracuse, 114–118,
     208(n129)
  of Ten Thousand, 124–127, 209(nn
     6, 9, 11)
Rhodians, 135
Romans, 15, 20, 99, 205(n63)

Sacae, 54

Sacred Band, 144, 159, 162, 171,
     212(n64)
St. Jacob, Battle of, 49
Samos, 28
Sardis, Battle of, 139, 140–141, 171,
     211(n57)
Sargon II, 34
Sarissa, 156, 172, 214(n2), 215(n17)
Sarissophoroi, 155, 156–157
Schulman, A. R., 12
Sciritae, 97, 98
Scouting, 203(n31)
  fourth-century, 146
  during Peloponnesian War, 94, 96,
     104, 107, 171, 203(n44)
Screening
  infantry movements, 145, 148, 151,
     165, 213(n69)
  retreats, 57–58, 61, 106–107, 109,
     191(n11)
Scythas, 139
Scythians, 31–32, 157
Second Lateran Council, 27
Second Messenian War, 26
Selinuntians, 106, 110
Sennacherib, 34, 186(n49)
Shalmaneser III, 34, 186(n49)
Shields, 188(n68, 71)
  Archaic period, 25, 48
  Dark Age, 14–15, 16
  Middle Ages, 180(n30)
  Mycenaean period, 9
Sicels, 107, 110, 206(n91)
Sicilian Expedition, 100, 102–119, 131,
     171, 206(nn 71, 74, 91)
Sitacles, 154
Sitoi, 71, 74, 81, 196(n69)
Skirmishes/raids
  Archaic, 38–40, 56–57
  Battle of Plataea, 190(n94)
  Epaminondas and cavalry, 146, 150–
     151
  fourth-century Greek-Persian, 128

Peloponnesian War, 92–93, 120–121
  See also Cavalry charge; Tactics
Slingers
  effectiveness against cavalry, 27,
    125–126, 127
  Xenophon's use of, 135
Snodgrass, A. M., 9, 14, 15, 27, 64
Sociopolitical organization
  Athens, 49–50, 67, 72, 74, 193(n31),
    197(n77)
  Ionia, 129
  Sparta, 26
  Thessaly, 29, 185(n37)
Socrates, 65
Solon, 63, 64, 193(n30)
Spartans
  Archaic period cavalry, 24–26,
    183(nn 10, 11), 184(n12)
  and Battle of Leuctra, 141–145, 171,
    212(n58)
  and Battle of Phalerum, 51–53,
    189(n83)
  and Battle of Plataea, 56, 57
  and Battle of Tanagra, 68–69
  cavalry development during
    Peloponnesian War, 89–91, 91(fig.),
    134, 171, 202(nn 25, 26, 27, 28)
  446 B.C. invasion of Attica, 70
  Messenian Wars, 23–24, 26
  military tactics, 77
  military training, 131–132, 142
  and Peloponnesian War, 83–90, 97–
    100, 110–122, 202(n20), 205(nn 55,
    56)
Spartulos, Siege of, 90–93, 203(n38)
Spears, 188(n70)
  cavalry sarissa, 156, 172, 215(n17)
  Dark Age, 15
  long infantry sarissa, 156–157, 172
  Mycenaean period, 9–10
  use during Archaic period, 33
  See also Equipment/weapons;
    Javelin

Sphodrias, 145
Squires/servants, 22, 35–36, 186(n45)
  Macedonian limit on, 158, 189(n79)
Strabo, 27, 36, 184(n19)
Swiss confederation, 49
Swords, 185(n28)
  Dark Age, 15
  kopis, 156
  from Mycenaean period, 10–11
  use during Archaic period, 28
  Xenophon on, 139
  See also Equipment/weapons
Syracusans
  and Siege of Syracuse, 100–102,
    104–119, 121–122, 171
  troop organization and formation,
    100–102, 101(fig.), 205(nn 67, 68)
Syracuse, Siege of, 83, 99, 100–119,
    105(fig.), 171, 206(nn 86, 88),
    207(nn 93, 115), 208(nn 119, 129)
Syria, 12–13, 169

Tactics
  Alexander at Issus, 166–167
  Athenian, 201(n6), 208(n135)
  coordinated infantry-cavalry attack,
    140–141, 145, 152, 153, 159, 162,
    163, 167, 171–172, 204(n53),
    213(n70), 214(n2), 216(n37)
  effect of phalanx on, 21
  flanking and rear attacks by cavalry,
    95–96, 111–112, 120, 154, 171
  infantry, 123
  used by Assyrians, 32, 33, 34–35
  Xenophon's Asian, 135
  See also Cavalry charge; Defense,
    cavalry for; Fighting style;
    Formation, troop; Harassment;
    Scouting; Screening; Skirmishes/
    raids
Tanagra, 61, 94
Tanagra, Battle of, 68–69, 177(n4)

Ten Thousand, the, 123–127, 128, 135, 152, 209(nn 6, 9, 11)
Thasos, 36, 37(Fig. 3.3)
Thebans, 210(n38), 216(n37)
  and Battle of Chaeronea, 159–162
  and Battle of Leuctra, 141–145, 171, 212(nn 59, 64)
  and Battle of Mantinea (362 B.C.), 171–172, 213(n75)
  and Battle of Plataea, 55, 56, 57, 60, 61, 190(n94)
  and Boeotian Confederacy, 61, 192(n18). *See also* Boeotian Confederacy
  cavalry, 2, 22, 170, 195(n62)
  cavalry equipment, 192(n21)
  and Peloponnesian War, 85, 94, 95, 96, 121, 171, 204(nn 46, 51)
  See also Boeotia
Theodorus of Samos, 26
Thespis, 61, 94, 95
Thessalians
  and Battle of Issus, 163–167, 218(n44)
  and Battle of Mantinea, 146–151
  and Battle of Phalerum, 51–53
  and Battle of Plataea, 54, 55
  and Battle of Tanagra, 68–69
  casualty rates during Archaic period, 49
  cavalry of, 3, 22, 28–32, 31(fig.), 185(nn 34, 37, 40), 192(n21), 195(n62)
  and Lelantine War, 26, 28, 170, 185(n31)
  and Peloponnesian War, 85, 86
Thibron, 136
Thracians, 29, 154, 165, 215(n11)
Thucydides, 28, 69, 73
  on Peloponnesian War, 26, 84–119, 201(n13)
Timagenides, 190(n94)

Timesis, 71, 74, 81
Tiryns, 15
Tissaphernes, 171
Tolimedes, 69
Training, 199(n105)
  of Agesilaus mercenary cavalry, 133–134, 136
  Athenian cavalry, 77–80, 199(n103)
  Boeotian cavalry, 144
  of horses, 60, 138–139, 191(n6)
  Macedonian, 157, 159, 216(n28)
  mercenary, 210(n31)
  Spartan military, 131–132, 142
  Xenophon on, 138–139
Trierarchy, 72, 73, 197(n81)
Trireme, 59, 72, 73
Troop organization, 195(n62)
  Archaic Athenian cavalry, 65–66, 194(n39)
  Boeotian Confederacy, 61–62, 63, 201(n9)
  Classical Athenian cavalry, 69, 70, 195(nn 58, 63), 196(nn 64, 65)
  Macedonian, 155–156, 157, 215(n12)
  Peloponnesian War and Spartan, 89–90, 202(n27)
  Spartan Archaic period, 24–25, 183(n11), 184(n12)
  Syracusan, 100, 205(nn 67, 68)
  Thessalian, 29–30
  Xenophon's works on, 137
Tukulti-Ninurta, 32, 186(n45)
Tyrtaeus, 26, 182(n5)

Ugarit, 12–13, 180(n23)
Urartu, 34

Vases/amphoras
  Archaic period, 21–22, 22–23, 36, 37(Fig. 3.4), 40–45, 42(figs.), 43(fig.), 44(fig.), 45(fig.), 64–65, 193(nn 32, 33)

Dark Age, 13–15, 14(fig.), 16–17, 16(fig.)
Mycenaean period, 8–9, 12–13
Virgil, 28

Warship. *See* Trireme
Weapons. *See* Equipment/weapons
William the Conqueror, 59

Xanthippos, 65
Xenocles, 139
Xenophon, 84
  and Asian campaign, 27, 124–127, 128, 135–136, 152, 171, 209(n13), 211(nn 42, 43, 51)
  on Athenian cavalry, 71, 73, 75, 77–78
  background of, 130–131
  on Battle of Mantinea, 148–149
  on Boeotian cavalry, 144
  and Siege of Spartulos, 90–92
  on Spartan cavalry, 142
  works on cavalry, 74, 136–139, 198(n91), 211(n44)
Xenophontos Hipparchikos (Xenophon), 74, 211(n44)
Xenophontos peri Hippikes (Xenophon), 211(n44)
Xerxes, 59